Karting

Leroi "Tex" Smith

arco
New York

First Edition, Eighth Printing, 1982

Published by Arco Publishing, Inc.
219 Park Avenue South, New York, N.Y. 10003

Library of Congress Catalog Card Number 70-77893
ISBN 0-668-01939-5

Printed in the United States of America

Contents

Preface

IT MAY seem strange to the reader that a preface to any karting book would be written by the publisher of a hot rod magazine. However, it really isn't so unusual. *Rod & Custom* was karting's top booster in the early days of the sport and has continued in this editorial interest through the past decade, promoting the sport whenever and wherever possible. In recent years when the karting sport had no magazine of its own, *Rod & Custom* tried, if only in a small way, to expose the fun and excitement of the sport to a national audience that knew nothing of its existence. My own interest in karting dates to the first Kart Nationals in 1959 and has continued to the present day. My teenage son and I run karts in both Sprints and Enduros.

Over the years the sport has undergone a number of radical changes, from the first simple and underpowered sit-up Sprint karts to the highly sophisticated lay-down Enduro machines of today. The very slippery full-bodied FKE machines remind one of fantastically expensive road racing automobiles.

The first Enduro machines were merely Sprint karts with larger fuel tanks added for up to an hour of running time. The addition of higher gear ratios accommodate the $2-2\frac{1}{2}$ mile sports car courses. In the quest for quicker lap times on these longer tracks, the lay-down kart came into being. The lay-down concept went through many changes until the present day off-set Enduro machine is every bit as sophisticated for racing as the finest Indy car.

Modern karts feature such goodies as 4-wheel disc brakes, oil bath slipper clutches, mag wheels, tuned exhaust systems, exhaust temp heat probes and special tires for high speed work. Even with all of these advancements and changes, the basic kart is still there. It has just been re-arranged. Therefore the main purpose of this book is to bring the reader up to date on karting as it is today, with its changes and advancements. Karting has survived and grown for over a decade. From all indications, the 1970's will find the sport bigger and stronger than ever. Give it a chance and it will find you.

Tom Medley
Publisher,
Rod & Custom Magazine

Introduction

WHEN KARTS came charging into the automotive sport I was an editor at *Hot Rod Magazine*, concerned more with supercharged dragsters and chromeplated street roadsters than with diminutive two stroke "tinker toys." It was easy to dismiss karting enthusiasm as some kind of childhood carryover, a kid's game played with coasters on a vacant parking lot. I'd built my share of soap box and two-by-four pushcars and one or two had even used a discarded Maytag washing machine engine. That anyone, particularly a car enthusiast, could become totally engrossed in the small poppers was incomprehensible. Where karts gained ready acceptance from the general public, the hardcore automotive sport generally regarded these four-wheeled chain saws as a noisy nuisance. Not for long.

One day our magazine schedule was interrupted by a raucous noise in the parking lot; the alien, stacatto blatt of an unmuffled two-stroke engine and squealing tires. There, perched atop some sort of four-wheeled thing, sat *Rod & Custom Magazine* editor Lynn Wineland. Everyone stared distrustfully at the oil and smoke belching mini-monster and politely asked, "What's that"? Lynn called it a Go-Kart, and said there were eight or ten just like it being used for impromptu races on weekends over at the Rose Bowl parking lot. Everyone was offered a ride.

"Careful of the steering," he cautioned, "it is cat quick. And hang on good; even in the cramped, nearly fetal driving position it is snappy and prone to unload the driver in hard corners." We hot rod types were skeptical, but game. Surely we must have destroyed the agile little engine, thrashing around the parked cars and having a ball playing with a bundle of mechanical spice. All were immediately converted kart nuts, a malady that has spread throughout the automotive sport. We had been wrong about karting; it is perhaps the most refreshing aspect of four-wheeled adventure.

The name "go-kart" was coined by Wineland simply because the machines had to be called something, and that seemed most descriptive. The "k" was added for kart to separate the fledgling vehicle from its washing machine powered predecessors. That karting could and would evolve into some sort of organized competition seemed obvious, but the main interest was, and remains, a fun machine the entire family may enjoy.

The exciting kart story was spread by enthusiastic automotive publications, but only personal contact could convince anyone this was a worthwhile sport. As a commercial enterprise, karting mushroomed nationwide. The first official manufacturing plant was aptly titled Go-Kart, but other plants were soon in production throughout the country. Small engine manufacturers finally gave in to demand and began supplying the new market. Special accessory items like tires and wheels were designed and produced; hop-up equipment for the engines appeared; lawnmower repairmen became karting experts; an entire industry was spawned.

That karting would crest in popularity and then level off into a stable segment of the automotive scene was also predictable. That it has maintained such a high level of enthusiasm has been the major surprise. As karting spread across the land, requirements for special facilities grew. Local supermarket parking lots were literally overrun with karters. City streets were alive with the little screamers, although this was illegal traffic if the kart was not equipped with muffler, lighting, etc. Competition became the focal point of interest, with emphasis on a road race type circuit which accents the kart handling qualities.

But karts were still for fun. Wally Parks, President of the National Hot Road Association and at that time Editor of *Hot Rod Magazine,* showed up one day with a bright yellow kart. We took it to an abandoned World War II airfield, long since overgrown with sagebrush and tumbleweed, where hours were spent bumping through the weeds with abandon. My own kart was one of the first produced by Go-Kart, with a single West Bend engine and racing "slicks" for rear tires. It never was painted, and served for mom and the kids to tool around vacant lots as well as for amateur competition for dad. One day a fellow turned up at the local parking arena with two West Bend engines and soundly trounced everyone. Next week, we all had two engines.

This is what has made karting so very popular. A small change here, some adjustment there until performance was a tiny fraction better. Enough better to maybe win a few races. In karting the changes were for more power, better traction in corners, chassis handling for twisty courses, better brakes, increased driver comfort. This sophistication, which began with Art Ingel's first kart, continues today. Taken gradually, the changes seem matter of fact, almost insignificant. Taken in one lump they can be awesome.

Following a one-year separation from karting in 1959-1960 (more college), I returned to Southern California and an invitation to try out the new Go-Kart factory race track. My mount was a recently introduced three-engined kart with live rear axle and four-wheel disc brakes. The experience was frightening. I hurtled into corners at impossible speeds and braked with impossible ease. A touch of excess throttle would send great, billowing clouds of white smoke from tortured tires. Enthusiasts who had been with the sport the past year took this drastically improved performance for granted; for me it was traumatic. It also underscored a hard fact. The cost of karting was soaring.

Where the original karts had been available in kit form for under $200, the price was edging steadily upward in the more exotic, and desirable, racing classes. Sport governing bodies like the International Kart Federation (IKF) had been formed, with instructions from the membership to keep costs in control if possible. Karting was for everybody. To this end, the organizations instituted special classes for the less expensive karts and placed a claiming tag on many classes. The unlimited classes had no cost restrictions. Although production costs have skyrocketed since 1956, a Fun kart can still be purchased for under $200. From the backyard to the local Sprint track is even less costly.

In terms of manufacturers, karting is not as big today as it was six or seven years ago. Those manufacturers that remain, however, are now solidly entrenched as part of the performance automotive industry. Where once there were over 150 companies offering karts of some type, there are now a dozen. Where the original companies were generally small with limited production, modern companies are large and diversified. Karts are shipped in quantity, along with minibikes and related accessories. Lightweight motorcycles are considered relative to the same general audience.

The number of karts in existence is pure guesswork, but figures released by engine manufacturers and the larger chassis builders indicates a total United States production of something over 200,000. This would include all karts produced since mid-1956 and assumes a very low attrition rate. A kart lifetime is endless, partly because of the basic sound construction technique in quality metal tubing and partly because of the design. The modern kart differs only slightly from earlier machines, the obvious difference being in laydown seating for long distance Enduro karts. It is possible for an enthusiast to utilize modern engines on a ten-year-old chassis and have a very good chance of winning races.

Art Ingels had a great idea back there in Fifty-six.

1. What Is Karting, Anyway?

KARTING, spelled with a "K" on purpose, is not the same as the little washing-machine-motor powered putt-putts and nonpowered coasters that have chugged around the neighborhood streets for decades. The kart is a highly sophisticated, miniature car particularly suited to maneuverable, high-speed competition. As much a thoroughbred as a Kentucky Derby runner, the kart can also be utilized for any number of nonracing purposes. Karts are used as transportation in very large storage facilities, often equipped with electric motors for power. They make outstanding training devices for driver education classes; interstate highway marking crews use them for reflector installation; they have been seriously considered as Moon travel machines. They are not a toy!

While most Americans and many foreign people (the sport is big across the world) know what a go-kart is, few enthusiasts know the origin. Some think of karts as stripped versions of three-quarter and quarter midgets, these being racing cars with full oval-track-type bodies. While such

1

cars were popular with a small group of enthusiasts, they were not really adaptable to diverse competition, nor were they real family vehicles. Karts were not an evolution of these midget-type racers, although they do have a race car heritage.

The kart was invented in 1956 by Art Ingels, a craftsman working at the time for Frank Kurtis of Indianapolis racer fame. Art was engrossed with building Kurtis Roadsters for the annual Brickyard 500-mile race, cars generally conceded the world's ultimate in quality workmanship. At his disposal was a considerable amount of salvage tubing, and in the corner a surplus two-stroke West Bend single-cylinder engine originally intended for a lawnmower. The idea persisted that this engine could be utilized on some kind of little car, a tiny vehicle that could be used to putt around race track pits or the garage parking lot.

The result was much more spirited than expected. Vehicle weight was well under 100 pounds and Art tipped the scales right at 210 pounds. The little 2½ horsepower engine scooted Art over the pavement at 30 miles per hour, a speed that seems more like 60 when the driver is so close to the ground. Barely long enough for an adult to double up in, the kart didn't turn a corner, it darted around. Other Kurtis workmen and friends took rides on the popper and immediately began construction of their own karts, carbon copies of the original. The sport was born.

At first Art tried to convince Kurtis of the commercial prospects of the little kart, but Kurtis wasn't listen-

The man who started it all, Art Ingels, aboard the very first go-kart with a surplus West Bend two-stroke engine. Shown with Art is Lou Borelli, partner in what became Caretta Kart Manufacturing.

Caretta

APRIL 1968

Evolution of karting is graphically shown here. First Ingels' kart had flat frame, hand brake, very simple construction.

ing. True, the kart could be sold for less than $150 at the time; but shop production was already overtaxed just with racing cars. Art continued building full-sized racing cars.

Meanwhile Bill Rowles, a Southern California surplus dealer, had seen the little car and the crowds it invariably gathered. He knew where there were plenty of inexpensive West Bend engines, brand new, but listed as surplus. Acquaintance Duffy Livingstone, with partner Roy Desbrow, had a successful muffler shop going along. The three built cars for themselves first, but friends kept a steady flow of orders going. Obviously some kind of production was needed. Rowles, Livingston, and Desbrow became Go-Kart Company, an organization that

snowballed into a million dollar industry.

Meanwhile, Art Ingels also saw the production possibilities and left Kurtis to form another new kart company named Caretta. Others followed quickly, with plants everywhere in the country—this was one automotive sport not confined to sunny Southern California.

While production karts were relatively similar in overall appearance and chassis dimensions, close inspection revealed myriad differences. Some used dropped frames, others dropped axles—some both. Steering, although direct in all cases, was modified for quicker or slower response. Bars alongside the seat, called sissy bars, were added to keep the driver

As competition progressed, Caretta kart introduced sissy rails beside seat, dropped axle, lowered frame, racing slicks.

from sliding over the frame during hard cornering. Manufacturers kept racing teams going year around just to test new ideas and gain publicity.

Then there was an entire army of individual karts, built from everything including water pipe and wood. As a rule, the home design failed to compete well with the factory design, simply because the individual builder could not rack up the hundreds of experience hours necessary for rapid evolution. The individual also tended to create rather weird machinery, often far afield from the basic kart concept. Organization was needed, both to promote the sport and to control it safetywise.

In December of 1957 the Go-Kart Club of America (GKCA) was started. Competition regulations were issued, and for the first time individual and factory designers had a framework of building reference. At first, there were only three classes of karts. The emphasis was on low cost and fun.

GKCA was joined shortly by another organization, called the United States Kart Association, with the purposes of insuring competition events, spreading the good word about the sport, and assimilating track specifications. Both these organizations have been superceded by the International Kart Federation, with offices at 529 South Second Avenue, Covina, California 91722. In addition to all the necessary regulations and public relations necessary for such an organization, the IKF also supplies a monthly magazine *Karter News* for members. There is another karting group called the Enduro Karting Association, at P. O. Box 118, Monrovia, California, which concentrates entirely on Enduro and Formula, or full-bodied, karts. Regulations of the IKF are in effect at EKA meets.

Organization of any automotive sport has a rapid stabilization effect upon the type of vehicles involved, whether karts or sports cars or dragsters. In karting, it tended to reduce the number of fun karts, or those units sold strictly for banging around neighborhood streets, while increasing the number of karts in competition. Most cities have rules forbidding unlicensed vehicles on public roads, laws which keep karts off streets and on racing tracks. Today these strictly for fun cars, now called yard karts, are in the great minority.

The great splurge in kart production is also now over, with production in the hands of a dozen or so companies. The original Go-Kart company is gone, although the name has been purchased by another old-line company, and emphasis has shifted to a steady output of maximum quality competition karts. The under-$200 competition kart doesn't exist anymore, either, even for the talented homebuilder. Material prices have risen steadily during the last decade, until a typical modern Sprint kart, single engine, will cost about $500. The more elaborate Enduro kart will run at least $700 in single engine trim. Really competitive karts can cost over $1,000.

Compared to regular automobile racing, however, karting is a penny proposition. An Indianapolis racer will start at around $60,000; a Trans-Am road racing sedan will cost at least $40,000; a supercharged dragster will cost over $25,000; even the so-called low-cost Formula V (Volkswagen power) road racer will require at least $5,000 to be competitive. Much to the chagrin of many automotive racing purists, a good twin-engined kart will lap most race tracks faster than a car. Kart top speeds are in excess of 120 mph, yet the safety factor is the envy of all automotive racing organizations.

There are five basic kinds of karts now in existence: Sprint, Enduro, Fun (or yard), Concession (rental), and FKE. All are similar, and all are different, each created for a definite purpose.

Jimmy Yamane, an early McCulloch Corp. employee, came to National Championships with single-engine kart, and won the first single-engine classes at the original Go-Kart private raceway.

It was called "run what you brung" at the early Eastland Shopping Center impromptu races in 1958. Parking lot races were fantastically successful. From this meager beginning came a world-wide sport.

For those who participated, there was nothing like the Tecate, Mexico, street endurance races. There was mass confusion but this type of action bred a tremendous following for the sport.

The Tecate race had everything from smooth asphalt to dirt back alleys among houses. Spectators could watch from front yard.

Sprint Karts

Karts for very short tracks (usually no longer than ½ mile) are all lumped into the Sprint category, and generally look almost identical to karts of the late 1950's. The driver sits upright with legs tucked back and body english may or may not be part of the driving style. Up until 1964 all karts were of this nature, but then the laydown configuration came along for the long-distance events, the driver position an obvious concession to aerodynamics.

Sprint tracks may be either oval or road race type, and the surface may be macadam or dirt. In any case, the emphasis is on correct gearing for the track, engine rpm's up in the maximum power range, driver technique, and chassis handling. There are usually more Sprint tracks in a specific area than Enduro locations, because Enduros are run on big sports car tracks, while Sprint tracks are often privately owned. Sometimes the Sprint track is set up in the infield of a fairgrounds horse racing track or even a

portion of the local stock car track. Spectators seem to like Sprint racing, especially on the dirt, as it resembles flat track motorcycle competition with great noise and lots of visual action. Karts can be run on indoor tracks, too, but the problem of ventilation overcomes the fantastic accoustical thrill.

Because of the general similarity between the modern Sprint and the earlier kart, it is possible to make a few relatively inexpensive changes to the early kart and be competitive. Most Enduro kart enthusiasts have a Sprinter chassis available to fill in on weeks where there are no long events scheduled, often using the same engine on both karts with different tuning and gearing. As in all facets of karting, the family is encouraged to participate, so classes are set up for youngsters, men, and women. Light and heavyweight categories are also listed for calorie conscious (or unconscious) drivers.

For anyone just beginning in kart-

TOP: **Talk about hairy, the Tecate straight featured karts going in both directions, speeds up to 70 mph during early days.** BOTTOM: **State of the sprint art today, with tiny machines huddled together at Adams sprint track in San Bernardino, Calif. Nationals events like this draw upward of 500 entries.**

ing, the Sprint-type machine is highly recommended. It has the advantage of being most versatile, since it is basically a competition-type Fun kart and can be used for teaching the family members how to drive with an inexpensive, low horsepower 2- or 4-stroke engine. As driver confidence increases and ability is sharpened, making the transition to competition is a weekend labor. It must be emphasized that competition is not the all-important part of karting, but it is the most glamorous and has great appeal to youngsters. In this respect it is a superb bonding agent among family members.

7

Enduro Karts

An Enduro kart can immediately be spotted by its reclining driver position and large fuel tanks alongside the frame. These karts are designed for larger race courses, usually sports car tracks with a minimum lap distance of 1.5 miles. The track curves are generally not as tight as Sprint tracks, but the straights are very long and speeds get well above 100 mph in the unrestricted classes. Endurance is the test here, which is a direct reflection on the early two-stroke's reputation for dependability (or lack of it).

Karters seemed to just naturally drift to the wide-open endurance contests, since the time involved (an endurance race is usually a time maximum, with one-hour being standard) allows considerably more competition and a chance to make up for a driving

TOP: **First attempt at streamlining, with frame stretched ahead of front axle with metal covering: BOTTOM: Streamlining developed the FKE closed body classes, which require roll bars and safety belts, and are capable of 135 mph.**

mistake. The karts may make pit stops for fuel, tires, or repair, which brings the family members and friends into play as pit crew. At one time, before the rules outlawed it, engines were even changed in less than 30 seconds through use of quick-change mounts. Now the Enduro kart must run the distance on the original engine(s), thus proving the reliability of a well-tuned two-stroke.

Because the Enduro kart has more things on it, it naturally costs more money. Fortunately, most of the accessories of distinction, such as aluminum gas tanks, can be built by the home craftsman. If the enthusiast happens to be a machinist, he can make practically every other speed item, from disc brakes to slipper clutches. While the Enduro and Sprint chassis fit within the same general measurements (see Chapter 3, "Clas-

ses and Regulations"), it requires a good deal of frame modification to change a Sprint to an Enduro.

The home builder can save some money by creating his own design, but he is still faced with the same materials cost as the manufacturer so the end result will be similar in terms of cost. As a guide, the unskilled builder should not attempt making an entire kart for serious competition unless he is using the vehicle as an experience aid only. On the other hand, once an enthusiast has spent many hours driving a kart and knows intimately exactly how a kart must behave, he can then consider personal design changes. Most current kart manufacturers have evolved from the earlier industry with this hard-won experience as a guideline.

Long-distance Enduro racing gained in popularity in early 1960. Attempt at reducing wind resistance is shown here. Front driver is in a full upright position, number two man is in a semi-laydown position.

First full lay-down Enduro was run by Larry Eyerly of Salem, Oregon. A sensation in sport, it featured a long frame and big fuel tanks.

Formula Karts

Formula, or FKE, karts are relatively new to the karting scene and tend to transcend the area between a true kart and a true automobile. FKE karts have bodies, plain and simple, with emphasis on lightweight and streamlining. Without the body, they are Enduro karts, with the same kind of laydown driver position.

Running within the framework of IKF or EKA, these specialized machines were created to give more automotive identity to the sport, an identity attended by some controversy within karting. In essence, Formula karts are an extension downward of the automotive formula series, being miniature versions of road circuit sports and racing cars.

Although aerodynamically more streamlined than the open kart, they are somewhat heavier, by about 30 pounds, and are often slightly slower. Apparently there is very little difference in aerodynamics between the open and closed cars, particularly at the fluctuating speeds of road racing. With such a small amount of horsepower available, the difference in weight seems to be more of a contributing factor. However, for all-out top speed attempts, where tuning and gearing are considerably different, the full-bodied Formula karts would begin to show an advantage. Bonneville racers of very nearly the same size, shape, and weight, but with twice the horsepower, have recorded speeds over 200 mph. Without the streamlined bodies, the same cars were 40 mph slower.

Formula karting is still in its infancy, with few full-bodied cars at any particular event. Whether or not this segment of karting can survive will depend on competition developments in the early 1970's. With bodies the karts are quite attractive, and it is highly possible that given a public showing before crowds more accustomed to sports cars, where the Formula karts can turn lap times and speeds quite competitive with cars costing thirty or forty times as much, KFE's might generate an entirely new outlet for karting. Of course, owners of very expensive race cars don't take kindly to being "put on the trailer" by a lowly kart. To this end, some sports car groups have legislated against karts for hillclimbs, gymkhanas, and road racing. FKE's could change this attitude simply because they *look* like expensive cars.

10

Woman's national champion Kathy Harman shows the very low seating in a modern dual-engine kart.

Fun Karts

At one time these were the bulk of the karting industry, with sales in the multiple thousands. Emphasis was on casual parking lot use, competition being impromptu and disorganized. As most karts were nearly identical in size, and engines were constant for all builders, it was easy for sport organizations to set standards to include all manufacturers. Because karts were simple to construct, there were many factories started, but only those with the best business foundation survived.

Originally, everything produced was really a Fun kart, with competition the special attribute of karts with better tires, aluminum alloy wheels, more powerful engines, etc. That has changed somewhat today, with a Fun kart (called a Yard kart by some) usually a very simple chassis of the Sprint design powered by a 4-stroke engine. This engine is essentially the difference, since it is considered better for use where little or no maintenance is likely. In this respect, the Fun kart harks back to the old washing machine cart days.

Fun karts are the least expensive of the lot, and must be considered as a good starting point for anyone not entirely sure he will like the sport. Terminal speeds are in the 30 mph area, enough to hone driving ability but not fast enough to scare the fledgling driver. Most kart manufacturers list a Fun kart, with either two- or four-stroke power. While the four-stroke may be best for someone not likely to take good care of the engine, the four-stroke will encourage experience with tuning and even the least powerful two-stroke can be modified at home to produce extra horses.

Concession Karts

Concession, or rental, karts are not normally considered a part of the general sport, although there are many thousands of them in use. They are essentially a heavy-duty version of the Fun kart, with emphasis on ruggedness and low-cost maintenance. Such small concession cars have been in existence for years longer than karting, usually included in carnival or spa attractions. When the kart came along, it offered an economical vehicle for the same purpose, with the added advantage of being identified with a popular sport.

Rental karts usually have four-stroke engines, are considerably heavier than ordinary karts, and are made to be bashed around, literally. Top speed is restricted to under 30 mph, but with the low seating the impression of speed is great. While a concession kart is neither fish nor fowl, it does serve to whet the appetite for a true kart, and as such is a service to the sport.

A kart is something very special to a young boy or girl. It gives them invaluable car training and teaches respect for speed. As a bond for family members it is excellent, with dad turning the wrenches and son driving.

The beginning of karting fun begins with a fun kart. This is the HumBug from Bug Engineering which features the simplest accessories, and a four-stroke engine. The basic frame can be made more sophisticated to make a competition machine.

2. Choose Your Kart

"DON'T LOOK for karts under C"! Enthusiasts are emphatic about the difference between a kart and a cart, yet they've seldom been able to convince telephone officials that karts, and kart parts, shouldn't be listed under "C." While most larger cities will have at least one kart shop, or a speed shop with karts and parts, the new enthusiast may need as much basic information on the subject as possible. This information will come faster through karting publications than by word-of-mouth. *Karter News,* the magazine from IKF is a good start. *Street Rodder Magazine* has a section on karts.

For the beginner, trying to choose a kart will include the assimilation of information from the following sources: other owners, magazines, books, and the kart shop. Everyone will have specific views about what is best, leaving the buyer with some tough decisions. The beginner will have an easier time of it if he knows what the kart is to be used for. If it is to be only a learning tool, then it can be a very inexpensive design, and the type engine is not vital. If it may eventually become a race kart, then chassis design and engine mounting is important. If it is for racing only, the prospective buyer should have second thoughts.

A Fun kart has all the inherent agility of a racing kart, but top speeds are drastically limited. For this reason, it is recommended for the youngster who has yet to learn to drive, and for the female driver. The man does not approach a powered vehicle so timidly, but time spent putting around in a Fun kart is invaluable when learning to race. Since the Fun kart is the least expensive, it can serve as an "attrition machine"; if the family is not going to immediately like karting, and few seldom can resist the enjoyment, the test will have been inexpensive. The used kart can then be sold and most of the investment recaptured.

If the kart remains in the family, it is still an attrition device. Someone new to any kind of vehicle is likely to be hard on the equipment during the learning period. Curbs and cement walls have a way of jumping in front of the new driver, while exhuberant driving is likely to overshadow finesse. A Fun kart is likely to see action on every kind of rough surface, and generally will give rides to at least two-thirds of the people in a given neighborhood.

Because a new kart in the family is likely to receive yeoman duty, it is essential that quality be a major factor during purchase. There are a few, very few, manufacturers who sell inexpensive karts or kart kits at extremely low prices. Beware of the super bargain. As a guide, most karts will be very similar in cost, with the usual difference in brakes and engine type. The very cheap kart will include most of the items sold with the better kart, so the price is a direct relationship to workmanship and material quality. Generally, the cheap kart will have inferior wheels and tires, scrub brakes, poor construction, and poor tubing. It seldom survives.

When shopping for a Fun kart, look to the racing kart manufacturers, or those builders who have been in business for a long time. In one case, the manufacturer started out making a competition kart, but dropped that more expensive line and continued only with the Fun kart. Local builders may be capable of producing a good kart, but the proof will be in their competition karts. If they don't make a good racing machine, chances are they don't make a quality Fun kart either. The difference, in cost, between a poor and a good Fun kart will be less than $30, but the difference in vehicle life span is considerable. The quality Fun kart may ultimately become a competition kart.

Most Fun karts are made to the same specifications as competition karts, with the cost differential being in accessories. However, in most cases the Fun kart chassis is made of heavy-duty thick-walled seamless steel tubing, while the competition chassis is of better chromemoly tubing. If there is a possibility the Fun kart might be changed to racing soon, the customer may initially order a premium steel or chromemoly frame for a slight price increase.

The same things hold true with brakes, rear axles, wheels, tires; everything that begins to make up a competition kart. Obviously the new owner will not know exactly what accessory items are required. The only way to find out, if competition is contemplated, is to attend race meetings and take careful note of what is being used.

It is entirely possible to buy a good used kart, either the Fun or the competition type, at considerable savings, but it must be expected the engine will not be as sharp as when it was new. This is particularly true of the Fun kart that has been banged around for several months. Unfortunately,

ABOVE: This is what racing can bring over and above the mere enjoyment. Because there is such a wide spread of classes, and competition success depends on the driver as well as the kart, trophies are spread around. BELOW: Proof that karting is a family affair is Karen Reed of Garden Grove, Calif., who runs a sprint kart in A Open class. Girls are especially fond of this form of competition.

private owners with no background in karting will expect to receive at least three-quarter of the new price. It must be pointed out in this case that the tired engine, when replaced, is worth at least half the kart price alone, not counting the worn tires, brakes, etc. Bargain, in a word, and you get the kart at a fair price.

Before shopping for a used kart, know in advance what new kart prices are, what the individual accessories will cost, and what areas of repair may be involved. If the kart has been crashed, chances are the front or rear axle is bent, and perhaps a wheel or

two. These are easily repaired by any local automotive shop at low cost. Be careful of any broken engine parts, as they must be replaced.

Sometimes, local kart enthusiasts will want to sell a smaller (slower) class kart to advance. This can be a definite advantage to the beginner, especially if the enthusiast will fit a low horsepower engine and in essence create a Fun kart. The rest of the kart will be ready for the track when the time for transition comes. In some cases, a completely used ensemble may be purchased, including helmet, leather jacket, etc. In this case, the

Safety is essential to karting, and because of helmets and jackets driver injury is rare.

price is normally below what a new Fun kart alone would cost and makes it a good bargain.

The decision to buy a competition kart should be tempered with reason. There is absolutely no sense in paying the extra money for a kart that may be raced seldom, if ever. At the same time, it is wise to understand that kart racing can become almost a mania, often with the entire family.

Never start out youngsters or women on a kart that is likely to scare them. This can, and does, happen when the man does not realize that driving reaction is a learned, and not inherited, habit. Until a boy is fifteen or sixteen years old, he is likely to be timid about speed, or any condition where he does not realize absolute control over the vehicle. A good indication of his confidence are bicycle riding habits. If he is pulling "wheelies," broadsliding in dirt, and in general pushing his bike hard, he will have little trouble learning how to handle a really hot kart. Men are already accustomed to velocity situations, and find it simple to master the kart, at least well enough to be competitive while learning.

A high-performance kart will tend

Selecting a kart depends primarily on what kind of racing is immediately available. Specially constructed sprint tracks, usually private ventures, are located throughout the country. Sprint karts are the least expensive of competition types, and offer three chances to win in Moto—Cross heat system.

In some places dirt sprint racing is run as a professional competition for money prizes. Tracks are usually clay, and the action is wild and wooley.

to be quick, to have a high speed, and to stop on a dime. All this is much more pronounced than with a car, requiring a finesse that can only come with practice. At first the new driver will zig-zag because of harsh over-control, and throttle/brake manipulation is likely to be erratic at best. For this reason, it is wise to fit even the competition kart with a smooth low-horsepower engine at first. A high-powered engine is not suitable for learning, since it tends to produce power in a rather narrow rpm band high on the scale. At other rpm's it will be difficult to control, and may not even run. A good used engine for learning is often available for $15 or $20 and is worth the extra money.

When buying a competition kart, it is necessary to decide what kind of racing is to be done. As mentioned earlier, there is a definite difference between Sprint and Enduro karts. As

a guide, it is advisable to start out with the upright Sprint kart. The laydown Enduro kart is more difficult to master for the beginner, as the head is often no more than 18 inches off the surface, sometimes the knees are higher. This gives some unusual sensations at high kart speeds and experience in sprint kart driving helps the transition.

Trying to pick an instant winner in any particular kart design may be difficult. The best start is by watching what the local competition is doing. Generally there will be a particular kart that is doing better than the others, as well as a specific engine, certain tires and wheels, etc. Don't be misled into thinking this combination is the best across country. What usually happens is that some local karting shop dominates competition, or some knowledgable enthusiast is helping owners of simi-

Enduro racing costs more than sprinting, but it is possible to buy some used early enduro karts at low prices and have much fun while learning to drive. Sprinter karts can be run on enduro tracks with the addition of larger gas tanks.

lar equipment. But don't knock the equipment either, since it is getting the job done. Compare what local winning karts are doing relative to the national scene, and this can be done through results listed in IKF's *Karter News*.

Since competition is going to be local, at least for a season or two, select one of the faster karts and try to duplicate the basic machine. Keep in mind that a fast stock class machine using a 120-pound rider is going to be faster than one with a 220-pound driver. Using the heaviest potential driver (usually old dad) as a gauge, select the fastest equipment in that category.

In chassis, there is considerable difference of opinion as to just what is necessary for a winner. While the frames may look alike, they are quite different in the little things that mean handling. One-inch difference in

wheelbase or tread width can make a world of difference in handling. Location of the driver, forward or aft, will drastically effect handling, as will tires and wheels. Using the potential driver as a yardstick, look for duplicates who are successful. Don't be afraid to ask questions, either, since most karters are eager to advise newcomers.

The kart shop will always try to steer the customer onto a winning combination, because new success will tend to sell more karts. Do not argue with an expert until you've become one! No other advice will save so much time and money.

And here enters a basic problem of any competition. By the time a beginner buys a good kart chassis equipped with good accessories and has learned how to drive, other seasoned drivers may be using advanced equipment. He is already obsolete and

If you really want to get way out, the ultimate is FKE classes with Grand Prix type bodies. This is the most expensive form of karting.

he hasn't even run a race. This can and does happen, that's why the minimum competition equipment should be purchased at first. Add as you race and the cost of karting is within any budget.

The type of racing prevalent in any area will determine what kind of kart is purchased, obviously. But most areas are strongest on Sprint racing, with enough Enduro events thrown in to make life interesting. FKE events are still considered as part of Enduro racing and are scheduled accordingly. As a rule, the Sprint kart will be adaptable to most local races.

The Enduro and FKE karts are the most expensive of all, and their price can easily top $1,000. These are the most professional and certainly appear more like a race car than all of the karts. It is a natural evolution for

the Sprinter to go into Enduro racing, in some cases Sprint karts are equipped with large gas tanks and run with the laydown designs. If you become engrossed with karting, which you will if you give it half a chance, you'll find yourself wanting both a Sprinter and an Enduro machine. Futhermore, you'll think about a kart for other family members, so it isn't unusual to see three and four kart families. In some cases, the teenage son gets the ball rolling and then the family follows suit. Even with multiple karts, it is still an inexpensive sport, as compared with skiing, boating, flying, snowmobiles, and the such.

Although the engines are not a prime factor in choosing a kart, they should be considered. The imported rotary valve two-strokes are more expensive than the American engines, but they put out considerably more power and have been designed for karting. Most karts can be adapted to foreign engines if originally equipped with American designs; making the reverse switch may be more difficult.

In review, the Sprinter is upright seating; the Enduro is laydown seating; the FKE uses a body; the Fun kart is a low-performance Sprinter. Classes, or divisions within a general karting style, are determined by both driver and engine. Trying to choose a kart is a very personal matter. What works for your friend may not work for you. It is advisable to drive a specific kart before buying it, if possible. Shop for a kart the way you would for a new car, by comparing what is available. Following is a list of manufacturers, all with literature explaining their product in detail.

Manufacturers

Bird Engineering
Box 427
Omaha, Neb. 68101

Bonanza Industries
1775 South First St.
San Jose, Calif. 95112

Fox Corporation
P. O. Box 797
Janesville, Wisc. 53545

Hartman Engineering
3731 Park Place
Montrose, Calif. 91020

Inglewood Kart Shop
1307 North LaBrea
Inglewood, Calif. 90302

Jan Ho Industries
16131 Gothard
Huntington Beach, Calif. 92647

Kendick Engineering
6737 Sepulveda Blvd.
Van Nuys, Calif. 91401

K & P Engineering
330 S. Irwindale Ave.
Azusa, Calif. 91702

Margay Products
3185 South Kings Highway
St. Louis, Mo. 63139

Michrina Enterprises, Inc.
11865 Levan Road
Livonia, Mich. 48150

P & R Enterprises
P. O. Box 5190
Waco, Texas 76708

Red Devil Engineering
400 West Moore St.
Walla Walla, Wash. 99362

Rupp Manufacturing
P. O. Box 1095
Mansfield, Ohio 44903

Shoemaker Motor Sports
R. D. 2
Ford City, Penna. 16226

Steen's Inc.
Box 2276P
Alhambra, Calif. 91803

3. Classes and Rules

KARTING is an international sport. From its modest California beginnings, it spread from one nation to another until now it even reaches behind the Iron Curtain. Perhaps it would never have become so universally popular had it not enjoyed such a simple, relaxed set of rules and regulations in its formative years.

Karters Don Boberick and Marvin Patchin wrote the original rules. In those early days, karts were to have a wheelbase of 40 to 50 inches with a track minimum two-thirds that of the wheelbase, and engines could be anything from 84 to 270 cc's. Well, today the maximum engine size is still 270 cc's and the wheelbase rules remain much the same. Apparently, Boberick and Patchin were close to the optimum.

Kart racing and kart racers, though, have changed considerably. Karting has become one of *the* prime training grounds for the auto racers of tomorrow. Many famous racers—from Ferrari's Jody Schecter to two-time Grand Prix champion Emerson Fittipaldi—got their start in karts. Now there are two racing federations running a variety of high-speed events across the country and around the world. They are the International Kart Federation and the World Karting Association. Both sanction events, issue competition licenses and instruct officials in organization and safety practices. Also, they both guarantee good clean competition and lots of fun!

So, if you're ready to do more than just read about racing, contact either the International Kart Federation, 416 South Grand, Covina, California 91724 or the World Karting Association, Post Office Box 2548, North Canton, Ohio 44720.

International Kart Federation

ELIGIBILITY

Only members of IKF may drive in events sanctioned by IKF.

LIABILITY/WAIVER: All drivers shall sign a waiver of liability before being allowed to participate at any IKF member track.

The entrant and/or driver, in signing the entry form for any IKF event, elects to use the track at their own risk, and thereby releases and forever discharges the International Kart Federation, Inc., together with their heirs, assigns, officers, representatives, agents, employees and members, from all liability from injury to person, property, employees and/or reputation, that may be received by said entrant and/or driver, and from all claims of said injuries to parties listed above growing out of, or as resulting from the event contemplated under the entry form, or caused by any construction or condition of the course over which the event is held.

MINORS LIABILITY WAIVER: It is mandatory that all minors complete the "Parents Statement of Health for Minor(s)" form and the IKF "Release of Liability and Hold Harmless Agreement" before being allowed to participate on any IKF member track. The liability waiver is related to the competition insurance program and since the program provides nationwide coverage to states with differing legal age requirements, anyone under twenty-one (21) years of age shall be considered a minor.

AGE: A driver's age on or before July 1, shall be considered their karting age during that competition year. The competition year begins the day following the Grandnational event and ends with the following year's Grandnationals. For example, a 15-year-old Junior will be considered a 16-year-old Senior if they are going to be 16 on or before July 1 of the current competition year.

ROOKIE JUNIOR STATUS: A Rookie Junior driver who once enters an IKF sanctioned Championship Sprint in Junior One or Junior Two cannot return to Rookie Junior class. However, this does not apply to the Rookie Junior sprint driver who enters a sanctioned Road Racing event as a Junior class driver (based upon eligibility) since there is not a Rookie Junior Road Racing class under the present rules.

80cc MAC SENIOR STATUS: An 80cc Mac Senior driver competing in 80cc Mac Senior class, at any given event, shall not receive IKF race credit for any other class at that event.

PREGNANT WOMEN: Pregnant women are not allowed to compete. This restriction applies to practice, family days, tests, qualifying and competition.

DRIVING ABILITY: All drivers shall demonstrate their driving ability to the satisfaction of the race officials during a mandatory practice period, before being allowed to compete.

APPEARANCE: All members competing in IKF events shall maintain a clean, neat appearance.

OFFICIAL ENTRY: The kart frame, not the driver, is the official entry in an IKF event and there shall be no substitution of the frame without permission of the Race Director.

The entrant must be present at pre-race technical inspection with all equipment necessary to substantiate legal entry for all classes entered. If a chassis is presented with an engine which is legal in one class entered, but not another, the engine(s) to be used in the additional class(es) should also be available for inspection at pre-race tech.

ENTRY REFUNDS: There shall be no entry fee refunds at sanctioned events after the entrant registers and has successfully completed pre-race tech inspection.

ENTRY BY MAIL: No race credit shall be given a mail-in entrant who does not appear at the track ready to race.

NUMBER OF CLASS ENTRIES: Only one entry per entrant per class shall be allowed in a given IKF-sanctioned event. No entrant regardless of circumstances or conditions, shall be permitted to register a second entry in a given class in which they have been previously registered as an entrant.

RELIEF DRIVERS: The driver of record shall qualify the kart in which they entered and complete at least one lap in competition before a relief driver may assume that entry. Alternate or relief drivers who meet all class requirements shall be officially registered as a relief driver for that class. Sprint relief drivers may register for a class, prior to any given heat race for that class. If a relief driver is used, both or all drivers shall meet minimum post-race weight requirements.

SAFETY

Safety is one of the prime considerations of IKF. Methods of operation, vehicle construction, track facilities and competition practices are under constant review to protect the karter and to raise the safety standards of the sport.

ACCIDENT INSURANCE: Accident insurance is provided for member participants of the International Kart Federation.

Any IKF member who purchases a valid IKF pit pass shall receive spectator bodily injury liability and property damage liability in the amount of $1,000,000.00 (single limit) per accident (less $100.00 deductible) and excess medical coverage in the amount of $3,000.00 blanket accident medical expense (less $25.00 deductible).

ACCIDENTS: Karts involved in an accident may be required to stop for inspection by the officials.

Accidents shall be investigated by the track officials only. No pit personnel are permitted on the track while the race is in progress.

ACCIDENT REPORTS: An IKF accident report must be completed by the Race Director or their representative, any time an injury occurs during the conduct of an event.

Accident report should be submitted to the IKF office with the event recap, or sooner, if possible.

EMERGENCY EQUIPMENT: An emergency vehicle or ambulance, with a stretcher shall be on hand during *every* racing program. If a state-licensed ambulance service is not used, the emergency vehicle shall fully enclose the injured person and provide sufficient room for the person to be stretched outright, in a prone position.

A physician, paramedic or qualified attendant and first aid kit shall be present during all racing events. Each entrant shall have an adequate first aid kit.

FIRE EXTINGUISHER: It is mandatory that each entry in the event have a minimum of one operable 2½-pound dry powder fire extinguisher on the starting grid at the start of each race, in the hot pit area or have same securely attached to the vehicle during the race event. CO_2 (carbon dioxide) type extinguishers are not an acceptable substitute for the dry powder type.

PROTECTIVE BARRIERS: No person, race official or other, shall be permitted on the racing surface at any time during a race. Two haybales should be provided at corners for the protection of corner marshals.

SPRINT GRANDNATIONAL APEX CURBINGS: Apex curbings will be mandatory at all corners at the Sprint Grandnationals and will be subject to the approval of IKF.

PROTECTIVE CLOTHING: Crash helmets of approved design and which are specifically manufactured for racing shall be compulsory for all racing and practice. The outside structure of the helmet shell shall provide full ear protection. Only those helmets meeting the following standards may be used: American Standards Association Z90.1-1971, Safety Helmet Council of America, Snell-70 and any Federal Standard which may take precedence over the existing standards. The wearing of suitable goggles or face shield is compulsory. In addition, all drivers shall be required to wear jackets of heavyweight leather or heavyweight vinyl material, full length pants, and shoes or boots to prevent or minimize abrasions. The Race Officials may modify or supplement this rule to require any additional protective clothing deemed necessary for the drivers. Crash helmets, goggles, face shields, and jackets to be used by the drivers must also be available for the technical committee's inspection.

Nomex, or equivalent material is mandatory for closed body FKE karts and undergarments of nomex or equivalent material are recommended for drivers of all classes.

EAR PLUGS: The use of ear plugs by participants, both drivers and pit crews is *strongly* recommended for drivers of all classes.

MEDICAL INFORMATION: Drivers competing in IKF-sanctioned events shall display their first and last name, blood type and RH factor and any allergic reaction to medication on their helmet, an identification bracelet or dog tag.

LONG HAIR: Drivers with long hair are strongly recommended to tie the hair back and place it under jackets to keep it from being caught in the mechanical components of the kart.

HYDRAZINE FUELS: The use of hydrazine fuel is illegal in all classes.

ENGINES

The basic engine standard for all competition classes is an internal combustion engine of the two-stroke/cycle type unless otherwise stated or specified.

ELIGIBILITY: Eligibility of all engines, except open classes, is based upon approval of the IKF National Board of Directors.

CLASSIFICATION: In all cases a kart shall be classified by total displacement of engine(s) mounted on the kart regardless of whether all engines are connected to the axle sprocket or not.

CALCULATING ENGINE DISPLACEMENT: Use the following equation to compute displacement. Displacement = bore diameter × bore diameter × .7854 × stroke.

EXHAUST SYSTEMS: All exhaust systems shall be equipped with a silencing can meeting the following specifications:

1. No minimum or maximum length (L) or diameter (D) for exhaust silencing can.

2. The expansion chamber must outlet (1) into the rearward half of silencing can (A), that portion farthest from the header pipe.

3. The exhaust gas outlet hole to atmosphere (2) must be in the forward half of the silencing can (B), that portion closest to the header pipe.

4. The exhaust gas outlet hole to atmosphere (2) may be of any number or shape, but may not exceed .7854 square inches (the area of 1″ diameter circle).

5. There may be no physical connection between the expansion chamber outlet (1) and the exhaust gas outlet hole to atmosphere (2).

6. A single cylinder 270cc Open may have two 1″ diameter or smaller outlet holes.

7. Sprint exhaust systems cannot be adjusted while the kart is in motion.

ROOKIE: Engines under 5.04 cu. in. maximum displacement. Modifications or alterations are prohibited with the exception of over-boring for wear up to, but not exceeding 5.04 cubic inches displacement. Engines to have a single cylinder, single carburetor, single ignition, and single reed assembly. Unless otherwise specified, all parts are to be of original manufacture and stock appearing. The following engines have been homologated for this class: Mac MC-49C, MC-49E, 100cc Piston Valve (restricted).

100cc/200cc MAC: Mac engines 6.218 cu. in. maximum displacement. Modifications or alterations are prohibited with the exception of over-boring for wear up to, but not exceeding a maximum bore size of 2.200. Maximum cubic inch displacement is 6.218 cu. in. The engine to have a single cylinder, single carburetor, single ignition, and single reed assembly. Unless otherwise specified, all parts are to be of original manufacture and stock appearing. The following engines have been homologated for this class: Mac MC-91, MC-91A, MC-91B, MC-91B/1, MC-92, MC-91-MC, MC-93.

125cc MAC: Mac engines 7.745 cu. in. maximum displacement. Modifications or alterations are prohibited with the exception of over-boring for wear up to, but not exceeding a maximum of 7.745 cu. in. displacement. The engine to have a single cylinder, single carburetor, single ignition, and single reed assembly. Unless otherwise specified, all parts are to be of original manufacture and stock appearing. The following engines have been homologated for this class: MAC MC-101A/A, MC-101B, MC-101MC.

100cc PISTON VALVE: Engines under 6.183 cu. in. maximum displacement. Engines to have a single cylinder and single stock carburetor. Unless other specified, all parts are to be oF original manufacture and stock appearing. The following engine has been homologated for this class: Yamaha KT-100S.

100cc STOCK ROTARY VALVE: Engines under 6.216 cu. in. maximum displacement. Engines to have a single cylinder and single stock carburetor. Unless otherwise specified, all parts are to be of original manufacture. The following engines have been homologated for this class: BM-SS96. Corsair T-80, Corsair T-80A, Komet K-78 and Komet K-88.

100 cc STOCK REED VALVE: Engines under 6.216 cu. in. maximum displacement. Engines to have a single cylinder and single stock carburator. Unless otherwise specified, all parts are to be of original manufacture. The following engines have been homologated for this class: Komet K-55 GHR and LMR-100.

100cc STOCK APPEARING: Engines under 6.216 cu. in. maximum displacement. Engines to have a single cylinder and single stock carburetor. Internal modifications allowed. External modifications which do not in any way affect a performance gain are allowable. The following engines have been homologated for this class: BM-FC, BM-104, BM-SS, BM-SS96, Corsair T-80,

Corsair T-80A, Komet K-77, Komet K-77TA, Komet K-79, Komet K-79TP, Komet K-88, Komet K-88TP, Parilla TG14, Parilla BA13-A, Parilla BA13-B, Parilla BA13-C, Parilla SS20, Parilla TP22, Saetta V18 (rfight and left), Yamaha KT-100S, Hewland, Manx 100, Parilla SS21, Komet K55GHR, LMR-100.

OPEN CLASSES

100cc MODIFIED REED VALVE: The only permissible engines are Mac MC-7, MC-8, MC-9, MC-10, MC-20, MC-30, MC-40, MC-45, MC-90, MC-91, MC-91A, MC-91B, MC-91B/1, MC-91MC, (cylinder P/N 91039), MC-92, MC-93. Reed valve induction systems only. No water cooling. The following parts must be of original manufacture: Crankshaft, cylinder, cylinder head, ignition system w/flywheel, and sidecover. No restriction as to modification. Maximum stroke length of 1.650. Maximum cubic inch displacement of 6.218 cubic inch.

100cc OPEN: Engines under 6.216 cu. in. displacement with no restrictions to modifications. This class is limited to single engines with single cylinders.

135cc OPEN: Engines under 8.30 cu. in. displacement with no restrictions to modifications. This class is limited to a single engine with a single cylinder.

270cc OPEN: Engine(s) over 8.30 cu. in. and under 16.60 cu. in. displacement with no restrictions to modifications, number of cylinders, or forward speeds.

SUPERCHARGING: All supercharged (forced induction) engines shall be advanced to the next higher displacement class. 270cc class cannot be supercharged.

WATER-COOLED ENGINES: In addition to the specifications for construction and classification of all karts, the following special rules and classifications shall be adhered to by all karts using water-cooled engines.

a. Classification: Legal in all open classes.

b. Construction: (1) No frame members shall be permitted as an integral part of the cooling system. (2) A protective shielding must be provided between the driver and the cooling system so as to preclude the possibility of coolant reaching any portion of the driver's body. (3) All parts of the circulatory system shall be placed in protected areas not normally susceptible to damage in case of an accident, etc.

c. Cooling System: (1) Water only shall be permitted as a cooling agent. (2) A pressure system shall be mandatory for water circulation with a "catch" or "expansion" tank an integral part of such pressure system. (3) All hose and hose fastening devices of the cooling system shall be of the "high pressure" type and of the minimum quality required for aircraft.

TIRES

RACING TIRES: Applicable to all IKF classes. Amateur and Professional maximum overall mounted width of the tire is not to exceed 8″ (measured while the wheel and tire are suspended. Manufacturer's suggested retail not to exceed $35.00 *excluding* F.E.T.) All tires must be readily available through normal marketing channels to the general membership. The Board reserves the right to disallow any tire at any time which they feel does not meet the above requirements. The Board further reserves the right to change these rules.

SPRINT COMPETITION CLASSES

Each National Sprint class listed below, must maintain an average of 2.6 entries per IKF-sanctioned event to remain a national caliber class. Any class which does not maintain said average, will be placed on probation. If the class does not reach the base participation figure a second consecutive year, it will become a local option class.

SPRINT CLASS WEIGHT: All sprint class weights are the minimum combined kart/driver weight before and after the race.

MAXIMUM NUMBER OF CLASSES A DRIVER MAY ENTER AT ANY IKF-SANCTIONED SPRINT EVENT: Three

FOUR-CYCLE STOCK (LOCAL OPTION) 5 H.P. BRIGGS TYPE 130-202, 1501, 130-232, 36-01.

a. Driver age 6-12 years.

b. No minimum combined kart/driver weight, except kart alone shall not weigh less than 85 lbs.

c. Not a Nationals class.

JUNIOR

JUNIOR: To be run at all IKF-sanctioned sprint events.

ELIGIBILITY: All IKF members with the karting age of nine through fifteen.

LOSS OF ELIGIBILITY: All Juniors, move to Amateur class when their karting age becomes 16 if they have 2 years experience, if less than 2 years they may go to Novice for the remainder of the two years.

NUMBER PANEL COLOR: White.

Class	Engine Type	Fuel	Weight	Age
Rookie	80cc Stock Mac	Open	215	9-12
	100cc Stock Piston Valve (Restricted)	Gas-Oil	235	9-12
	100cc Mac 93 (Restricted)	Gas-Oil	235	9-12
Junior I	100cc Stock Mac	Open	265	12-15
	100cc Stock Piston Valve	Gas-Oil	265	12-15

25

Junior II	100cc Stock Mac	Open	265	12-15
	100cc Stock Piston Valve	Gas-Oil	265	12-15
	100cc Stock Reed Valve	Gas-Oil	295	12-15
	100cc Stock Reed Valve	Gas-Oil	295	12-15
	100cc Stock Rotary Valve	Gas-Oil	295	12-15
Junior III	100cc Stock Appearing	Gas-Oil	280	12-15
	125cc Mac	Open	280	12-15

NOVICE

NOVICE: To be run all IKF-sanctioned sprint races except the Grandnationals.

DRIVER ELIGIBILITY: Any driver who after the 1979 Sprint Grandnationals, elects to run novice class, other than those excluded by expert class rules. All new members are encouraged to start in the novice division and then move up as the rules or their experience warrants.

LENGTH OF ELIGIBILITY: Two years maximum from the date of the first IKF-sanctioned race run as a novice.

LOSS OF ELIGIBILITY: A novice immediately moves up to amateur if:

1. He enters any other class at an IKF-sanctioned sprint event.
2. He enters any pro karting event

CLASS AGE: 16 years and up.

NUMBER PANEL COLOR: Black

Class	Engine Type	Fuel	Weight
Light	100cc Stock Mac	Open	280
	100cc Stock Piston Valve	Gas-Oil	280
	100cc Stock Reed Valve	Gas-Oil	310
	100cc Stock Rotary Valve	Gas-Oil	310
Heavy	100cc Stock Mac	Open	320
	100cc Stock Piston Valve	Gas-Oil	320
	100cc Stock Reed Valve	Gas-Oil	350
	100cc Stock Rotary Valve	Gas-Oil	350

AMATEUR

AMATUER: To be run at all IKF-sanctioned sprint races.

DRIVER ELIGIBILITY: All sprint drivers, other than those excluded by expert status, who elect to run amateur class or those who move up from novice class.

LENGTH OF ELIGIBILITY: There is no maximum time a karter may compete as an amateur. He may also compete in expert and professional races.

LOSS OF ELIGIBILITY: An amateur moves up to expert if:

1. He wins two IKF Grandnational class championships combined whether they are sprint, speedway or road race.
2. He places in the top three at a $3,000 plus Pro-Race, sanctioned or non-sanctioned event. (Whether or not he accepts the money.)
3. He wins one expert class at the Sprint Grandnationals.

CLASS AGE: 16 years and up, with the exception of 80cc Mac Amateur which is 13 and older.

NUMBER PANEL COLOR: White

Amateurs *must* run white number panel when competing in expert classes.

Class	Engine Type	Fuel	Weight
Sportsman	80cc Stock Mac	Open	290
	100cc Stock Piston Valve (Restricted)	Gas-Oil	310
	100cc Mac 93 (Restricted)	Gas-Oil	310
100cc Stock Light	100cc Mac	Open	280
	100cc Piston Valve	Gas-Oil	280
100cc Stock Heavy	100cc Mac	Open	330
	100cc Piston Valve	Gas-Oil	330
100cc Super Stock Light	100cc Mac	Open	280
	100cc Piston Valve	Gas-Oil	280
	100cc Stock Reed Valve	Gas-Oil	310
	100cc Stock Rotary Valve	Gas-Oil	310
100cc Super	100cc Mac	Open	320

Stock Heavy	100cc Piston Valve	Gas-Oil	320
	100cc Stock Reed Valve	Gas-Oil	350
	100cc Stock Rotary Valve	Gas-Oil	350

EXPERT

EXPERT: To be run at all IKF-sactioned sprint races.

DRIVER ELIGIBILITY: All drivers whose karting age is 16 and up and have either or:

1. Won 2 or more IKF Grandnational class championships combined, whether they are sprint, speedway, or road race.

2. Placed in top three in a $3,000 or more pro race.

3. Elected to be an expert.

4. An amateur may run expert class and retain his amateur standing but must run with a white number panel.

5. An expert can compete in amateur classes but is not eligible for awards or points if there are no other entrants in his class.

NUMBER PANEL COLOR: Yellow for IKF listed Experts *only*. . .all other competitors are required to use white panels.

Class	Engine Type	Fuel	Weight
I	100cc Stock Mac	Open	300
	100cc Stock Piston Valve	Gas-Oil	300
	100cc Stock Reed Valve	Gas-Oil	330
	100cc Stock Rotary Valve	Gas-Oil	330
II	100cc Stock Appearing	Gas-Oil	290
	100cc Modified Mac	Open	290
	100cc Open	Open	330
	125cc Stock Mac	Open	300
	100cc Stock Mac	Open	265
	100cc Stock Piston Valve	Gas-Oil	265
	100cc Stock Reed Valve	Gas-Oil	265
	100cc Stock Rotary Valve	Gas-Oil	265
III	100cc Open	Open	280
	135cc Open	Open	330
	100cc Open	Gas-Oil	264
IV	200cc Stock Mac	Open	350
	200cc Stock Piston Valve	Gas-Oil	350
	200cc Open	Open	375
	270cc Open	Open	400

SPRINT CHASSIS SPECIFICATIONS

The responsibility of meeting all IKF specifications rests with the driver.

The eligibility of all karts to compete shall be determined by their meeting the requirements, as set forth in this section.

MINIMUM KART WEIGHT: Race ready; Dry: Single Classes—85 lbs. Dual Classes—105 lbs.

WHEELBASE: Maximum 50 inches; minimum 40 inches as measured from the axle wheel centers.

MAXIMUM OVERALL KART LENGTH: 72 inches.

NO OVERALL KART WIDTH

MAXIMUM OVERALL KART HEIGHT: 26 inches.

MINIMUM TREAD WIDTH: 28 inches, measured from the centerline of right tire to the centerline of left tire.

TIRE SIZE: Maximum diameter 19.5 inches, minimum diameter 9 inches. Only pneumatic type tires shall be permitted.

WHEELS: Shall be void of any defects. Maximum number of four wheels.

WHEEL BEARINGS: Ground ball or roller type only. Split-race bearings not allowed.

AXLE NUTS: Front and rear, shall be safety wired or cotter keyed. Snap Rings okay for slippy wheels.

WHEEL WEIGHTS: Clip-on type wheel balancing weights shall not exceed one-fourth ounce each.

FRAME: The main frame shall be void of any type body shell above the wheel centers. Main frame members shall be not less than one inch outside diameter by .083-inch wall thickness, cold roll steel tubing or other material of equal strength.

No projection from the vehicle which constitutes a hazard to other vehicles or drivers will be permitted.

DRIVER'S COMPARTMENT: The driver's compartment shall be equipped with side rails, side panels or similarly effective lateral support. All parts of the driver to be limited to the confines of the width and length of the kart. If driver's feet extend beyond leading edge of front tires, an adequate bumper protection shall be incorporated within the overall maximum length. Driver's feet shall not extend beyond bumper when pedals are fully depressed.

SEAT BELTS: The use of seat belts is prohibited.

SEAT BACK AND FLOOR PAN: No void large enough for any part of the driver's body to inadvertently pass through, shall be permitted.

SEAT STRUTS: The point where the seat strut attaches to the seat should be adequately reinforced or protected to prevent the strut from piercing the seat and causing driver injury on impact.

FUEL SYSTEM PROTECTION: Any fuel tank, which is the highest portion of the kart, shall be protected by a rollbar. The rollbar shall not exceed 26 inches in height and shall be of suitable strength and design to prevent the tank or cap from having contact with the ground, in the event of an upset.

FUEL: Generally, as class allows, no fuel restrictions, except Hydrazine, which is banned as either a base fuel or an additive, regardless of the amount used.

FUEL CAPS: All flip type fuel caps shall be safely fastened during an event.

BALLAST: All weight added to meet minimum kart/driver weight requirements shall be bolted to the kart. Carrying of ballast on the driver's person is prohibited. No weight shall be bolted to the underside of the kart.

SPOILERS/WINGS: No spoilers or wings permitted.

THROTTLE: Karts shall be equipped with foot operated throttle incorporating a return spring which closes the throttle when pedal is released.

BRAKES: All karts shall have pedal operated brakes oeprating in such a manner as to brake both rear wheels equally and adequately. No scrub-type brakes permitted. Dual brakes are recommended for karts entered in the 200/270cc classes. Master cylinders must have the roll pin on the pivot arm safety fastened or cotter keyed to prevent loss.

Dual brakes consist of two individual braking systems on separate brake discs or drums.

CLUTCHES: The use of clutch(es) is not mandatory. The use of a wet-type clutch is permitted only if the unit is sealed to prevent leaks.

STEERING SPECIFICATIONS: The steering shall be direct acting and of suitable design for maximum safety. Steering design shall be such that the pitman arm cannot rotate over center.

The steering shaft shall be solid steel. Minimum diameter 5/8-inch, of equal or greater strength to cold rolled steel.

The steering wheel hub shall be attached to the shaft by a taper and key or serrated surfaces, and shall be secured to the shaft by a nut. The nut shall be either safety wired or cotter keyed to prevent loss. A bolt passing through the steering hub and steering shaft, to hold the hub to the shaft is illegal. It is not permissible to weld the hub to the shaft, or the steering wheel to the hub. Recommended shaft taper: 5 to 10 degrees, with the taper starting at the full 5/8-inch diameter.

The center hole in the steering wheel must be smaller in diameter than the diameter of the solid steering shaft. A washer may be placed between the steering wheel and the center nut and a washer between the steering wheel and the steering shaft to prevent the steering wheel from moving up or down the solid steering shaft in case of hub failure.

All collars and other devices used to retain the steering column in upper and lower guides shall be secured to prevent possible loss of the collar.

All bolts used in the steering system shall be of aircraft standard quality (grade 5 or better) and shall be a 3/16-inch minimum diameter. This does not pertain to king pins or wheel spindles.

All steering assembly bolts and nuts, including spindles and king pins, shall be safety wired or cotter keyed.

All rod ends shall have universal type swivel joints and jam nuts.

The chrome plating of all components of the steering assembly (spindles, steering shaft, tie rod end bearings, steering wheel hub, drag links, and miscellaneous nuts and bolts) is not permitted. Chrome plating of the steering wheel is permitted.

CHAIN GUARD: Karts shall be equipped with a chain, belt or gear guard designed to eliminate the possibility of personal injury. Outboard drive systems shall be allowed only if the chain and sprockets are completely enclosed from front, rear, top, and outside. An exhaust header is not considered a chain guard.

EXPOSED SPROCKETS: An axle sprocket not fitted with a drive chain shall have a device to prevent tooth exposure from any angle or have the unused sprocket encircled with a chain.

CHAIN OILER: The use of any type chain oiler is not permitted.

SPRINT NUMBER PANELS: Maximum width 14″, maximum height 18″, minimum width 9″, minimum height 7″, as measured on surface of panel. Panels made from cloth, leather or other fabrics shall not be acceptable. All edges shall be rolled or folded under or protected with rubber or comparable material edging for maximum protection. All panels shall be attached in a safe manner and shall be subject to rigid technical inspection.

The front number panel shall be mounted forward of the front wheels, within the maximum overall height, width and length specifications as established for sprint karts.

The use of side number panels in sprint events is considered optional. If a side panel is used, it shall be a 7″ high, 9″ long minimum, flat, rectangular panel. The side number panel shall have a 1″ maximum radius rounded corner. Approved Speedway panels may be used.

SELECTIVE GEARBOX: No transmission, gearbox or other device which permits a change of gear or sprocket ratios while the vehicle is in motion is permitted, except in 270cc Open class.

SPEEDWAY COMPETITION CLASSES

Class	Engine Type	Fuel	Weight	Age
Rookie Junior	80cc Mac	Open	215	9-12
	100cc Piston Valve (Restricted)	Gas-Oil	235	9-12
	100cc Mac 93 (Restricted)	Gas-Oil	235	9-12
100cc Junior	100cc Stock Mac	Open	265	12-15
	100cc Stock Piston Valve	Gas-Oil	265	12-15
	100cc Stock Reed Valve	Gas-Oil	295	12-15
	100cc Stock Rotary Valve	Gas-Oil	295	12-15
100cc Stock	100cc Stock Mac	Open	305	16-up
	100cc Stock Piston Valve	Gas-Oil	305	16-up
100cc Super Stock Light	100cc Mac	Open	280	16-up
	100cc Piston Valve	Gas-Oil	280	16-up
	100cc Stock Reed Valve	Gas-Oil	310	16-up
	100cc Stock Rotary Valve	Gas-Oil	310	16-up
100cc Super Stock Heavy	100cc Mac	Open	320	16-up
	100cc Piston Valve	Gas-Oil	320	16-up
	100cc Stock Reed Valve	Gas-Oil	350	16-up
	100cc Stock Rotary Valve	Gas-Oil	350	16-up
100cc Open	100cc Mac	Open	300	16-up
	100cc Piston Valve	Open	300	16-up
	100cc Reed Valve	Open	320	16-up
	100cc Rotary Valve	Open	320	16-up
135cc Open	125cc Mac Stock	Open	310	16-up
	125cc Mac Open	Open	330	16-up
	135cc All Open Motors	Open	350	16-up

(100cc and 135cc Open Classes may be combined on a local option basis for separate credit but combined trophies.)

(Local Option)

200cc Stock	2 x 100cc Stock Piston Valve	Gas-Oil	350	16-up
	2 x 100cc Stock Mac	Open	350	16-up
	2 x 100cc Stock Reed Valve	Gas-Oil	380	16-up
	2 x 100cc Stock Rotary Valve	Gas-Oil	380	16-up

IKF listed experts must run yellow number panels. All others *must* run white number panels.

SPEEDWAY CHASSIS SPECIFICATIONS

All chassis specifications will be the same as the sprint chassis specifications with the following exceptions:

CHAIN OILER: The use of a chain oiler is permitted on dirt tracks only.

SPEEDWAY NUMBER PANELS: Maximum width 14", maximum height 18", minimum width 9", minimum height 7", as measured on surface on panel. The front number panel must be mounted forward of the front wheels. Panels made from cloth, leather or other fabrics shall not be acceptable. All edges shall be rolled or folded under or protected with rubber or comparable material edging for maximum protection. All panels shall be attached in a safe manner and shall be subject to rigid technical inspection.

The use of side number panels in speedway events is considered optional. If a side panel is used, it shall be a 7" high, 9" long minimum, flat rectangular panel. The side number panel shall have a 1" maximum radius rounded corner. Approved speedway panels allowed.

SELECTIVE GEARBOX: No transmission, gearbox or other device which permits a change of gear or sprocket ratios while the vehicle is in motion is permitted.

ROAD RACING COMPETITION CLASSES

Each National Road Racing class listed below, must maintain an average of 6.36 entries per IKF-sanctioned event, to remain a national caliber class. Any class which does not maintain said average will be placed on probation. If the class does not reach the base participation figure a second consecutive year, it will become a local option class.

1. 100cc STOCK JUNIOR
   a. Approved Mac and 100cc Yamaha Piston Valve
   b. Driver age 12-15 years.
   c. Combined kart/driver weight before and after race, 290 lbs. minimum.
   d. Gas and Oil Only (Yamaha)

2. 100cc SUPER STOCK JUNIOR
   a. 100cc Approved Stock Rotary Valve and 100cc Approved Reed Valve.
   b. Driver age 12-15 years.
   c. Combined kart/driver weight before and after race, 290 lbs. minimum.
   d. Gas and Oil Only (Yamaha)
   e. Any legal Junior I will be allowed to run this class.

3. 100cc MODIFIED—REED VALVE
   a. Approved Reed Valve engines only.
   b. Driver age 16 years and up.
   c. Combined kart-driver weight before and after race, 325 lbs. minimum.
   d. No restrictions as to modifications.
   e. No water cooling.

4. 100cc MAC—LIGHTWEIGHT
   a. Approved Mac engines only.
   b. Driver age 16 years and up.
   c. Combined kart/driver weight before and after race, 280 lbs. minimum.

5. 100cc MAC—HEAVYWEIGHT
   a. Approved Mac engines only.
   b. Driver age 16 years and up.
   c. Combined kart/driver weight before and after race, 330 lbs. minimum.

6. 100cc STOCK
   a. 100cc Approved Stock Reed Valve & 100cc Stock Rotary Valve Engine
   b. Driver age 16 and up.
   c. Combined kart/driver weight before and after race, 330 lbs. minimum.
   d. May not be run by anyone who has won more than one Grandnational championship, (sprint, speedway, or road race).
   e. To be run with 100cc Modified Reed Valve for separate points and trophies.

7. 100cc PISTON VALVE AMATEUR
   a. Approved piston valve engines only.
   b. Driver age 16 years and up.
   c. Road Racing weight: 330 lbs. combined kart and driver weight.
   d. Gas and Oil only.
   e. No IKF or WKA National champion or listed Expert may compete in this class.

7A. 100cc Piston VALVE EXPERT
   a. Approved piston valve engines only.
   b. Driver age 16 years and up.
   c. Road Racing weight: 330 lbs. combined kart and driver weight.
   d. Gas and Oil only.

8. 100cc STOCK APPEARING—LIGHTWEIGHT
   a. Driver age 16 years and up.
   b. Combined kart/driver weight before and

after race, 300 lbs. minimum.
   c. Gas and Oil only.

9. 100cc STOCK APPEARING—HEAVYWEIGHT
   a. Driver age 16 years and up.
   b. Combined kart/driver weight before and after race, 350 lbs. minimum.
   c. Gas and Oil only.

10. 100cc OPEN — LIGHTWEIGHT
   a. Driver age 16 years and up.
   b. Combined kart/driver weight before and after race, 300 lbs. minimum.
   c. No restrictions as to modifications.

11. 100cc OPEN — HEAVYWEIGHT/FKE I
   a. Driver age 16 years and up.
   b. Combined kart/driver weight before and after race, 350 lbs. minimum.
   c. No restrictions as to modifications.

12. 135cc OPEN/FKE II
   a. Driver age 16 years and up.
   b. Combined kart/driver weight before and after race, 340 lbs. minimum.
   c. No restrictions as to modifications.

13. 125cc MAC
   a. Approved Mac engines only.
   b. Driver age 16 years and up.
   c. Combined kart/driver weight before and after race. 325 lbs. minimum

14. 200cc STOCK
   a. Approved Mac engines and Yamaha 100cc piston valve engines.
   b. Driver age 16 years and up.
   c. Combined kart/driver weight before and after race, 350 lbs. minimum. Yamaha 375 Gas/Oil only.

15. 270cc OPEN
   a. Driver age 18 years and up.
   b. Combined kart/driver weight before and after race, over 200cc 375 lbs. minimum, under 200cc 350 lbs. minimum.
   c. No restrictions as to modifications, number of cylinders, or forward speeds.
   d. Body work is permitted. If body covers driver as set forth in the FKE section of the Rule Book. FKE safety and chassis regulations will be enforced.
   e. Supercharging is not permitted.
   f. No maximum length.

Wings and spoilers shall be allowed with no overall length restriction. The 26-inch overall height requirement will be enforced. Front wings/spoilers shall not extend above the top of the front tires or past the rear of the front tire, nor cover the driver's feet. They shall not interfere with the front or rear tires at any time or in any position. Overall height shall not exceed 26 inches. (Only applies to Class 15.)

ROAD RACING CHASSIS SPECIFICATIONS

The responsibility of meeting all IKF specifications rests with the driver.

The eligibility of all karts to compete will be determined by their meeting the requirements as set forth in this section.

For information pertaining to FKE equipment, refer to section Formula Kart Experimental.

MINIMUM KART WEIGHT: Race Ready; dry: Single Classes—95 lbs.; Dual Classes—115lbs.

WHEELBASE: Maximum 50 inches; minimum 40 inches as measured from the axle centers.

MAXIMUM OVERALL KART LENGTH: 80 inches.

MAXIMUM OVERALL KART WIDTH: No limit.

MAXIMUM OVERALL KART HEIGHT: 26 inches.

MINIMUM TREAD WIDTH: 30 inches, measured from the centerline of right tire to the centerline of left tire.

MAXIMUM NUMBER OF WHEELS: Four, void of any defects.

All chassis specifications will be the same as the sprint chassis specifications with the following exceptions:

ROAD RACING BUMPERS: All Road Racing karts shall be equipped with front protection in the form of a bumper, to provide foot and ankle protection for the driver.

FUEL AND LUBRICATION SYSTEM PROTECTION: Any fuel or chain oiler tank, which is the highest portion of the kart, shall be protected by a rollbar. The rollbar shall not exceed 26 inches in height and shall be of suitable strength and design to prevent the tank or cap from having contact with the ground in the event of an upset.

WINGS/SPOILERS: Devices termed "wings" or "spoilers" when mounted on a kart shall not cause the overall length or height of the kart to exceed 80 inches, and 26 inches respectively. Front wing/spoilers shall not extend above the top of the front tires or past the rear of the front tire, nor cover the driver's feet. They shall not interfere with the front or rear tires at any time or in any position.

They shall be mounted securely to the kart in a safe manner. Movable or adjustable surfaces which may be moved or adjusted while the kart is in motion are not permitted.

WING AND SPOILER CONSTRUCTION: All wings/spoilers shall be constructed of metal or plastic materials only, and shall be void of any sharp edges.

REAR FENDERS: It is permissable to add fenders which cover the rear tires of a road racing kart. The fenders may not project from the kart causing a hazard to fellow competitors.

CLUTCHES: The use of clutch(es) is mandatory in all classes. The use of a wet-type clutch is permitted only if the unit is sealed to prevent leaks.

SELECTIVE GEARBOX: No transmission, gearbox or other device which permits a change of gear or sprocket ratios while the vehicle is in motion is permitted, except where specified.

CHAIN OILER: Chain oil reservoir capacity shall not exceed eight ounces (1/2 pint) for single engine machines and 16 ounces (one pint) for dual engine machines.

ROAD RACING NUMBER PANELS: A 10" diameter round or 7" x 9" minimum/8" x 10" maximum rectangular panel may be used in front, as long as the panel is flat and does not exceed 80 square inches. The front number panel shall be mounted forward of the front wheels, within the maximum overall height, width and length specifications. The panel may be leaned rearward to not more than a 45 degree sloped position. Any additional front number panels, not mounted forward of the front wheels shall constitute illegal body work.

A flat 7" high, 9" long rectangular number panel shall be used on the side. If the side tank of a kart has this minimum area and is flat or has a relatively flat surface that will not distort the paper numbers, then the tank may be substituted. If the side tank is round or is so shaped that the number is not legible, the required number panel shall be attached. The side number panel will have 1" maximum radius rounded corner.

FORMULA KART EXPERIMENTAL

FKE I—(Class name: 100cc Open Heavy/FKE I) Those vehicles having a maximum engine displacement under 100cc's or 6.216 cubic inches. Minimum combined vechicle and driver weight before and after event shall be 350 lbs.

FKE II—(Class name: 135cc Open/FKE II) Those vehicles having a maximum engine displacement under 135cc's or 8.30 cubic inches. Minimum combined vehicle and driver weight before and after event shall be 340 lbs.

SPECIFICATIONS: All construction practices and specifications which appear under Road Racing Chassis Specifications, shall be applicable to FKE machines, with exception of the following items. These, as listed, are peculiar to all FKE classes and vary from the like item shown under Road Racing Chassis Specifications.

MAXIMUM OVERALL VEHICLE LENGTH: No limit.

MAXIMUM OVERALL VEHICLE HEIGHT: No limit.

MAXIMUM OVERALL VEHICLE WIDTH: No limit.

WHEELBASE: Maximum 55 inches, minimum 40 inches as measured from the axle centers.

TREAD WIDTH: Minimum of 30" tire center to tire center.

BODY: A body which surrounds the driver and covers the driver from the knees forward, or shell which is sat upon and no part of the driver's body is covered or enclosed, shall be required in the FKE classes. It may be of the open or covered wheel type. Only metal or fiberglass materials shall be accepted for the body or shell construction. Enclosed or covered driver compartments shall not be allowed. The body or shell shall extend from the front of the vehicle to at least the seat hoop or rear rollbar. It need not cover the engine compartment. Any floor or belly pan utilized in the engine compartment shall be adequately vented and equipped with drain holes.

FKE BUMPERS: A body shell, covering the driver's feet shall constitute a bumper for FKE karts.

FIXED WINGS/SPOILERS: If a spoiler is used, it shall be an integral part of the body, and shall not extend above the rollbar, or beyond the maximum legal overall width.

NUMBERS: Each entrant in the FKE class shall be assigned identifying numbers which will be displayed at all times during the event in three locations on the vehicle; one on right side, one on the left side and one showing forward, all clearly visible for scoring purposes.

DRIVER'S COMPARTMENT: All FKE classes shall have a full belly pan with no openings large enough for any part of the driver's body to inadvertently pass through. Enclosed bodies shall have an operating kill switch to be located in the driver's compartment. Vehicles shall be so constructed as to permit easy entrance and exit for the driver, in assuming the driving position, without the removal or moving of any part of the vehicle.

FIREWALLS: Required to separate engine compartment from driver's compartment.

ROLLBARS: On closed-bodied karts a one (1) inch minimum diameter, 0.083 wall thickness steel rollbar shall be placed directly behind the driver and welded to the main frame rails and be adequately braced forward or rearward. It shall extend at least one inch above the driver's helmet when in a driving position. The steering hoop is also considered a rollbar and shall be a minimum of 3/4 inch diameter steel and of suitable wall thickness. The driver's legs shall pass under the steering hoop in closed body vehicles.

SEAT BELTS: Aircraft quality seat belts are mandatory in closed body vehicles. Seat belts shall be securely anchored to main frame rails. Shoulder harnesses are recommended. Seat belts are not permitted in shell body FKE karts where the driver is not enclosed.

STEERING WHEEL: Full circle not mandatory. Shall have a minimum grip length of 11 inches. Wheel must turn lock to lock with driver in place.

TRANSMISSIONS: Permissible.

BRAKES: Shall be pedal operated. FKE I and FKE II vehicles shall have a minimum of one brake system operating in such a manner as to brake both rear wheels equally and adequately. Two system, 4-wheel brakes, operating from one brake pedal, are recommended in all FKE classes. No scrub brakes permitted in any division.

THROTTLE: Vehicles to be equipped with foot or hand operated throttle having a return spring which shall close the throttle when released.

FUEL: No restrictions.

FUEL SYSTEMS: No limit to fuel capacity. Fuel tank caps shall be exposed and accessible on the outside of the vehicle. The body section under the tanks shall be vented in such a manner as to permit fuel from a ruptured or leaky tank to drain outside of body. All fuel lines shall be adequately safety wired or secured with hose clamps. No pressurized fuel tanks permitted.

EXHAUST SYSTEMS: Shall be carried rearward and to the outside of any body panels.

BATTERIES: Wet cell batteries shall be located outside the driver's compartment.

FIRE EXTINGUISHERS: Each entry shall have a minimum of an operable 1-1/2 pound dry powder fire extinguisher at the start of each event on the starting grid or have same securely attached to the vehicle during race event.

CLOTHING: The wearing of fire protective garments shall be mandatory for the driver of an FKE I or II machine when the driver sits within and is enclosed by the body of the machine. The driver shall wear an outer suit/garment made of Nomex (or similar material).

Leather or heavy vinyl jackets and full length pants shall be required in open-bodied FKEs.

Shoes or boots shall be worn by drivers of either closed or open bodied FKEs.

WORLD KARTING ASSOCIATION:

COMPETITION RULES AND REGULATIONS

A driver's actual age as of January 1st, will establish his karting age during that calendar year. One exception: If a driver turns 16 during his racing year and wishes to move to a senior class he may do so by a written request to the W.K.A. office. The driver will lose all of his points that he accumulated in any junior class that he participat-ed in during that year. Once a driver has moved up a class he may not return to a junior class. If the Enduro Grand National is at the end of the season, a junior driver may finish his junior racing year and if eligible, he may also begin his senior year if the race is the first point race of the following year.

To determine Competition Age:

2 Cycle Sprint	4 Cycle Sprint	Enduro	Age
Junior Sportsman	Rookie Box Stock		8-12
Reed Junior	Jr. Box Stock	Reed Junior	12-15
Yamaha Junior			12-15
Stock Junior	Junior Modified	Stock Junior	13-15
Reed Lt. & Hvy.	Modified Lt & Hvy.	Reed Lt & Hvy.	16 min.

125cc Reed	Stock Appearing		125cc Reed	16 min.
100cc Cont. Lt & Hvy.	Box Stock Lt & Hvy.		100cc Cont.	16 min.
Yamaha Senior	Open		Yamaha Senior	16 min.
Senior Sportsman-14	Sportsman		Stock Lt & Hvy.	16 min.
Unlimited			Open Lt & Hvy.	16 min.
			Open Reed	16 min.
			B Limited	18 min.
			B Stock	18 min.
			B & C Open	18 min.
			Super Kart	18 min.

Each racing division, 2 Cycle Sprint, 4 Cycle Sprint, and Enduro will be independent of each other as to competition age requirements. All other rules and regulations will remain in force.

PROTECTION CLOTHING

Full coverage crash helmets of approved design and which are specifically manufactured for racing use are compulsory wear for all racing and practicing. The outside structure of the helmet shell must provide full ear protection. (It is recommended that only those helmets meeting the following standards be used. American Standards Association Z90, 1-1966 Testing Standards, Snell—68, S.H.C.A. (Safety Helmet Council of America), Snell—70 Approved). The wearing of suitable goggles or visors is compulsory. In addition all drivers shall be required to wear jackets of heavy weight leather or vinyl material and full length pants, to prevent or minimize abrasions. The Race Officials may modify or supplement this rule to require any additional protective clothing deemed necessary to the safety of the drivers. Full coverage crash helmets, goggles, visors and jackets to be used by the drivers must also be available for the technical committee's inspection. Any mirror like finished or plated safety headgear, regardless if the headgear meets the standards as stated above, will not be permitted.

KARTS

Each entrant kart shall be assigned an identifying number which will be carried at all times during the event either on the helmet or kart, depending on local regulations, in a clearly legible color that is highly contrasting to the vehicle's or helmet's paint work.

The eligibility of all karts to compete will be determined by their meeting the minimum requirements below:

a. WHEELBASE: Maximum 50 inches, minimum 40 inches as measured from the axle centers.

b. MINIMUM TREAD WIDTH: 28 inches for Sprints, 30 inches for Enduros as measured from the top of the centerline of left tire on each axle.

c. OVERALL MAXIMUM WIDTH: 46 inches Sprint, 50 inches Enduro

d. OVERALL MAXIMUM LENGTH: 72 inches Sprint, 80 inches Enduro

e. HEIGHT: Maximum of 26 inches.

f. TIRE SIZE: Maximum diameter 19.5 inches, minimum diameter 9 inches, pneumatic type only. Or as specified in class specification.

g. WHEELS: To incorporate bearings of ground ball or roller type only. Split race bearing not allowed. All axle nuts (front and rear) must be safety wired, cottered, or snap rings. Maximum rim width in all classes 8 inches. Wheels must be devoid of any defects.

h. FRAME: All metal devoid of any type body shell above the wheel centers. Main frame members minimum strength shall be no less than one inch outside diameter by .083 wall thickness cold roll electric welded steel tubing or other material of at least equal strength.

i. SEAT BACK AND FLOOR PAN: No void large enough to permit any part of the driver's body to pass through will be allowed. Front Porch maximum length 24″ from wheel center.

j. STEERING: Direct and of a suitable design for maximum safety. All steering assembly bolts and nuts, including spindle bolts, must be cottered and/or safety wired. All bolts must be a minimum of 3/16 inch diameter aircraft bolts with a shear strength of no less than 1400 pounds. All rod ends must have universal type swivel joints. Jam nuts recommended on tie rod ends. Steering assembly cannot pass beyond center, even when reasonable force is exerted.

k. STEERING SPECIFICATIONS: MINIMUM SHAFT DIAMETER 5/8 inch. Shaft material steel only, cold rolled steel. Wheel attachment must be secured with Aircraft quality nut or cap screw in an axial position with center line of the shaft. Welding the steering wheel to the hub, or the hub to the upper shaft is prohibited.

BRAKES: All karts must have brakes working in such a manner as to brake both rear wheels equally and adequately. Caliper and Master Cylinder mounting bolts must be safety wired or keyed.

FUEL AND LUBRICATION SYSTEM: Any fuel tank or chain oiler portion thereof which is the highest portion of any kart must be protected by a rollbar not to exceed 26 inches in height and of suitable strength and design to prevent the tank or cap from having contact with the ground in the event of an upset. No pressurized fuel tanks permitted. Any member using any fuel other than gas & oil in the gas & oil only classes any nitro in the fuel of the 4 cycle classes will be given a 6 month suspension.

MINIMUM KART WEIGHT: Dry weight, fully equipped including engines. Single Class: 85 lbs., Dual Class; 105 lbs.

ALL WEIGHT: All weights added to meet minimum Kart / Driver weight requirements must be properly secured to the kart. CARRYING OF WEIGHTS ON THE DRIVER'S PERSON PROHIBITED. Clip-on wheel balancing weights are not to exceed ¼ oz. each. Additional security is required when using stick on weights.

THROTTLE: Karts to be equipped with throttle having a self returning spring which will close throttle when released.

CHAIN GUARD: All chain, belt or gear driven karts must be equipped with a chain belt or gear guard designed to eliminate the possibility of personal injury. Outboard drive systems will be allowed only if the chain and sprockets are completely enclosed from front, rear, top and outside.

EXPOSED SPROCKETS: Karts starting a race or practice which is equipped with an axle sprocket not fitted with a drive chain must provide a device to prevent teeth exposure from any angle, or encircle the unused sprocket with a chain.

SELECTIVE GEARBOX. No transmission, gearbox or other device which permits a change of gear or sprocket ratios while the vehicle is in motion is permitted with the exception of the Enduro "Super Kart" class.

DRIVER'S COMPARTMENT. The driver's compartment shall be equipped with side rails, side plates or such other similarly effective form of lateral support for the driver.

SEAT BELTS: The use of seat belts is PROHIBITED.

MUFFLERS: All kart engines must be equipped with quiet mufflers. They may be the type being manufactured and distributed by various suppliers that certify them not to exceed 85 decibels or any style chamber muffler may be used, provided it does not exceed 85 decibels.

No sideways projection is allowable beyond the outer edge of the tire or shell. Muffler tips in front of rear axle must be below axle center as well as inboard of outside of rear tire or wheel.

All exhaust system requirements in general must have a blunt end closed or rolled surface end. Any projection over ¼ inch in length must have a minimum 2 inch O.D. blunt surface.

No Kart shall be passed at tech inspection unless it meets the minimum specifications as set forth in this rule. This applies to both Sprint and Enduro Karts.

SPRINT AND ENDURO KARTS: All parts of the driver to be limited to the confines of the width and length of the kart. If driver's feet extend past leading edge of front tires, and adequate bumper protection must be incorporated within the overall maximum length. Feet not to extend beyond said bumper when pedals are in fully depressed position. Roller type bumpers are illegal. Grease or lubricants are not allowed on tires or kart.

CHAIN OILER: Enduro machines only. Chain oiler not legal for Sprint classes. Physical size of chain oil reservoir shall be such that actual capacity of reservoir does not exceed eight ounces (½ pint) for single engine machines. Maximum capacity for twin (dual) engine machines shall not exceed sixteen ounces (1 Pint)

CLUTCHES: The use of clutch(es) is mandatory in all three divisions, Sprint, Enduro & 4 Cycle.

CHAIN LUBES: The Sprint chain lube must be liquid. Grease is NOT allowed.

ENGINES

All engines specifications and legal modifications are in the North American Tech Manual, which is available through W.K.A. Below are some general rules.

SUPERCHARGED ENGINES: All supercharged (forced induction) engines shall be advanced to the next higher displacement class. C Open class cannot be supercharged.

EXHAUST SYSTEM: Exhaust system must be such that exhaust gases are carried away from and rearward of the driver.

FUEL: No restrictions except hydrazine will be prohibited, or as otherwise stated in a class specification. All fuel or anything else entering engine other than atmospheric air must pass through the inlet needle and seat of the carburetor(s). No Modifications to carburetors permitted in Stock Appearing and 100cc Classes, or as specified in the Tech Manual.

WATER-COOLED ENGINES: Water-cooled engines are illegal in all classes.

RESLEEVED BLOCK ILLEGAL in American Reed Classes.

FUEL PUMPS: Are not legal in Stock Appearing, American Reed and 100cc Controlled classes unless pump is integral part of engine.

NUMBER PANELS

NUMBER PANELS ARE MANDATORY IN ALL W.K.A. EVENTS

Sprint: Maximum width 14 inches, height 18 inches, as measured on surface of panel. Minimum width 9 inches, height 7 inches as measured on surface of panel. Panels made from cloth, leather or other fabrics are NOT acceptable. All edges must be rolled or folded under or protected with rubber or comparable material edging for maximum protection. It is recommended that a plastic material be used. It is mandatory to have one front number panel and suggested to place one on the side and one in the rear.

Enduro: Only one front number panel is legal and should be mounted either in front of either wheel or in the center of the front bumper. The panel may be leaned rearward from 90 degree upright position to not more than a 45 degree sloped position. It is mandatory to have one front number one side number panel. If the tank of the kart is flattened and meets the standards it may be used as a substitute. The size and material specification are the same as the sprint.

COMPETITION CLASSES— TWO CYCLE SPRINT

Class	Age	Weight
Junior Sportsman	8 thru 12 years	215 lbs.
Reed Junior	12 thru 15 years.	255 lbs.
Yamaha Junior	12 thru 15 years	265 lbs.
Stock Junior	13 thru 15 years	265 lbs. (100cc Cont.) 285 lbs. (Stk. Appr.)
Senior Sportsman	14 years & Up	315 lbs.
Reed Light	16 years & Up	275 lbs.
Reed Heavy	16 years & Up	335 lbs.
Yamaha Senior	16 years & Up	300 lbs.
100cc Controlled Light	16 years & Up	285 lbs. (Yamaha) 310 lbs. (100cc Cont.)
100cc Controlled Heavy	16 years & Up	325 lbs. (Yamaha) 350 lbs. (100cc Cont.)
125cc Reed	16 years & Up	315 lbs.
Unlimited	16 years & Up	270 lbs. (100cc Mac Open) 300 lbs. (100cc For. Open) 300 lbs. (125cc Mac Open) 335 lbs. (135cc For. Open)

JUNIOR SPORTSMAN
1. Approved American Reed engines only.
2. Age 8 thru 12 years old.
3. Minimum combined kart/driver weight 215 lbs. before and after race.
4. Claiming allowed.

REED JUNIOR
1. Approved American Reed engines only.
2. Age 12 thru 15 years old.
3. Minimum combined kart/driver weight 255 lbs. before and after race.
4. Claiming allowed.

YAMAHA JUNIOR
1. Approve Stock Yamaha engines only.
2. Any Clutch and stock pipe.
3. Minimum combined kart/driver weight 265 lbs. before and after race.
4. Age 12 thru 15 years old.
5. Claiming allowed.

STOCK JUNIOR
1. 100cc Stock Appearing engine, Approved Yamaha engines and 125cc Box Stock American Reed engines.
2. Age 13 thru 15 years old.
3. Minimum combined kart/driver weight: 100cc Controlled engines 265 lbs., Stock Appearing engines 285 lbs., before and after race.
4. Claiming allowed.

SENIOR SPORTSMAN
1. Approved McCulloch engines only.
2. Tire Maximum: Front: 350x5, Rear: 11x600x5. American made tires that are in production as of August, 1979.
3. Minimum combined kart/driver weight 315 lbs. before and after race.
4. Age 14 years old and up.

5. You are not eligible if you have placed in the top five at a National/Olympic event or National Point Standings.

REED LIGHT
1. Approved American Reed engines only.
2. Age 16 years old and up.
3. Minimum combined kart/driver weight 275 lbs. before and after race.
4. Claiming allowed.

REED HEAVY
1. Approved American Reed engines only.
2. Age 16 years old and up.
3. Minimum combined kart/driver weight 335 lbs, before and after race.
4. Claiming allowed.

YAMAHA SENIOR
1. Approved Stock Yamaha engines with Stock Pipe.
2. Age 16 years old and up.
3. Minimum combined kart/driver weight 300 lbs., before and after race.
4. Claiming allowed.

100cc CONTROLLED LIGHT
1. Approved 100cc Controlled engines and Approved Yamaha engines with open pipe.
2. Age 16 years old and up.
3. Minimum combined kart/driver weight 285 lbs. for Yamaha engines and 310 lbs. for 100cc Controlled engines.
4. Claiming allowed.

100cc CONTROLLED HEAVY
1. Approved 100cc Controlled engines and Approved Yamaha engines with open pipe.
2. Age 16 years old and up.
3. Minimum combined kart/driver weight 325 lbs. for Yamaha engines and 350 lbs. for 100cc

Controlled engines.

4. Claiming allowed.

125cc REED

1. Approved American Reed engines over 6.1 cubic inches & under 8.2 cubic inches.

2. Age 16 years old and up.

3. Minimum combined kart/driver weight 315 lbs.

4. Claiming allowed.

UNLIMITED

1. Any Single Class engine.

2. Age 16 years old and up.

3. No restriction on price or modification.

4. Minimum combined kart/driver weight as follows:

    270 lbs.—100cc Open McCulloch
    300 lbs.—100cc Foreign Open
    300 lbs.—125cc Open McCulloch
    335 lbs.—135cc Open Foreign

All of the above two cycle classes will be run as a W.K.A. National Point class. There may be other classes on a local option classification. They will not be Point classes.

COMPETITION CLASSES— FOUR CYCLE SPRINT

Class	Age	Weight
Rookie Box Stock	8 thru 12 years	225 lbs.
Box Stock Junior	12 thru 15 years	265 lbs.
Junior Modified	12 thru 15 years	265 lbs.
Box Stock Lite	16 years & Up	280 lbs.
Box Stock Heavy	16 years & Up	350 lbs.
Modified Lite	16 years & Up	280 lbs.
Modified Heavy	16 years & Up	350 lbs.
Sportsman	16 Years & Up	325 lbs.
Stock Appearing	16 years & Up	325 lbs.
Open	16 years & Up	325 lbs.

ROOKIE BOX STOCK

1. Briggs and Stratton 5 HP stock engines as purchased by the manufacturer.

2. Minimum age 8 thru 12 years old.

3. Minimum combined kart/driver weight 225 lbs. before and after race.

BOX STOCK JUNIOR

1. Briggs and Stratton 5 HP stock engines, as purchased by the manufacturer.

2. Minimum age 12 thru 15 years old.

3. Minimum combined kart/driver weight 265 lbs. before and after the race.

JUNIOR MODIFIED

1. Any 5 HP engine.

2. Minimum age 12 thru 15 years old.

3. Minimum combined kart/driver weight 265 lbs., before and after race.

BOX STOCK LITE

1. Briggs and Stratton 5 HP stock engines as purchased by the manufacturer.

2. Minimu age 16 years old.

3. Minimum combined kart/driver weight 280 lbs. before and after race.

BOX STOCK HEAVY

1. Briggs and STratton 5 HP stock engines as

purchased by the manufacturer.

2. Minimum age 16 years old.

3. Minimum combined kart/driver weight 350 lbs. before and after race.

MODIFIED LITE

1. Any 5 HP engine.

2. Minimum age 16 years old.

3. Minimum combined kart/driver weight 280 lbs., before and after race.

4. Carburetor $70.00 maximum suggested list price. This excludes intake manifold.

MODIFIED HEAVY

1. Any 5 HP engine

2. Minimum age 16 years old.

3. Minimum combined kart/driver weight 350 lbs., before and after race.

4. Carburetor $70.00 maximum suggested list price. This excludes intake manifold.

SPORTSMAN

1. Briggs and Stratton 5 HP stock engine with Walbro LME series, 25, 34, or 37.

2. Minimum age 16 years old.

3. Minimum combined kart/driver weight 325 lbs., before and after race.

STOCK APPEARING

1. Briggs and Stratton 5 HP stock engine.

2. Minimum combined kart/driver weight 325 lbs. before and after race.

3. Minimum age 16 years old.

OPEN

1. Any 5 HP engine

2. Minimum age 16 years old.

3. Minimum combined kart/driver weight 325 lbs., before and after race.

All other rules and requirements, except as listed under 4 cycle classes, and the following will be the same as stated in our Competition Rules and Regulations.

Box Stock Light and Box Stock Heavy classes may be combined at local option with minimum combined kart/driver weight before and after race at 325 lbs. This will not be a point class.

Clutches are mandatory and limited to a centrifugal automatic dry type.

Exhaust extensions if used must extend rearward past the carburetor to a minimum of one inch. If the extension is exposed, it must have a two inch O.D. washer welded on the exposed end and *not to exceed 85 decibels.*

All 4 Cycle engines specification and modifications, please refer to the current North American Technical Manual, available through W.K.A.

ENDURO CLASSES AND ENDURO LICENSES

An application for a W.K.A. Enduro driver's license must be filled out. A new driver must wear an X on the rear of his helmet for his first two (2) races.

REED JUNIOR

1. Approved American Reed engines and ap-

proved Yamaha engines only.

2. Age 12 thru 15 years old.

3. Minimum combined kart/driver weight before and after race 275 lbs. for American Reed engine & 295 for Yamaha engine.

4. Claiming Allowed.

STOCK JUNIOR

1. Any Approved Stock Appearing engine and 125cc American Reed engine.

2. Age 13 thru 15 years old.

3. Minimum combined kart/driver weight before and after race 295 for Rotary valve, 275 lbs. for American Reed valve of 6.1 cubic inch, and 305 lbs for 125 cc American Reed valve.

4. Claiming Allowed.

REED LIGHT

1. Approved American Reed engine.

2. Driver's age 16 years old and up.

3. Minimum combined kart/driver weight before and after race 290 lbs.

4. Claiming Allowed.

REED HEAVY

1. Approved American Reed engine.

2. Driver's age 16 years old and up.

3. Minimum combined kart/driver weight before and after race 340 lbs.

4. Claiming Allowed.

STOCK LIGHT

1. Approved Stock Appearing engine only.

2. Driver's age 16 years old and up.

3. Minimum combined kart/driver weight before and after race 300 lbs. for Rotary valve & 270 lbs. American Reed Valve.

4. Claiming Allowed.

STOCK HEAVY

1. Approved Stock Appearing engines only.

2. Driver's age 16 years old and up.

3. Minimum combined kart/driver weight before and after race 360 lbs. for Rotary valve & 340 lbs. American Reed Valve.

4. Claiming Allowed.

OPEN LIGHT

1. Any 100cc (6.240 cu. inch) engines.

2. Driver's age 16 years old and up.

3. Minimum combined kart/driver weight before and after race 300 lbs.

4. No restrictions as to price or modifications.

OPEN HEAVY

1. Any 100cc (6.240 cu. inch) engines.

2. Driver's age 16 years old and up.

3. Minimum combined kart/driver weight before and after race 360 lbs.

4. No restrictions as to price or modifications.

OPEN REED

1. Approved American Reed engines only.

2. Driver's age 16 years and up.

3. Minimum combined kart/driver weight before and after race 320 lbs.

4. Reed induction system only.

5. No restrictions as to price or modifications.

125cc REED

1. Approved American Reed engines only over 6.1 cubic inches and under 8.2 cubic inches.

2. Driver's age 16 years old and up.

3. Minimum combined kart/driver weight before and after race 330 lbs.

4. Claiming Allowed.

100cc CONTROLLED STOCK

1. Approved 100cc Stock engines.

2. Driver's age 16 years old and up.

3. Minimum combined kart/driver weight before and after race 340 lbs.

4. Claiming Allowed.

YAMAHA SENIOR

1. Approved Yamaha engines.

2. Driver's age 16 years old and up.

3. Any Pipe and any clutch.

4. Minimum combined kart/driver weight before and after race, 320 lbs.

5. Claiming Allowed.

B LIMITED

1. Any engine under 8.25 cubic inch displacement (single engine, single cylinder).

2. Driver's age 18 years old and up.

3. Minimum combined kart/driver weight before and after race, 350 lbs.

4. No restrictions as to price or modifications.

B STOCK

1. Any approved engine over 6.1 and under 12.2 cubic inch.

2. Driver's age 18 years old and up.

3. Minimum combined kart/driver weight before and after race, 360 lbs. 200.c.c. McCulloch, 380 lbs. 200c.c. Controlled Stock at 400 lbs.

4. No adjustable pipe on any foreign engine.

5. Claiming Allowed.

B OPEN

1. Any engine(s) under 12.2 cubic inch.

2. Driver's age 18 years old and up.

3. Minimum combined kart/driver weight before and after race, 355 lbs. American Reed valve, 385 lbs. Rotary valve.

4. No restrictions as to price or modifications.

C OPEN

1. Any engine(s) under 16.5 cubic inch.

2. Driver's age 18 years old and up.

3. Minimum combined kart/driver weight before and after race, 355 lbs. American Reed valve., 385 lbs. Rotary valve.

4. No restrictions as to price or modifications.

SUPER KART

1. Approved engine of a minimum of 195 c.c. and a maximum of 250c.c. Series production air-cooled engines only.

2. A transmission providing a minimum of 3 speeds with a maximum of 6 gears and 2 cylinders.

3. Minimum combined kart/driver weight before and after race, 400 lbs.

4. No restrictions as to price or modifications.

For further information on the Super Kart Class contact the W.K.A. office. This being a new class not all of the rules have been formulated as of this printing.

ENDURO DRIVER'S LICENSE

The enduro licenses shall be issued by W.K.A. The application shall be subject to final review by W.K.A.

CLASSES OF LICENSES. There shall be two classes of Licenses:

Class A: engines under 7.5 cubic inch displacement.

Class B: engines over 7.5 cubic inch displacement.

The holder of a Class "B" license may drive in either the single or the twin engine class, but the owner of a Class "A" license shall be limited to driving in classes with under 7.5 cubic inch displacement, until such time as he may qualify for a Class "B" license.

ELIGIBILITY. Only W.K.A. members in good standing may apply for drivers licenses, either by direct application, based on their previous Enduro experience, or by fulfilling the requirements as explained covering the Novice Driver. It is understood that the applicant must further satisfy all rules and regulations pertaining to classes, age and weight as defined in the W.K.A. Competition Rules and Regulations.

NOVICE DRIVERS. If the applicant is preparing to drive his first W.K.A. Enduro Point Race he shall be required to attend a special Driver's School, and to participate in a special practice session.

1. Drivers School: The W.K.A. representative shall be responsible for the handling of this school, or he may designate a responsible representative. All novice drivers shall be required to attend this school before being allowed on the track. The school will explain procedure, flags, officials, rules, etc. . . .

2. Practice Session: A special practice session of at least 20 minutes for Class "A" Novice applicants, and a separate 20 minutes for Class "B" Novice applicants shall be held, providing that the sponsoring club has sufficient available track time. Drivers School is mandatory.

3. Separate practice sessions must be held for Sprints and Rookie classes.

SPECIAL NOTE: The race director, or his designated representative, shall provide one (1) qualified Enduro driver to act as a pace driver in each practice session and provide one qualified Enduro driver to be placed at the rear of the practice pack to test the applicant's skill and reaction and be observed under actual competitive conditions, and have a special track official to observe the applicant's behavior.

After the practice session, the race director, or his designated representative will meet with the track official, pace drivers and applicants to discuss in detail the applicant's performance. If it is the judgement of this committee that any applicant fails to qualify the representative must refuse the applicant's entry and return the entry fee, except pit pass cost, to the applicant. If the committee is satisfied with his performance the race director or alternate may then allow the driver to compete, providing he starts at the rear of his class and has the rear color to be visible to all overtaking drivers. At the conclusion of the event, the director may approve the applicant's application for Provisional license, provided the applicant has shown satisfactory driving ability, attitude and conduct both on and off the track.

Once an Enduro driver has received his license, he will then be eligible to compete in an W.K.A. Enduro, subject to the following limitations.

1. He will be allowed to start with the Qualified drivers, but must have the rear of his helmet marked with two parallel stripes of sufficient size and color contrast to be visible to all overtaking driver.

2. At the conclusion of the event, the presiding official may certify the Provisional driver "Qualified" providing the race officials are satisfied with his driving ability, attitude and conduct, both on and off the track.

ENDURO RACING REGULATIONS:

TECHNICAL INSPECTION: inspection should be in accordance with regular W.K.A. competition regulations with the following additions.

1. Fuel Tank. No restrictions on size, other than that the tanks must not impair the operation of the kart and shall not exceed the legal overall length or width of kart. All tanks must be securely fastened to the kart frame.

2. Gas Lines: Must be safety wired or properly secured at tank carburetor and any other connection(s). Lines must be run or held in position(s) so that it is impossible to touch the track surface.

3. Chain Oilers: Must be securely fastened to kart. 8 ounces maximum per engine per race.

4. Tires: Maximum outside diameter 19.5 inches. Must be new or in good condition. Retreads are not allowed in Enduros.

5. Wheels: To incorporate bearings of ground ball or roller type only. Split race bearings not allowed. All axle nuts (front and rear) must be safety wired or cottered. Wheels must be devoid of any defects.

6. Clutch Oilers: The use of a wet type clutch is permitted only when the unit is sealed and does not leak.

DRIVER WEIGHT AND WEIGH IN: All drivers are subject to a minimum combined kart/driver weight check before the race, at discretion of race officials and a mandatory weighing in the impound area immediately following each race. Points will be awarded to only those that weigh in.

BRAKES: Dual brakes or four wheel brakes are recommended for all karts entered in the B Open, B Reed and C Open Classed. Dual brakes should consist of two (2) individual braking systems on separate brake discs or drums.

KART NUMBERS: Numbers shall be assigned and furnished to each entrant by the sponsoring club. The numbers shall be of such size and color as to promote good scoring. The entrant must accept the assigned number and affix these numbers to his kart in a manner acceptable to the chief scorer.

STARTS: The placing of all entries on the starting grid shall be conducted in the following manner.

1. Each class may be gridded separately.

2. If classes are combined, the fastest shall be gridded in front.

3. Inspection of all spoilers mandatory in a B & C Open and the Super Kart Classes only.

4. Standing starts. No pushing allowed. Oiling of clutch on the starting grid is prohibited.

5. Drip pans are mandatory at the starting grid for karts using chain oilers.

6. Green flag to be raised one minute before race starts so that karters may start their engines.

7. At the end of one minute, green flag drops, the time begins. No pushing allowed at start.

8. The karts are to be lined up along side of the track with a minimum of two (2) feet between karts. The lineup (or starting) area to be determined by the local officials.

9. The use of clutch(es) is mandatory in all classes.

TECHNICAL INSPECTION MANUAL

The technical inspectors in both karting associations are looking for much the same thing—a well-built, well-cared for kart—and so their tech inspections are much the same. With that (and an eye toward saving space and getting rid of redundant material) in mind, we've given you a best of the tech manuals here.

Suitability for competition—The basic design of the vehicle shall be suitable for high performance with emphasis on safety. The opinion of the inspectors and the race officials shall be binding.

Appearance—The vehicle shall be neat and clean.

Tires—Shall be new or in good condition without visible flaws.

Wheels—Void of any defects.

Wheel Bearings—Ground ball or roller type only. Split race bearings not allowed. Wheel bearings should be properly adjusted so that there is no excessive wheel play.

Axle Nuts—Both front and rear shall be safety wired or cotter keyed, and self-clamping wheels are allowed snap rings instead of nuts.

Brakes—Checked for proper operation and stopping ability. All hydraulic connections shall be tight and free from leaks. All brake caliper bolts, master cylinder bolts, and master cylinder roll pins must be cotter pinned or safety wired.

Wheel Weights—Clip-on or tape-on wheel balancing weights shall be securely fastened.

Throttle—Karts to be equipped with foot operated throttle having a spring which shall close throttle when released.

Fuel Tanks—No restrictions on size, other than the tanks shall not impair the operation of the kart and shall not exceed the maximum legal length or width of kart. All tanks shall be securely affixed to kart.

Fuel Lines—Shall be safety wrapped at all connections.

Chain Oilers—Shall be securely fastened to kart. (Enduro only). Eight oz. maximum capacity.

Clutch—The use of a wet type clutch is permitted only when the unit is sealed to prevent leakage.

Front Suspension and Steering— Shall be of a suitable design, in proper working order, and adjusted for maximum safety. All steering bolts, nuts, and linkage shall be tightened, and safety wired or cotter keyed, and shall be easily exposed for inspection purpose.

Frame—Of safe design, void of defects which would impair the safety of the vehicle. Particular attention should be given to all welds.

Bumpers—May not constitute a hazard to other competitors.

POST-RACE INSPECTION: At the end of competition, all cars and drivers shall proceed directly to the designated impound area to be checked for minimum class weight, maximum kart size, engine legality, ballast weight bolted to kart, legality of exhaust system and silencer, and fuel only.

Engine legality shall be determined according to specifications contained in the Technical Inspection Manual. All engine parts should be teched at ambiant temperature, not "hot."

Drivers may not add any weight to themselves or their karts between the finish of competition and weigh in.

MUFFLERS: All karts must be equipped with a silenced exhaust system. Any extended/extending tip (stinger, outlet pipe, etc.) of any muffler, chamber, or exhaust system that could puncture, penetrate, cut or otherwise cause injury to other competitors must be fitted with a safety guard. Said safety guard shall be a metal washer having a minimum thickness of 0.125-inch and a minimum outside diameter of 2.0 inches welded or brazed to the immediate end of the tip.

The exhaust system must be completely intact at the start and through the entirety of the race. An entrant whose exhaust system or silencer becomes disconnected from the engine and is no longer operable, shall be automatically black flagged. The competitor may resume racing when the exhaust system is repaired.

4. The Kart Chassis

SINCE THE invention of the wheel, a vehicle chassis has most often been regarded as nothing more than a platform for motive convenience. The great majority of vehicles produced down through the ages have been strictly utilitarian, nothing more than a means of moving freight and/or people from point A to point B. Deviation from this pragmatic approach to travel is dictated by only two small groups of users—those who want to travel in more comfort and those who want to travel at the limit of vehicle performance. Ninety-five percent of all karters eventually fit into the second special category. A kart is a very specialized piece of motorized equipment, and the transition from neighborhood putt-putting to organized competition is decisive.

Maximum performance, therefore, must be introduced into the vehicle. In thoroughbred race cars, this is the

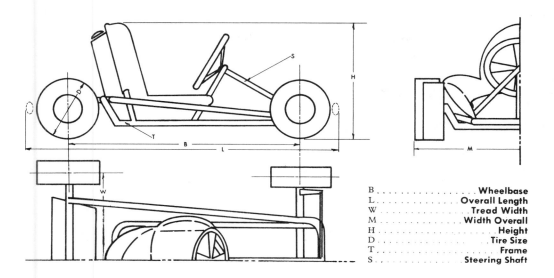

B	Wheelbase
L	Overall Length
W	Tread Width
M	Width Overall
H	Height
D	Tire Size
T	Frame
S	Steering Shaft

General dimensions of a kart are figured as shown, and will vary with each different manufacturer.

effect of experience. The same holds for karting, as most kart manufacturers have been deeply involved in competition and seldom fail to include all lessons learned in production practice.

Increased performance starts by whetting the engine to razor-sharp tune, and modifying it until the very last ounce of dependable power is secured. With this new power comes the requirement for superior brakes and tires. Almost as an afterthought, the average karter then begins to consider chassis refinement. Fortunately, many frames have been created for ultimate performance, the assumption being that most karters will end up racing anyway. A Fun kart may not have the small refinements of a pure racer, but it can usually be converted by the home craftsman and will normally do a respectable job in competition.

The essential difference between kart and car chassis is in the suspension. Karting simplicity demands an unsprung chassis, but special builders have experimented with suspended frames with some success. While the kart may not have a suspension, it is still subjected to the same forces effecting any automobile. Chassis design must take these forces into account.

The kart frame has only one purpose: to connect the four wheels and provide a riding platform for engine and driver. The requirements are for something that is rigid in bending and torsion moments and will not have excessive sag or twist. While it must support all the component kart parts as well as the driver, the frame may or may not absorb all the loads of competition. In a well-designed kart, the frame is the last thing to be considered. The driver is the first

ABOVE: Next up the line is the fun kart, made for family enjoyment in large, private areas. It is illegal to drive karts on the streets. Prices of fun karts start at $150, less engine. BELOW: Note similarity between Bug sprint and fun kart. Sprint karts emphasize light weight (this kart weighs 89 lbs. with engine) and flexible chassis.

thing to consider, then the engine and accessory parts followed by wheels, etc. The frame should be as simple as possible for the expected loads.

The development of performance chassis in the automobile is relative to kart chassis design, in that the first kart was built by a race car engineer. The very lightweight chassis for racing cars is a fairly recent development; most early racers used extremely heavy frames with little emphasis on weight saving and torsional stiffness. The earliest race cars used a girder-type frame with live axles front and rear. The twin-tube chassis was introduced to competition by Germany's Auto Union in 1934 and followed shortly by Mercedes Benz. Success caused imitation and most racing cars used this type chassis into the late 1950's. The space tube frame, which has been used in karting homebuilts, came to the automotive scene in big numbers with the small, lightweight, rear-engined race cars introduced in the early 1960's. There were a few space frames previous to this, but they weren't popular. The next step was a true unit-construction framework, wherein the body and frame are one piece. This chassis type is used by most American passenger car factories and is very successful in automobile competition. It has been tried with karts, but hasn't proven superior enough to warrant the extra cost over a con-

Super Bug sidewinder sprinter places foreign-make engines alongside driver. Seating still gets major attention even for short races. Four wheel brakes are used for maximum speed control into corners.

ventional tubing frame. It is possible, however, that the Enduro karts might make excellent use of a monocoque chassis with built-in fuel tanks and seating.

In karting, the twin-tube ladder frame is almost universal. The great advantage is ease of mass production which means low cost, and economics is a definite factor in this sport. The typical kart frame with twin side rails of round tubing may have diagonal or lateral bracing (or both) which will increase torsional rigidity, but this rigidity will never be very great simply because of the tubing cross-section. The ability to withstand central loading, or resistance to bending, could be increased by use of oval tubing, but then torsional rigidity would suffer even more. The stiffness of any frame can be increased by using a larger diameter tubing, but in karting a diameter of 1 inch has proven a practical minimum.

Kart frames are made of either round or square tubing, with the round section in preference. Electric resistance welded tubing is common, and does not cost as much as the solid drawn tubing, but for severe competition chromemoly tubing is selected. The IKF competition rules call for frame main members of 1-inch minimum outside diameter by .083-inch wall thickness cold roll steel tubing, or other material of at least equal strength. The qualification leaves the door open for those advanced engineers who can work effectively with chassis material, thus some competition frames are of the more costly chromemoly tubing with the same diameter but a reduced wall thickness of .065-inch.

While chromemoly is better than mild steel, it also requires special welding techniques during construction. This normally means some sort of Heli-Arc welding and controlled cooling. An improperly welded chromemoly frame will have localized stress points that eventually fracture under severe use. To overcome this stress, it is possible for the non-professional builder to have the chassis "normalized" by heating the entire chassis in an oven and then slowly cooling.

Structurally, any kind of chassis must be judged on two criteria: strength-to-weight ratio, and stiffness-to-weight ratio. It is here the kart justifies the very basic approach to frame design and construction. For a vehicle that may have a total running weight of only 350 pounds or so, the minimum frame diameter of 1-inch by .083-inch wall thickness is considerably above the minimum strength of the tubing. In this respect, then, the kart has sufficient safety margin built in by the rule book. However, in the business of stiffness the kart chassis could be better.

The typical Sprint kart will have a static flexibility of about 1½-2 inches at a front wheel. With a driver on board, a wheel will deflect more before the opposite wheel lifts and under competition conditions where the weight transfer causes greater loads, the deflection will be even more.

A suspension will counteract some of this stiffness problem. The Kendick Avenger kart, which is a chromemoly frame, has a front suspension of rubber in shear (a form of torsion) which allows front wheel movement of around 4 inches. This

TOP: Bug Enduro Scarab sidewinder with large fuel tanks. This kart is built to accept either American or European engine. CENTER: Margay Products twin West Bend powered sprinter will accept any engine; features dual rear spot brakes. BOTTOM: Margay karts have rubber insulated rear suspension, are noted for excellent handling. Note position of fuel tanks.

particular design uses a reaction link between front suspension arms. When one wheel goes up, the action transfers across the chassis and forces the other wheel into the pavement.

Working within the framework of the rules book, the chassis must have a maximum wheelbase of 50 inches and a minimum of 40 inches, with Enduro laydown karts taking advantage of an additional overall length maximum of 14 to 16 inches. It is interesting to note that not many constructors go to the wheelbase maximum. As an example, the Kendick Sprint karts have a 44-inch wheelbase and the Enduro design is only 3½ inches longer.

The minimum tread width of a Sprint is 28 inches; 30 inches for Enduros. Maximum for both is 40 inches. The same Kendick Sprint karts have a 32-inch front tread and 33-inch rear. Enduro design is different, with a narrow rear tread of 31 inches and a front tread of 33 inches.

Kart frame rails have been produced in just about every conceivable form, more as an effort to be different than from an engineering standpoint. However, the original straight rails soon gave way to the dropped rails because of center of gravity. With a straight rail the ground clearance will likely be 5 inches or more and the CG will be quite high. Dropped rails cure this, but so does a formed seat/belly pan which holds the driver down inside the straight rails. The double bend frame rails take care of the CG problem and double as sissy bars for body control. A dropped front axle is used for the same purpose of lowering the CG.

For several years there has been contention among racing chassis men that a center of gravity can be too low. That this is incorrect is practically demonstrated by karts, and is explained by the following equation:

$$WG \times \frac{H}{T}$$

W = total weight of vehicle
G = cornering rate
H = center of gravity weight
T = track

The center of gravity of a typical Sprint kart with driver and having a total weight of 350 pounds will be roughly 12 inches above the ground and 26 inches behind the front wheels. Obviously these figures will change through a wide margin, but they serve to demonstrate how low the kart CG actually is. Next consider the Enduro kart with laydown driver position. The total height of driver will be about 20 inches from the ground, and the CG will be approximately 9 inches high and 30 inches behind the front wheels.

There is a condition of roll center that is involved in any chassis utilization, but because the kart is not

TOP: **Caretta chassis modified by Hartman Engineering to run Saetta imported rotary valve engines. Driver is offset to left, requiring outboard chain drive for left engine.** BOTTOM: **Modified Caretta twin with outboard drive. Chain guards are required by rules.**

suspended the roll center is considered to be near ground level and thus there is little the enthusiast can do about this specific. Weight transfer will have a great effect on kart performance however, and is pronounced in the Sprint race with an upright driver. If the center of gravity were at ground level, there would be no weight transfer and each pair of wheels would develop more cornering force than possible when the inner wheels are getting less traction than the outer wheels due to weight transfer in a turn. Chassis manufacturers try to keep the CG as low as possible, controlling weight transfer somewhat by driver position. While the weight ratio of any given kart must consider the many variables of tire sizes, rubber composition, CG, etc., an average of 55 percent weight rear and 45 percent front is typical (static).

There is no question but that the live, or locked, rear end gives better performance than individual rear

TOP: **Unusual kart in enduro racing is Kendick Engineering machine. Offset engine uses single tank, four-wheel brakes. BOTTOM: Kendick kart has front suspension that allows up to 4 inches front wheel travel.**

wheel drive. While the live rear axle does present some problems, these are usually overcome with careful tire selection. If the rear tires are too wide, they will provide too much traction in a turn, and since the two rear wheels are trying to turn at a different rate of speed through the corner, the extra traction will tend to lug the engine. For this reason, karters prefer to run the narrowest tires possible so they will break loose before lugging the engine.

Most rear axles are secured by quality sealed bearings that ensure extended axle service with minimum care. Often the entire rear section of a kart, or that part generally comprising the axle mounting and sometimes the engine mount, is removable from the main frame assembly. It has become a widespread practice to sesure this sub-assembly in rubber bushings, a practice that gives a rather limited form of "suspension" to the chassis. Prime effect of such a

49

suspension is isolation of wheel and engine vibration, although mounts that are too loose produce a poor handling kart.

The front axle is built as an integral part of the frame (the exception being suspended chassis), usually with a 2—3 inch drop as a method of lowering the main frame rails. The axle is of the same material as the basic frame, with special spindle bosses jig-welded for front end geometry. While it is possible to select a piece of tubing that will accept a specific size bolt, race car mechanics have found it better to use heavy wall tubing of a slightly smaller size, then ream the tubing to size after any welding distortion.

The penchant for simplicity in kart construction carries through to the front spindles. These are vital parts of the entire structure, yet they are most often nothing more than premium quality bolts butt welded to a spindle bracket. Few failures are ever traced to spindles, unless the driver makes an unscheduled trip through weeds, and then the spindles bend rather than break.

All commercially produced karts include correct basic steering geometry, but not all include the Akerman theory. The front wheels must have three things for proper directional control: caster, camber, and toe-in. How well the front wheels work in a turn, then, is determined by the Akerman principle.

Caster is relative to the front axle king pin fore-aft inclination. A market shopping cart wheel is called a caster simply because the wheel axis is behind the cart attachment point. This causes the wheel to "follow" the cart in a reasonably straight line. When the spindle king pin is slanted,

the bottom forward of the top, the wheel centerline will intersect the king pin centerline slightly behind the load center. The wheel will then caster, or follow, and will tend to align itself. Turn the kart wheels slightly, then release the steering wheel and the kart will return to a straight line.

Obviously caster has a direct effect on how a kart will handle, and this effect can be modified by merely changing front wheel and/or tire sizes. Thus it is wise to use the front wheels and tires the kart was designed for. As an example, a 10-inch slick or smaller tire can use a 7-degree caster (angle of the king pin in fore-aft plane), but a 12-inch slick works better with only 5-degree caster. The bigger tire has more contact area, so it needs less caster for steering. Too much caster makes the kart hard to turn from straight ahead, and the recovery from a turn is violent. While some racers utilize different size front tires (one large, one small) for some specific track, this seems only to work well as a wedging factor on oval tracks. Front end alignment may not be so critical on Sprint karts, but it is imperative on the high speed Enduro machines.

From a front view, the king pin is also angled outward at the bottom, the optimum angle occurring when a line drawn through the king pin center intersects the wheel vertical centerline at the point of tire-road contact. This inclination is necessary to bring the wheel rotation plane on the same centerline as the king pin. When the front wheels are turned, the spindle end will rise and fall because of the inclined king pin, an action that raises the kart on a turn and lowers it in the straight ahead direc-

TOP: **National Enduro Champion Chuck Pittinger shows full belly pan of Kendick kart, a requirement in rules.** LEFT: **GP muffler sprint kart is made by Duffy Livingston of Go-Kart manufacturing fame.** RIGHT: **GP also makes outstanding FKE kart, including chassis and body. Shown here is the Mole body.**

ABOVE: Interior of GP kart shows different tubing frame arrangement, tiller steering. Motor platform is separated from rest of car. BELOW: Dart J Kart, twin-engined type, manufactured by Mickey Rupp of Mansfield, Ohio. Jim Whitehead is a past National Champion driver; pit crewman is Gil Horstman who makes kart speed parts.

Also from GP, with Livingston as defending FKE National Champion, comes the latest version of the Mole.

tion. In this manner, kart weight also helps to return the turning kart to a straight path. While earlier karts did not include this basic inclination principle, modern karts do. Some homemade front ends tend to go for excessive inclination—7 to 10 degrees is usually enough.

Camber is very important in a vehicle with independent suspension; it is not so important with a solid suspended axle; and even less important with a kart. The problem is that some karters try to use either negative or positive camber to improve handling but experience has proven the results negligible. When tires tilt outward, so they are wider apart at the bottom than at the top when viewed from the front, this is positive camber. The reverse situation is negative camber. When the wheel tilts outward, it is usually done to bring the wheel vertical centerline to intersect the king pin centerline. The combination of the king pin inclination angle and the wheel camber angle then becomes the included angle. The value of camber in karting is debatable, since both positive and negative camber force the tire into an out-of-square contact with the road and results in the tire having several rolling diameters. In karting, the most common type of camber is excessive positive in an attempt to "wedge" the front end, but this effect is cancelled in a turn and doesn't give a significant improvement.

Toe-in is utilized on all automobiles, and is the result of adjusting the steering linkage to cause the front edge of the tires to be closer than the rear edge, as viewed from above.

LEFT: Boone kart from Van Nuys, Calif. is in limited production as a custom enduro only; it features radical offset. RIGHT: Very few Fowler sprint karts have been made, but they have been extremely successful. BELOW: Dual West Bend-powered special, which was homebuilt by Jim Stroud of Tulsa, Oklahoma, is tremendously fast.

When a vehicle is rolling along, parallel tires tend to spread, which causes the driver to be constantly making small control corrections. By adjusting the linkage to give about 1/16-inch toe-in, the karter can cure this wandering tendency.

The Akerman effect comes into play when a kart is cornering. While going straight ahead, the wheels make parallel paths, but in a turn, the inside wheel must make a tighter radius than the outer wheel. If both wheels remain parallel in the turn, one of the two will skid sideways because it is being forced to make a radius that doesn't exist at that particular point.

Akerman is easy to determine. Draw a line from the center of the rear axle through each front king pin. To make the front tires work correctly through a turn, the steering arms must be attached to the spindle parallel with this imaginary line. Whether the steering arms are ahead of or behind the axle is not of major consequence, although more wheel-to-arm clearance is obtained by putting the arms behind the axle. Generally speaking, this little business of front-end geometry is a quick way to distinguish the quality kart chassis from the quickie. In an effort to get maximum performance, the best chassis will include these items, the cheap chassis will not.

It is possible to modify kart handling by changing the Akerman effect. If the kart should handle a bit quicker in turns, make the Akerman line intersect a point several inches ahead of the rear axle (in effect, spread the steering arms apart for leading designs, close them for trailing designs). The inside wheel in a turn

ABOVE: **Rick Paronelli shows his Caretta chassis with father Hank's body design. One-off's are popular in karting. BELOW: Homemade kart chassis can be quite successful, but the builder must observe all the rules of good construction used on any type of automobile.**

will now make a tighter corner. If the kart handles skitterish, or it has a short wheelbase, the steering can be slowed down by moving the Akerman point behind the rear axle slightly. It is possible to get the same kind of Akerman effect with straight steering arms and overlapping linkage connections at the steering shaft. In this method, the connection arcs will vary so that the inside wheel linkage travels more or less than the outside.

Since most karts do not have both front wheels on the ground during a hard corner, particularly the Sprinters, all the weight is on the outside wheel and there is a difference in slip angle between the front tires. Therefore it is possible to have negative Akerman on a kart with great weight transfer, and neutral Akerman with little transfer. It all ends up to be a matter of trial and error, but it is definitely worth experimenting with for quicker lap times.

Since practically all modern Sprint karts have the flexible frame construction that will allow the inside wheel to lift and put greater force onto the outside wheel, Ackerman may be ignored to some degree, but it must still be included in the basic design. At the same time, the karter must recognize the steering tendencies of a live rear axle.

The farther apart the rear wheels, the greater this steering effect. The wider the rear wheels, thus giving more tire contact, the greater this effect. In drag racing, where directional control is extremely critical, rear wheel steering was nullified to a great extent by bringing the wheels in next to the single-seat body. Sports cars sometimes narrow the rear tread for the same reason.

When a kart understeers and the front end "washes out" (goes straight ahead), a narrower axle will reduce rear end steering. If the kart over-

LEFT: Kendick four-engined dragster is for exhibition in acceleration trials only. It is not eligible for regular kart racing. RIGHT: Marauder kart from Hornet Mfg. in Texas, the popular enduro machine. It utilizes standard non-Akerman steering and four wheel brakes.

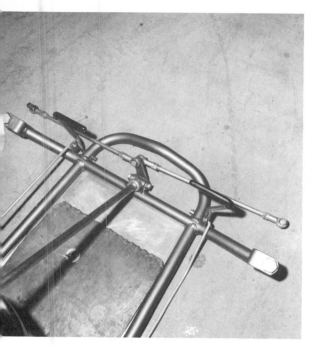 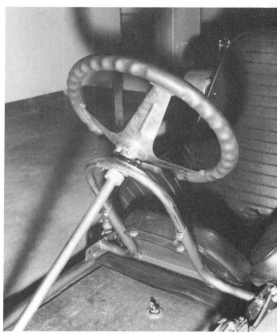

LEFT: **Rules call for strong steering shaft and adjustable steering rod ends.** RIGHT: **Hoop of Dart kart can be adjusted up and down for different drivers.** BELOW, LEFT: **Types of steering wheels available through kart shops.** BELOW, RIGHT: **Spindles should be well built. Wheel here has been spaced out for better control on dirt tracks.**

LEFT: **Two types of front spindles, one of which is for four-wheel brakes. Note spindle shaft is quality bolt welded to kingpin boss.** RIGHT: **Sidewinder motor mount is rubber mounted at axle.** BELOW, LEFT: **Saetta engine on the insulated mount.** BELOW, RIGHT: **Axles are made of quality steel, run in sealed bearings. Note the double yoke for disc brake caliper.**

ABOVE: **Two types of sprint kart seating—custom seat at bottom, commercial seat at top.** BELOW: **Laydown seating is as form-fitting as sprints. Headrest is necessary.**

ABOVE: An outstanding homebuilt is this Tom Spalding sprinter. The home craftsman can build superior kart with patience and planning. BELOW: From Texas is this sleek Hornet kart with bathtub seating. Sports car mirror housings are fitted with temperature gauges.

This bottoms-up view of Hornet Marauder shows full one-piece belly pan to accord with IKF rules. Engine is suspended in rubber with twin radius rods running forward to attachment point near front wheels.

steers and "spins out," a wider rear axle will help. This increase or decrease in rear tread may be only an inch, but it is usually enough to control the handling qualities. Obviously, wider or narrower tires will have a tread width effect, and tire composition will effect rear end steering (a sticky tire for understeer, a slick tire for oversteer).

Weight transfer in a turn is another consideration. If the rear tires are really effective, in a turn all the power can be transferred to the outside tire which has the weight transfer and gets a better bite. The combined effect may be a kart that goes through a turn very well power-off, but will spin out power-on. The extra rear traction and power is causing oversteer. The solution is to keep two or three axle and wheel combina-

tions for different tracks, or to have a wide axle that will allow a wheel to be adjusted in or out.

The final attribute of any good kart chassis is seating. How well the driver is held in the frame will determine how well he drives in a race. In both Enduro and Sprint chassis, the seating has continued to improve until current practice has the driver well supported up the sides of the back and along each hip. Seat padding may be soft or firm, depending on individual preference, but in all cases it is snug and does not allow the body weight to shift even slightly.

Since chassis handling is effected by weight transfer and distribution, the karter should experiment with different fore-aft seating (using pads) until the best handling configuration is found.

Tires and wheels are part of track tuning. John Hartman adds air to rear tires of enduro kart to adjust handling of machine through turns.

5. Wheels and Tires

WHEELS AND tires receive special attention in karting. Fortunately for the enthusiast, there is not a great deal of difference between the small kart and the larger race car, so the special problems of wheel strength and tire traction have often been solved by Indianapolis and road racing cars. While the engineering has been handled by the experts, the driver must still decide exactly what he needs for wheels and tires, and more important, how to use them.

Kart wheels are of two types, keyed and bearing. The keyed wheels are designed for use on live rear axles and are secured by a steel key and axle nut. Since most axles are 1-inch major diameter, stepped to a smaller thread diameter for the bolt, the wheels may also be tapered or stepped. The best wheels will include either tapered roller or ball bearings, usually with an inner race standard 5/8-inch or 3/4-inch to fit front spindle bolts.

During the early days, karting wheels were all steel stampings, units available through industrial outlets. Both bearing and bushing designs were used, but tire width and types were soon to dictate wheels of a better quality. The kart industry responded with a number of alloy wheels, but these were of rather limited width. Current karting catalogs list a variety of wheels made by several manufacturers, with sizes ranging from diameters of 4 to 8 inches and widths from 2½ to 5¼ inches.

The prime value of racing wheels is strength and light weight, areas where the aluminum and magnesium products are far superior to the original pressed steel. A set of four mag wheels can save as much as ten pounds in kart weight, and while this might not be extremely important due to overall class weight restrictions, the weight is at chassis extremities and does have an effect on handling. In the case of a suspended chassis, this effect is pronounced.

Strength is the main virtue of competition kart wheels. Unless the pressed steel wheel has been made specifically for kart use, it will be very weak in the flange and hub area with a tendency to crack a hub or bearing. Most modern alloy competition wheels are patterned after automotive wheels, with web and offset spoke sections for maximum strength and stress distribution between rim and hub.

No sand cast wheels are recommended for kart use, since they are fragile. Other types of casting are acceptable, and forgings or spanked castings are the best of all. Some wheels have been made up using a combination of steel and alloy—the steel for strength and the alloy for weight savings. Most of them are of the bolt-up design, with the halves separable for tire service. In at least one design there is a center spider and hub that is not disturbed when the two rim halves are separated.

There is a difference in the weight of wheels, which comes from both design and alloy. Magnesium is almost as strong as aluminum, and can be as much as 40 percent lighter for a given design. The average 6-inch diameter aluminum wheel with 3½-inch width will weigh about 1 pound 10 ounces while a similar mag wheel will be about 1 pound.

Since most carts use a ⅝-inch front spindle, most wheels come with hubs in this size. However, the larger ¾-inch size is available and suggested for extreme duty. Ball bearings are normally supplied for the smaller spindle while tapered roller bearings are common for the larger size. Ball bearings are not as good for side loads as are the taper rollers, but the roller bearings have more inherent drag. Further, tapered bearings are not sealed, must have a dust cover washer, and should be serviced often.

The type of lubricant used in wheel bearings isn't nearly as important as keeping the lubricant clean. Most any wheel grease is acceptable, although some purists go to great length with lubricants composed of bearing grease and an additive (STP, Bardahl, etc.). Not much adjustment can be given to ball bearing wheels, although the washer should be snug to the wheel. Tapered rollers are the same as those used in automotive front wheels, and should be adjusted in the same manner.

Current practice is to use the very narrow 2½-inch front wheels, by 5-inch diameter, for both Enduro and

Margay wheel uses pressed steel outer halves so alloy hub does not need to be removed for wheel/tire changes. RIGHT: Margay wheel with hub installed. Width can be modified by added spacer.

Sprint karts. At the rear, most Sprints are equipped with only slightly wider 3½-inch width rear wheels, Enduro's use the widest 5⅛–5¼ wheels. The 5-inch diameter is constant for most wheels since such a wide variety of tires are made for this size. FKE karts often use larger wheels, including 6- and 8-inch diameters.

A relative newcomer to karting is a wheel called Nylite, made in England and imported in America by Inglewood Kart Shop. This is a nylon wheel, weighing only 18 ounces, which uses design technique similar to alloy wheels. The two halves separate for tire changes like any kart wheel, and either ball or taper roller bearings are available. Impervious to any chemical common to karting, including the so-called special fuels and cleaners,

the synthetic material will only begin to melt at about 450 degrees. This is not significant, since tire compounds begin to vulcanize at around 300 degrees F. Weight of a front wheel is 18 ounces, the larger rear wheel is up to 24 ounces.

Compared to the more traditional wheels (forged casting, die casting, pressed steel), the Nylite will shatter at about the same destruction level, or roughly, 1,500 psi. It is interesting how these molded-injection nylon wheels are holding up, and it would seem only a natural step to similar wheels for full-scale racing cars.

All competition wheels make some provision for holding the tires in place. Because there is so much horsepower available, and because the tire compounds now used offer such outstanding traction, tires would rotate on ordinary wheel rims and break the inner tube valve stem. This problem is aggravated by very low tire pressures common for some types of racing. To cure this, competition wheels have small traction lugs integral with the tire bead side of the rim. When the tire is inflated, the bead seats against these small protrusions to eliminate unwanted rotation.

There has been a tremendous amount of refinement in kart tires since those knobby industrial units used on the first Ingels kart. Practically all tires are now of the "slick" design, or treadless to get maximum rubber on the ground. It was thought that slicks would not give good dirt traction, but experience has proven them more effective than groove or knobby tread patterns on dirt tracks that have a very hard packed surface.

The pneumatic tire was invented in 1845 by the Scottish civil engineer R. W. Thomson for use on horse-drawn carriages. Because the invention was so far ahead of time, its was virtually forgotten until reinvented in 1888 by a Belfast veterinary surgeon, J. B. Dunlop. Dunlop was interested in bicycles, and wanted a large tire which would overcome vibration and be fast on all kinds of surface. His "reinvention" came just as the automobile and motorcycle were being created. Interestingly, heavy trucks didn't use pneumatic tires until the 1920's, and tractors gained tires in the 1930's.

The kart tire is not unlike any other, in that it must carry a load, cushion the vehicle to some extent, transmit driving and braking forces to the ground, and control steering. Tires are standardized throughout the world, at least in sizes if not in design. Casing design has progressed from the original canvas to cotton to the modern Nylon, Rayon, and fiberglass. Synthetic tread compounds are fast replacing natural rubber throughout the world and are universal in America.

One of the most valuable properties of the pneumatic tire wasn't even considered by inventors, namely the ability of the tire to generate in itself the forces required to steer around corners. When the karter turns the wheels, forces are generated in the tires that cause them to make the turn as the centerline of the tread is deflected. As the tire is deflected from a given path, it acquires a slip-angle and generates a cornering force to oppose centrifugal force. This cornering force depends on tire inflation pressure, which is used to great advantage by karters.

The typical Sprint kart running on a hard-packed dirt surface will run something like 18 psi front and 20 psi rear, while the same kart on asphalt will run 25 and 30—35 psi, respectively. The Enduro kart, which usually runs on asphalt, will carry 25 psi front and 35 psi rear.

Understeer and oversteer are characteristics of karts (any vehicle, really) used to great advantage by seasoned drivers. Understeer is a state when the front axle as a whole has a greater slip angle under influence of a side force than has the rear axle as a whole. In effect, the driver must continually be steering more into the corner. Oversteer is the reverse, and the driver finds the kart trying to turn a tighter and tighter circle so he must constantly be taking steering motion out during the corner. Understeer is the most desirable. In some cases where the kart has little front end weight and poor front tire traction, the vehicle tends to "push" through turns. That is, while power is being applied to the rear tires, there is little turning force generated in the front tires, so the kart tends to go straight ahead, even though the wheels may be turned full-lock in direction of travel. This was the case with karts when slicks were first introduced at the rear and the small front tires still used industrial tread. Directional control was almost nonexistent.

The pneumatic tire is not perfectly elastic, so it consumes power as it rolls. While the tire must deflect and "work," only a small portion of this is desirable as a shock absorbing factor. As the tire flexes, heat is generated, so the high-performance tire must be much cooler running than a stock unit. In karting this is most difficult unless the tire has been designed from scratch and built for competition. However, if the tire is not subject to extreme heat problems, ordinary recaps are quite successful. As the tire flexes, it consumes some power (known as rolling resistance). As an example, the resistance may be 100 at 30 mph but will be over 200 at 100 mph.

The question of traction is of prime importance to the karter, more significant in Sprints than Enduros. Slicks have proven particularly useful with karts because the tread "pattern" is not on the tire but on the asphalt. Even when wet, a rough pavement will give good traction to a slick tire. Note the following table, which was a test between tires with and without tread pattern.

LEFT: **Custom wheels include very strong alloy centers if pressed steel rims are included. This is a Dart wheel.** RIGHT: **GEM spacers are available for all karts and wheels to bring width up to 5¼ tire maximum.**

	Rough Tarmac		Medium Tarmac		Smooth Tarmac		Smooth Concrete		Smooth Asphalt	
	dry	wet	dry	wet	dry	wet	dry	wet	dry	wet
Friction Coefficient New Tires	0.8	.66	.78	.66	.84	.71	1.0	.72	.62	.60
Used Tires	0.9	.69	.86	.56	.81	.34	1.0	.43	.58	.23

On the wet but rough surfaces where the water does not stand, the smooth tires cannot aquaplane, and since there is more actual rubber in contact with the road, the coefficient of friction is greater. Note however the difference in dry smooth asphalt. Because the slick racing tires for karts put so much more rubber on the road than an ordinary worn tire, the coefficient of friction must be assumed to exceed the traditional 1.00 used by engineers. In drag racing, where the slick gained prominence, it has been found that this coefficient and relative G force are almost doubled during hard acceleration. Even ordinary tires have been found to have a peak value of 1.3.

How the tire will perform is generally a cut-and-try method for racing, and the enthusiast is left to make do with whatever tires are on the market. Fortunately, most tire manufacturers (this includes the recappers) are in a highly competitive business, so they keep their homework up to date. Along these lines, therefore, the kart tire people keep in touch with tire developments for bigger race cars and utilize the improvements as they show. Consider the custom grooved slick.

When Firestone was running early tests on the wide-base Indianapolis tire, they found that special grooving would improve both straightaway vehicle stability and cornering ability. This was applied to karting tires by one manufacturer with some interesting results. The grooved tires ran considerably cooler than conventional slicks with equal wear. Cornering of a grooved slick was superior to a tread design tire, and reduction of the tire weight (cutting away the surface rubber) had an immediate effect on tire temperature and kart speed. High speed distortion was greater with 2-ply than with 4-ply but heat difference was small. The results of this kind of testing is a tire that looks like half industrial and half racing slick.

While so much importance has been placed on the type of casing to use, how big or little the tire must be, what kind of tread pattern to use if any and so on, the basic requirement for premium traction still rests a great deal with tire compounds. While the recapper may not have a tremendous influence on what kind of capping compound he may work with, the major tire companies are at liberty to experiment with compounds. For this reason some tires are called wet and others dry. Because karters reject the idea of driving around in the pouring rain, few so-called wet tire compounds are used in karting. They do give excellent traction on dry surfaces but wear rapidly.

Most racing slicks have been molded in such a way to give maximum foot pattern (amount of tire in contact with the road at reasonable tire pressures) with the minimum amount of rubber (to save weight). The actual shape of the unmounted wide tire may be drastically different from the mounted version, since the tire will tend to "sling out," or distort at higher rpm due to its own weight. The tire designer must consider this distortion and make the tire have maximum effectiveness at the desired speed range. Thus the Sprint tire may have a different shape from the Enduro tire, since the latter is running at sustained high speeds.

Most kart tires are available in sizes companion to wheels. That is, the narrow slicks are $2\frac{1}{2}$ inches wide, the super wide slicks are $5\frac{1}{8}$ inches wide. IKF has a limit to total diameter of tires, but most commercial racing tires are well within this limitation.

Before Enduro racing with its higher speeds became so popular, kart tire balancing was of little importance. Sprint tracks were short and the top speeds reached were limited. Emphasis was on acceleration. Vibrations caused by out-of-balance wheels at high Enduro speeds makes the steering wheel seem to grow until kart control is difficult at best.

There are two forms of wheel balance, static and dynamic. At certain speeds, the wheel and tire enter harmonics, caused by one of these imbalance conditions. Such harmonics will increase and decrease with speed changes. Static balancing will eliminate the fore-aft vibrations of the wheel as it turns on a given plane. When a wheel and tire are heavy on one side, this weight is thrown outward by centrifugal force, causing the vibration. Results are excessive tire wear, worn wheel bearings, and general poor kart handling at higher speeds.

Dynamic balancing eliminates the side-to-side wobble of wheels, and grows in importance in direct relationship to wheel and tire width. While static balancing is used to find the major heavy spot, and can be done with simple tools, the best dynamic balancing must be left to a wheel and tire company. Getting dynamic balancing done in an automotive establishment might be difficult, but most kart shops have arrangements with a garage for this service.

The recommended weight size for kart wheel balancing is the small one-quarter ounce passenger thin type. It is short and easily fits over the wheel rim with a large enough clip to retain the weight at high wheel rpm.

To find the static balancing point of a wheel, set the chassis on blocks so the wheels are exactly vertical. Check tire and wheel sideways run-out, which will seldom exceed .004-inch with racing equipment. Loosen the bearing so the wheel is very loose, but not sloppy. Spin the wheel slowly and allow it to come to a stop. Mark the bottom edge with chalk and spin the wheel again. If it stops with the chalked mark near the same spot, this is a good indication of the heavy spot. Place a quarter ounce balance weight exactly opposite the heavy spot, somewhere near the top of the wheel. Spin the wheel again. If it still stops with the heavy side toward the bottom of rotation, add another weight next to the first. Once the wheel will stop at any point of 360 degrees rotation, it is very close to static balance. If more than four quarter ounce weights are used, chances are there is a very bad spot in the tire or wheel. As most competition wheels are machined to exacting tolerances, they are very close to perfect static balance so suspect the tire. If three weights are required, it is possible to spread the two outside weights apart and eliminate the third weight. Once the wheel is balanced, paint a small mark next to the weights for future reference. If a weight is thrown or knocked off during a race, the new weight can be installed without going through the entire process.

Dynamic balancing can be done at home by mounting the wheel in a portable grinder and spinning it to high rpm. If the wheel vibrates excessively even after the static balance weights have been added, place similar weights on the wheel inside face (keep small, thin weights in here to clear steering and brake mechanism) opposite the outer weights. This should cure dynamic imbalance, but will be too much weight for static balance. Reduce all weights by one-half.

ABOVE: **Asuza full-alloy wheel is very light, is popular for competition.** BELOW: **New to karting is this full nylon Nylite wheel made in England.**

It is possible an out-of-round tire is causing the balance problems, or the tread rubber may be pulling loose from the casing at higher rpm. Check tire roundness and if it is out by an appreciable amount, any tire shop can cut it true.

While home balancing can get the wheel close, a tire shop with good dynamic balancing equipment (the bubble-level device is not good enough) can make the wheels nearly perfect. It is worth the extra effort to get professional results.

Tire Terms

Aspect ratio—the ratio of a tire's section width to its section height.

Bead—the inner band of each sidewall, that element which makes contact with and seals with the wheel rim.

Belt—a reinforcing band of tire fabric running around the circumference and strengthening the tread area.

Bias—the "conventional" tire, whose carcass is constructed of adjacent layers of fabric that run continuously from bead to bead.

Bias angle—the angle at which the cords in the tire fabric intersect the circumferential centerline of the finished tire.

Bias-belted—a tire type, similar to the bias type listed above, but with a circumferential belt of reinforcing fabric added.

Carcass—the main structure of a tire; as used in describing radial or bias-belted tires, that structure excluding the belt.

Cord—the structural part of tire fabric, generally straight fibers in the raw fabric.

Contact patch—the area of tire in direct contact with the pavement.

Cornering force—lateral force exerted by the tire on the pavement during cornering.

Green tire—a tire that has been built up on a cylindrical drum but

TOP LEFT: **Standard sprint tires are relatively narrow. Note how rear tire is curling under due to slightly lower air pressure. BOTTOM LEFT: Big and small tires are common on sprinters. Some drivers prefer wide tires for the rear with dual engines. There is less tire pressure in front than rear. BELOW: Enduro kart here uses tall, narrow tires; others prefer the tall wide tires. Driver must experiment to get best peformance.**

LEFT: Standard front, narrow, and wide rear recap tires are used mostly for Sprint racing. RIGHT: Balancing wheel statically (Go-Power alloy wheel). No more than four ¼-ounce weights should be required. BELOW: Difference between large recap tire, right, and concave Goodyear enduro tire. Centrifugal force throws center of Goodyear tire out to flat footprint at speed.

Different types of kart tires. Knobby tires are no longer used.

which has not been molded to its final shape.

Lug circle—the circle of bolts or studs that hold a wheel to its hub.

Nibbling—the jerking action which occurs in some tires as they are forced to traverse pavement ridges at a very slight angle.

Offset—the lateral distance between a wheel's vertical centerplane and the plane of its attachment to the hub; positive offset puts wheel centerplane outboard of attachment plane.

Pantographing—the change of bias angle that takes place as a tire is molded from the green state to its final shape.

Ply—a layer of structural fabric.

Radial—a tire type, characterized by flexible carcass with its cords running radially from bead to bead and a circumferential belt of high stiffness.

Rev/mi—the number of revolutions a tire makes per mile of travel.

Section height—the radial distance from wheel rim to surface of tread (unloaded tire).

Section width—the maximum lateral dimension of a tire, measured without load.

Slip angle—the angular difference between the direction of the wheel and that of the tire tread, in cornering.

Textile—tire fabric other than fiberglass or steel-reinforced.

Tread life—the number of miles covered by a tire until its tread is completely worn away.

Ultimate cornering force—maximum cornering force of which a tire is capable.

Brakes are as essential to winning kart performance as they are to normal size race cars. This is a typical four-wheel disc brake setup, with dual hydraulic cylinders.

6. Brakes

DURING THE early years of karting, emphasis was on making the machine go fast, and very little concern was directed toward the brakes. Most karts were being run on big parking lots, the top speeds were not very high, and the event courses didn't stress particular stopping ability. While some of the early karts used small drum brakes scrounged from industrial applications, there were no units designed specifically for the sport. Scrub brakes, or mechanically operated pads to rub against the tire were common.

As kart speeds increased and the competition became more sophisticated, the importance of good brakes was apparent. Some karting accessory manufacturers made up their own internal expanding shoe brakes; there were several mechanical disc brake designs tried; and one major brake company (Bendix) introduced

LEFT: **Bendix mechanical drum brake is in common use in eastern karting.** RIGHT: **Cable-operated mechanical drum brake on front of this kart has been added by homebuilder.**

a complete line of drum brakes for the sport. Today, Bendix is the major supplier of internal expanding drum brakes and Hurst/Airheart produces the bulk of disc brakes. Whatever type brake is used, there are very definite forces that limit braking effectiveness.

In engineering terms, a vehicle does not exceed a braking force of one G, which means that if the sum of the braking force at all wheels equals the weight of the vehicle, the deceleration force will be approximately 32.2 ft/sec/sec. Of course, the efficiency of any braking system is related to how much adhesion the tire has to a road surface, and once the tire is skidding on the surface, the traction factor is less. When maximum braking has been reached, it is considered 100 percent efficiency. It is very rare to exceed 100 percent.

Since braking is a vital part of any karting competition, it is essential the driver get maximum brake efficiency. In short, this means he can go deeper into turns before using the brakes, which allows him to gain valuable distance on opponents. A kart with superior brakes can often win races over karts with more speed and power. This is particularly true of the short, twisting courses. Unfortunately, only a minority of kart enthusiasts have learned the value of brakes, but they have put this knowledge to work in winning races.

The braking effort from any individual wheel is directly related to how much weight (and surface adhesion) that wheel has. If all four kart wheels used brakes, and all four had perfect traction, then braking would be optimum. It doesn't happen that way. Any time a kart decelerates or goes

75

into a corner, weight distribution on the chassis changes. This weight transfer has an immediate and direct effect on braking. The ratio of the center of gravity height (CG) to the wheelbase length determines the extent of weight transfer for a given deceleration. For the karter who really wants to get serious about stopping, the formula to determine weight transfer is:

W = total weight of kart

$$B = \frac{\%g \times W}{100} \text{ (g is 32.2 ft/sec/sec)}$$

W_f = weight on front wheels, static
W_r = weight on rear wheels, static
h = height of CG in inches
L = length of wheelbase in inches

The amount of weight transfer is $\frac{B \times h}{L}$, so front wheel weight becomes $W_f + \frac{B \times h}{L}$. Substitute W_r in this formula for rear wheel weight.

With this information, it is obvious that a kart and driver starting out with four wheel brakes and an equal weight on each wheel will decrease rear wheel weight and increase front wheel weight during deceleration. This means, in effect, the rear wheel braking becomes progressively less than the ideal 100 percent.

Staying with mathematical equations, consider the problems of distance and time to stop a kart. The distance required to stop any kart (any vehicle, for that matter) is:

$$\text{stopping distance} = \frac{V^2}{2a} \text{ feet}$$

V = initial velocity in ft/sec
a = deceleration in ft/sec/sec

Stopping distance thus varies as the square of the velocity. To find the stopping time, use the same figures where

$$\text{stopping time (seconds)} = \frac{V}{a}$$

This is a typical dual-caliper single-disc Airheart brake, when only one disc is used on rear axle of hotter karts.

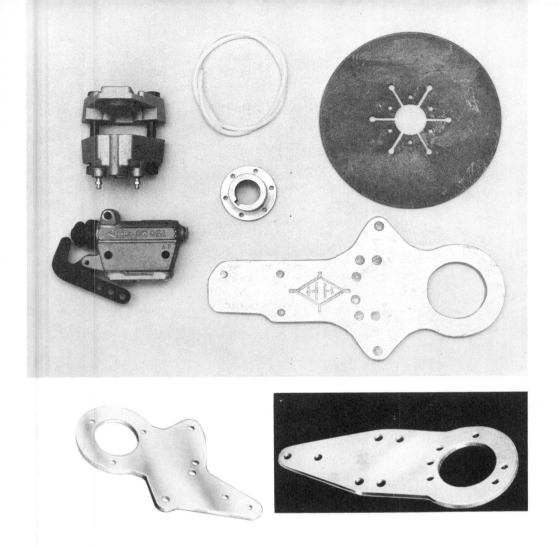

TOP: **H&H Products disc brake is made in Milwaukee, Wisc. It includes disc, master cylinder, and caliper.** BOTTOM: **Special GEM brackets fit disc brakes to practically any kart, are especially useful for the home craftsman.**

Braking ratio is the ratio of the braking drag forces between front and rear wheels. Again this can be turned to good advantage by the progressive kart enthusiast. The ratio is determined by the forces applied to front and rear brake assemblies, and includes diameter and width (as well as tire composition) of the wheel/tire combination. Thus the ratio will seldom be the same for two karts, because weight distribution will vary with driver weight, tires and wheels may differ, and brake components may change.

In practice, which ends up as the favorite engineering trial and error result, the braking ratio is designed to give maximum (100 percent ideal) individual wheel braking at maximum weight transfer. With a passenger car, engineers try to design about 60 percent of the braking power into the front wheels. Things are complicated when the same passenger car has a static weight ratio of about 60 percent front wheels and 40 percent rear wheels. For the typical Sprint kart (with driver) the ratio of wheel weight is about 50-50 and the Enduro kart ratio is about 40-60 (40 percent front). All this means that if the braking system has been designed to give maximum performance, and if that performance is approached, all wheels will skid at the same time.

It doesn't always happen that way. If too much weight is transferred to the front wheels, the rear brake(s) will lock up first, causing an uncontrollable skid. Karters have discovered this undesirable characteristic too often—the hard way.

The problem of heat, that is, when trying to determine the effect of heat upon braking and then designing around the problem, is not so easily calculated. As a rule, the diameter of kart wheels determines the size of drum brakes, which will in turn have more effect on design than heat considerations. Rarely can a drum brake be big enough to eliminate heat problems entirely, but the heat generated can be controlled. One independent kart manufacturer makes his own front drum brakes, using a finned wheel alloy casting with a pressed steel drum liner. This gives a bit more area to work with and is apparently successful. Because a disc brake can be nearly as big as the adjacent tire, and because of its very design, the disc unit will not suffer as much from heat as the drum design.

There doesn't seem to be any significant reason, but eastern U.S. karters tend to run drum brakes almost

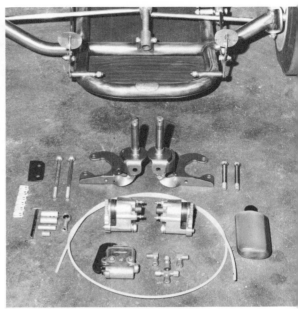

LEFT: Dual caliper support brackets mount single caliper to keep caliper from cocking and causing uneven puck wear. RIGHT: Complete Hartman-Airheart disc brake assembly for front wheels. Note extra strong front spindle brackets. BELOW: Margay uses clevice adjustment on Airheart master cylinders to get proportional hydraulic pressure between front and rear brakes.

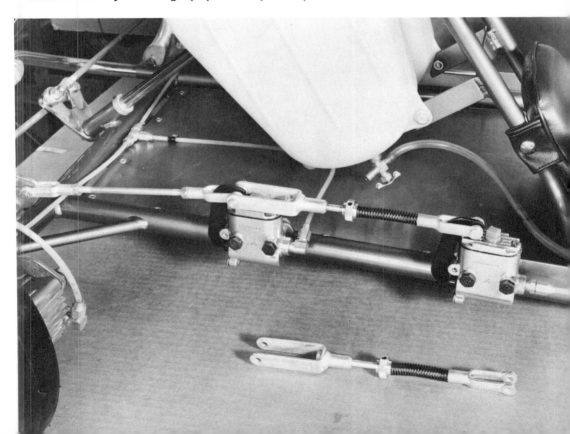

LEFT: When installing disc brakes on front, remove old spindle. Either include new spindle or rebuild old unit to accept caliper. RIGHT: Pound out kingpin with soft mallet. Pin bolt has serrations in head shank for interference fit with spindle. BELOW: Radius rods must be removed, since new rods must be shorter to fit new spindle steering arms.

exclusively while western karters have almost all traded for disc brakes. Both have certain advantages. First a look at the drum brake.

In one form or another, the internal expanding brake has been used on vehicles for decades. Such a design depends on brake shoe type and application for maximum performance. There are two types of brake shoes— the leading or servo shoe which rotates about its own pivot point, and the trailing or anti-servo shoe. For all practical purposes, the leading shoe will give $3\frac{1}{2}$ times the drag of a trailing shoe, and its stopping power will depend on the brake lining coefficient of friction, distance between pivot and drum center, and length of the lining arc. In essence, the leading shoe does most of the work.

Since the leading shoe is doing most of the stopping, it will wear much faster. In practice, therefore, the leading shoe may have a thicker, shorter lining. A cam-operated brake can overcome some of this unequal wear pattern, but it will put more force on the trailing shoe. The leading shoe will be constantly trying to assist itself (thus the servo name) by pulling the shoe into the rotating drum. Engineers try to design the leading shoe to give a coefficient of friction of at least 0.75 before this shoe will self-lock itself.

LEFT: **Difference in tie rod lengths. Shorter rods are used with disc brakes, are included in conversion kit.** RIGHT: **Holes are drilled in belly pan to hold pop rivets that position brake lines and fittings.**

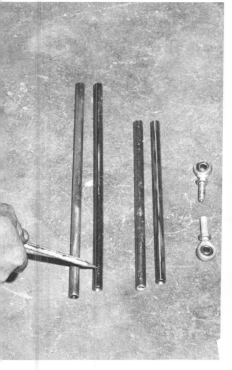

The average kart runs a Bendix brake with 6-inch drum diameter by $1\frac{3}{4}$-inch width. This is a leading-trailing shoe type, usually with a molded asbestos lining riveted to the shoe. Metallic linings are available as options. In use, the drum brake has proven entirely dependable through the years, particularly if the karter takes the time to include new linings periodically, turn the drum or replace it if necessary, and keep the shoes and linkage adjusted.

While the disc brake is not new to karting, it has only recently enjoyed a growing popularity with the intro-duction of a hydraulic system by Hurst/Airheart. As a rule, a small 6-inch disc and a single caliper will be used with a single-engine kart; a larger $7\frac{3}{4}$-inch disc and two cali-pers will be used with a twin-engine kart. Another popular option is use of two small discs with single calipers for each on the faster twin-engined karts. Four wheel discs are showing up in larger numbers as drivers learn how to use the greater potential of maximum braking.

The hydraulic discs also offer the possibility of separate systems for each brake. Thus it is possible for a single kart to have two or four in-dividual master cylinders; the extras used as backups in case one or two should fail.

The first disc brake patent was is-sued to Dr. F. Lanchester back in 1902, and the principle remains un-changed. Dr. Lanchester's initial idea

was to use mechanical calipers, a type of disc brake used during the early 1960's on karts, and the principle works remarkably well. American disc brake development has not been as rapid as that of European car builders, mostly because of total unit cost. Initially, there were some prob-lems with disc brake caliper pucks that wore quickly and caused noisy braking, a situation that a $20,000 sports car owner might consider ac-ceptable and a $2,000 passenger car owner would reject. It is interesting to note that while disc brakes had been installed in racing cars for many years, they were never really "bug-free" until the American and European passenger car builders in-troduced them into mass-production.

While the disc brake has some dis-advantages, it also has a host of advantages. The disc has excellent di-rectional stability when used at high speed; there is less brake fade; it is not as sensitive to speed as the drum design. There are several more tech-nical advantages, but these three are most important to the karter. Basic-ally, all disc design advantages come from insensitivity of the output torque to changes in coefficient of friction; ability of the brake to cool rapidly; and the lack of that mechanical fade.

Disc brakes take many different forms, but the spot (round puck) type is most common in America and is the type used in karting. In all kart disc brakes, a caliper is held rigidly to some portion of the frame or axle housing. The caliper is built to wrap over the rotating disc, something like the cupped hand. There are at least two friction elements in the caliper, one on either side of the disc, and when hydraulic pressure is applied to these pucks, they squeeze inward and grab the disc. Because of this hydraulic pressure which is trying to push the pucks apart, the caliper must be reasonably massive to retain its shape.

The rotating disc must be made of a good material, usually a malleable iron, that can withstand tremendous temperatures. During testing, engineers have literally burned the metal disc because of the extremely high temperatures, yet the system continued to work as a brake. This is not likely to happen in karting, but it does illustrate how effective this simple stopping system really is.

While the drum-type brakes will not seem to require as much pedal effort as the disc brakes, they will be more sensitive to pedal pressure. When the kart driver learns how to handle a drum-equipped vehicle, he finds the disc brake kart seems harder

to stop. This is only because the disc brakes do not have a self-assist capacity, but the more the driver pushes, the more the brakes work.

The amount of friction surface on any brake system, drum, scrub, or disc, will determine how effective the brakes are at high speeds. This is why four wheel brakes are becoming more popular in karting. It also explains the preference of larger caliper and disc, or multiple disc installations with the very fast karts. There is the matter of caliper position that has been overlooked by karters so far, though, and this will have an eventual effect on bearings. Since the frictional drag of the brake is acting at one point, and is not a pure couple, braking will alter wheel bearing load. If the brake caliper is located behind the rear axle, the drag force acts in opposition to the load applied by the weight of the car. However if the caliper is ahead of the axle, the drag force increases the load applied to the bearings.

Most kart shops have both types of brakes available, but no one uses the scrub brake for competition. It isn't

LEFT: **Brake accentuating rod uses Heim rod end to replace clevice.** RIGHT: **Install new spindle with bolt from bottom up for clearance next to inner diameter of disc.**

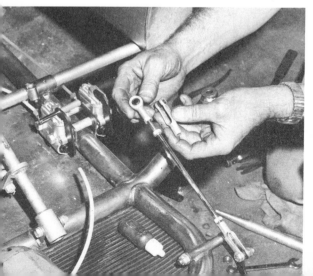

LEFT: Mount disc to wheel, install wheel on new spindle, check for clearance near kingpin. RIGHT: Use washer on tie rod end bolt to get clearance for steering pivot. CENTER: Fit caliper to spindle bracket as shown. Note the caliper fits with one-half on either side of disc. BOTTOM: Aluminum frying pans are cut to shape and mounted to rear of disc area for leg protection. Front attachment is by pop rivet.

Kathy Hartman fills hydraulic system with fluid and bleeds the individual calipers. Because braking force of front and rear wheels must vary, leverage on interconnecting link is adjustable with washers.

approved by IKF and it likely isn't going to be included on anything but the most inexpensive Fun kart. Drum brakes are not as expensive as the discs, so they are usually included as standard equipment on most commercial karts, with discs listed as optional.

The decision to run a single rear brake (which works to stop both rear wheels if a live axle is used) or front and rear brakes is up to the enthusiast. The rules require rear brakes only. However, as the driver gains driving finesse, he will find the additional braking to his definite advantage on tough tracks. Fortunately, they can be added to the existing system without a great deal of effort, thus cutting down the initial expense.

Stopping a kart with good brakes is almost as fantastic a driving experience as hurtling along at 120 mph.

Final drive can be exotic, as on this outboard Saetta/Caretta drive with Hartman slipper clutch.

7. The Final Drive

ALL THE power in the world does little good for the kart with an inferior final drive. The method of getting engine horsepower to the tires can seldom be too good, but it can often be just bad enough to neutralize an otherwise winning combination. While final drive isn't of much interest to the neighborhood karter, it is a vital concern for the competition enthusiast.

Final drive can be described as those mechanical components used to transmit crankshaft power to the tires, and may consist of (in part or total) : clutch, chain, gearbox, sprocket, axle. For competition, each component part must be of good quality, be entirely dependable, and be of reasonable cost. Most of the final drive equipment offered by kart shops fills those requirements.

Kart enthusiasts are constantly experimenting, changing this or that in an effort to get better performance. The centrifugal clutch has, through the years, been used and unused more than any other piece of kart equipment. The controversy of clutch value is as old as karting itself, but at least in the Enduro classes the value is well established. The Fun kart used for family driving will use the clutch as a convenience, especially important for female drivers.

The rise and fall of kart engine clutches can be traced almost exclusively to competition rules and clutch design evolution. The first clutches were anything but superior, designed for industrial uses where load conditions were low, constant, and predictable. In competition, they were undependable and seldom performed to requirements. Enthusiasts could still appreciate the advantages of a clutch and prevailed upon manufacturers to design a unit specifically for

BELOW: **Horstman dry clutch uses iron shoes. It is possible to oil temporarily through holes in housing.** BOTTOM: **Rules call for chains to be enclosed to prevent driver from losing a finger.**

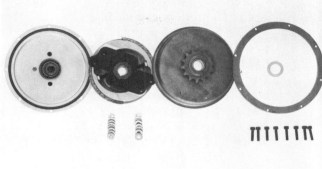

LEFT: **Burco oiler handled by Inglewood Kart Shop uses Horstman shoe assembly. It will fit both American and foreign engines.** RIGHT: **Exploded view of Hartman slipper clutch. Specialty of this clutch is non-leaking housing and aluminum shoes that can easily be adjusted for engagement speeds. It can also be non-energizing or self-energizing.**

karting. Initially, it was found that lap times with and without a clutch were almost identical, even with inferior clutches. As clutch improvements were made, lap times improved over direct drive karts.

Most kart clutches work on the centrifugal principle, and resemble a drum brake system to some extent. There is a backing plate, two, three, or four expanding shoes covered with a lining, and an outer drum. The backing plate, or driving portion of the clutch fits to the engine shaft with a woodruff key, a set screw, lock nut, taper wedge, or a combination of these methods. The drum is free to rotate over the backing plate and shoes, usually on a needle bearing hub. Because temperature will cause the drum to expand, just as with a drum brake, karters often fit specially machined expansion rings over the drum. These effectively reduce expansion and consequent clutch slippage.

The real heart of a good clutch, and the basic difference in most designs, is the clutch shoe and actuating mechanism design. In a typical design, pre-loaded springs are placed between the two shoes to pull them into a hub rest. While the engine is rotating at lower rpm the springs overcome centrifugal force trying to throw the shoes outward. As the engine rpm increases, centrifugal force overcomes the spring tension and the shoes are thrown outward to rub against the drum. The engaging action of the shoes multiplies the output torque as engine speed and torque increases. Rapid, full engagement is thus possible at lower rpm and the clutch will remain engaged below the rated engagement speed while it is under load.

The point at which the shoes expand enough to make solid contact with the drum is the engagement speed, regulated by weight of shoes and tension of the clutch springs. For this reason manufacturers offer a variety of springs so the enthusiast can modify engagement speed to suit his particular kart and use.

The two most popular clutch sizes are 3½- and 4½-inch diameter, the 3½ for smaller engines and the 4½ for large engines. Most small clutches with 4 shoes have a total lining area of approximately 12 inches, but the area is much less with 2 or 3 shoes. The large clutches with 2 shoes have similar area at 12 inches. Friction material for shoe facing is usually a replaceable, rivited fabric with iron or sintered metallic linings available on special request. Clutch diameter is important, since it is directly relative to horsepower transfer. A small clutch on a big engine will slip more, heat up quickly, and fail. A big clutch on a small engine may not allow enough slippage for the engine to run properly at lower rpm. Clutch engagement speed is equally critical.

Slower engines may require engagement at lower rpm while high rpm engines would stall with a similar low engagement. Since clutch engagement is a function of spring tension, clutch manufacturers usually offer a variety of springs for individual adjustment. Fairbanks-Morse springs are typical of the wide range of engagement speeds possible.

BOTTOM, LEFT: **Hartman slipper clutch installed on McCulloch American reed engine.** BELOW: **Aviation Industries slipper clutch built by Art Ingels is available for domestic and foreign engines.** BOTTOM, RIGHT: **Reinforced cooling ring slips over stock clutch housing to minimize drum distortion.**

3½-inch Diameter Clutch

Spring Number	Spring Color	Engagement Speed in rpm
20—67	White	3000—3100
30—63	Orange	2600—2700
20—60	Black	2300—2400
20—58	Brown	2200—2300
20—53	Grey-Green	1950—2000
20—50	Red	1900—2000
20—51	Plain	1750—1800
20—52	Dark Green	1700—1800
20—56	Light Green	1650—1750
20—55	Yellow	1500—1600
20—54	Maroon	1450—1500

In use, the clutch will be in full engagement when the engine is at maximum torque, a figure in rpm's that will be lower than peak horsepower rpm. This might be anywhere from 2300—7000 rpm depending on the engine, but usually American Reed engine peak torque is at a lower rpm than the imported rotary valve engine. The soft shoe lining allows some slippage in the marginal zones between clutch drum free-wheeling and shoe lockup. In use, the clutch then engages and partially disengages hundreds of times as kart speed goes from very fast to very slow. With a clutch, the enthusiast can gear for the track straights and let the clutch take care of the low speed corners. This means the clutch equipped kart can pull a slightly higher gear ratio than the direct drive counterpart, which must lug the engine around corners.

If the engagement speed of any clutch is to be a given rpm, say 4500, then it should engage at that speed under all conditions of load and temperature. It should also disengage within 100 rpm of that designed speed. To get strong acceleration the clutch must connect at the beginning of the best torque range. A dry clutch is operating with upwards of 400 degrees F heat during racing. Too much heat will cause the drum to distort and eventually fail, and the shoe lining will glaze (in the case of an organic lining, it will become brittle). This high temperature will also cause the springs to lose tension.

While the new clutches designed specifically for karts were vastly superior to the original modified industrial clutches, they continued to have a high attrition rate in maximum racing conditions. They all seemed to work well enough with stock engines, but failure was common with modified engines, especially in Enduro racing. The problem had to be licked someway, because IKF rules specifically require clutches for Enduro racing. The cure is the slipper clutch.

The slipper was successfully introduced in the 1960's by enterprising Texas karters. During a large National meet, the Texans managed to turn away most challengers simply because they could get through the Enduro corners faster. Now slipper clutches are almost universal.

Early clutch oilers were simple oil squirt cans attached to the kart frame, with a piece of tubing leading from can to clutch. The karter could squirt a dab of oil on the clutch at any time and cause it to slip. In this way the engagement rpm could be raised if necessary and the engagement shock could be lessened. Heat generated could be reduced significantly. This simple arrangement cured clutch reliability and engagement control factors, but it immediately led to oil-splattered tracks that made ice skating seem simple by comparison. Chain oilers drop tiny amounts of oil around the track, but clutch oilers were dumping large quantities at the wrong places, namely starting line and corners. IKF countered with a

LEFT: **Max-Torque clutch with two- and four-shoe design is available with various shoe material. Lining area is similar on both 3½- and 4½-inch designs.** RIGHT: **Axle-type dry slipper clutch uses steel balls for engagement race.**

rule banning clutch oilers that dump oil. The oiled clutch worked so well the idea was obviously worth pursuing. The result is the captive oil-immersed clutch, or a unit that is sealed in oil. The idea isn't new; it was used successfully as recently as the early 1950's when Hudson included oil-immersed clutches on passenger cars.

There are several different types of slipper clutches sold by karting shops, and all seem to work quite well. Some are made specifically for gear drive, while most are for chain drive. In all designs, the clutch revolves in a sealed housing, with just enough oil added to control the heat and engagement speed. However, if the oil clutch is not used correctly, it quickly becomes a disadvantage rather than an asset. There are two

areas of individual karter choice that make a really significant difference: the oil to be used and the clutch.

The oil selection is the most important decision, as experience has proven cooling more vital than lubrication of the shoes and drum. If the oil is too "slippery", the clutch will slip vigorously at first while there is an oil film on the drum. This causes too high an engine rpm, then as the oil film is burned away by the heat, the clutch will grab at too low an engagement speed. Iron shoe units sometimes cycle between this over- and under-slip condition several times during acceleration out of a single corner. Even under these undesirable conditions, the slipper clutch will improve kart performance.

The best common oil found so far

Akerman slipper clutch housing is used with Margay gearbox.

is type A automatic transmission fluid. It has a low viscosity which makes an ideal coolant; it does not break down readily under high temperature conditions; and it gives smooth engagement speeds. Kart shops sell special additives.

The selection of a perfect clutch is a bit more complicated. The idea is to get the clutch to hold engine speed just right to maintain maximum torque. Most stock engines give maximum torque at about 4000 rpm while most good modified engines give peak torque at about 7000—8000 rpm. The trick is to match the clutch to the individual engine torque characteristics.

Experience has shown the small iron shoe clutches work very well on the smaller A-stock engines. If the stock engine is weak at low rpm, two

of the shoes can be welded to the hub to increase engagement speed slightly. However, these iron shoes tend to wear out after several races and must be replaced. Particles from this destruction mix with the oil and thoroughly coat the clutch assembly and housing, which dictates a good cleaning during shoe replacement. These iron clutches also work reasonably well with the slightly larger modified B-engines, especially those with good low-end power.

A cleaner clutch is the fabric lining type (a phenolic block lining slips too much in the oil housing). This type gives a good deal of flexibility in engagement speed by spring tension adjustment and hub assembly rotation. With this type clutch on an A-stock engine, one thick and one thin spring combination works unless the engine is "high ported", then the two thick springs are needed. In some cases, the hub rotor must be reversed to provide a de-energization of the shoes.

Maintenance of a slipper clutch is simple, but the unit does require attention. A leaky seal on the engine power takeoff side will let clutch housing oil into the engine, which will lead to a fouled spark plug and burned clutch. A similar problem can arise with the gearbox seal, due largely to a dry condition of the seal. When a clutch housing is bolted to the engine, a combination of all the mating surfaces makes perfect production tolerances almost impossible to maintain. Occasionally, extra gaskets may be necessary to get proper alignment, particularly with gearboxes.

Do not put in "extra" oil over the recommended amount. This will vary from 4 to 8 ounces normally, depending on the type of clutch. Dynamometer tests show this is enough to cool the clutch and any more than the recommended amount tends to cause overheating and power loss. Sprint karters have found a larger vent desirable, since the severe service apparently causes some oil vaporization. An oil level dip stick can be added to the housing to check level between races.

During testing, it was found that an iron shoe clutch never exceeded 240 degrees F even under the worst possible conditions, which compares to a dry clutch temperature over 375 degrees F. In specifics of kart performance, the slipper clutch remains cooler for the entire race, therefore lap times will continue to remain constant. With the dry clutch, however, temperature will decrease the clutch effectiveness and lap times will begin to lag.

The most obvious advantage of the slipper clutch is keeping the engine rpm in the most effective range. This means the driver can use brakes to control the kart through a corner, zapping the throttle to keep the engine running clean. The slipping clutch allows this, and will pick up kart speed out of the turns amazingly fast. In terms of straightaway acceleration, the dry clutch will run the first 50 or so yards faster, but then the slipper clutch will fly by. Since the slipper clutch is running so much cooler, it will not wear out as soon, which means more completed races and less racing cost.

Getting the power from engine to axle is also a story in karting ingenuity. Chains are the most common type of transfer, but much interest is now being directed toward special gearboxes. While gearboxes didn't come into widespread use until the late 1960's, they were introduced to the sport before it was yet five years old.

Karters rejected the gearbox drive at first, although the manufacturers pointed out several obvious advantages. The typical reaction was "too costly and too heavy". At the time, when all races were of the Sprint variety, this weight consideration seemed to have some foundation. With the advent of Enduro contests the weight problem didn't seem so critical, especially when compared to the problems of chain friction losses and failures.

The specific problem of kart chains is in oiling. Even with oilers installed and constantly dripping a small quantity of oil on the chain, it will not operate as smoothly as a gearset running in oil. Karters report a very definite difference in the feel of a kart equipped with a gearbox, in that vibration is less at sustained speeds,

West Bend engine uses Akerman slipper clutch housing between power output shaft and Margay final drive gearbox. BOTTOM, LEFT: Akerman slipper housing with Maxi-Torque four-shoe clutch bolted to McCulloch engine. RIGHT: McCulloch 91 engine and Akerman slipper oil clutch housing bolted to Margay gearbox. Perfect alignment of engine and gearbox is critical.

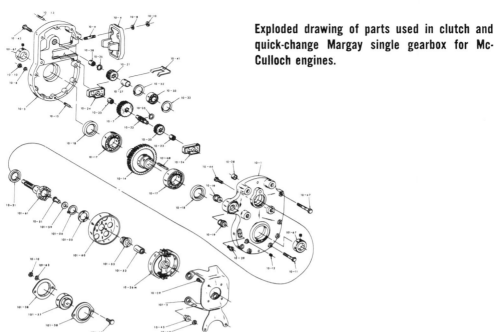

Exploded drawing of parts used in clutch and quick-change Margay single gearbox for McCulloch engines.

LEFT: A Margay quick-change gearbox attached to the rear axle with disc brake calipers mounted direct to gearbox. BELOW: Quick-change gears are spur-cut with needle bearing support blocks. All parts are matched for quick gear change. FAR RIGHT: Rear plate is removed; gears slip out as unit.

and some drivers claim the rpm is higher with gears.

Chief advantage is to the competition karter, where constant replacement will soon equal the cost of a gearbox. Gearboxes seem to last forever with minimal maintenance, but they are not to be recommended for the Fun kart from the simple expediency of economics.

There are two well-known gearboxes currently available—the Pro unit from Palitine, Illinois, and the Margay design from St. Louis. The Margay is a quick-change gearbox resembling quick-change rear end assemblies in large oval track race cars, and lists a tremendous number of gear ratios. For this reason alone it is desirable for Sprint karts when time between heat races is minimal and gearing must be changed.

While the early gearbox drives were for direct coupling only, the modern box is designed to be used with clutches and inboard mounted disc brakes.

Transmission type gearboxes, where there is the possibility to change gearing with a lever, are not legal in American karting classes except in the more sophisticated FKE category. European karters view this as a definite detrement to the growth of Stateside karting, but it has tended to keep speeds to a more controllable level and places emphasis on both American and foreign two-strokes. This in turn keeps the cost of racing down.

Chain drive is far and away the most common type of kart final drive coupling, a direct result of simplicity and initial cost. For a simple mechanical coupling, it has a minimum weight and a very wide gearing ratio. Number 35 chain is most common to karting, and as originally designed was intended for bicycles. Obviously the kart chain is rotating at a far greater rpm, and is therefore subjected to a greater wear rate than with a bicycle. Further, the chain is wrapping around the tiny engine sprocket in a very tight radius with

LEFT: **Margay gearbox can be set up for dual installation, as shown with two West Bend engines.** RIGHT: **Dyna-Drive final drive from Pro has interchangeable gears, but they are not quick-change.** BELOW: **Chain drive is most common kart final drive. Keeping chain in top shape is imperative.**

LEFT: **Dyna-Drive can be adapted for clutch use; it is most popular on sprint karts.** RIGHT: **Sprockets are available in many different ratios. Hubs allow movement on axle for alignment, and split sprockets allow gearing change without pulling a wheel.**

is apparent with motorcycles, where the primary chain runs in oil and as little as 3 or 4 tooth contact at the vital driving juncture.

Even under the most ideal karting conditions where dirt and temperature are controlled, and where maximum chain oiling common to karting is used, the chain will wear extremely fast. It takes very little time for kart chain to wear beyond use, thus a single weekend of racing might require two or more chains. As the chain wears, it becomes stiff, which increases friction power loss. A used chain will definitely cause higher lap times.

Lubrication is the prime problem with chain drive. Every joint in a chain is a plain bearing of steel working on another hardened steel surface. Lubricant must be at these points of contact at all times, something practically impossible with the exposed final chain drive common to karting. The importance of this oiling

seldom fails but the drive chain to the rear wheel is exposed and has a high failure rate.

Even with the semi-automatic chain oilers, the karter should periodically oil the chain at roller and link edges to ensure as much penetration as possible to the internal working surfaces. Although it is not common in karting, a fully enclosed chain drive will reduce the amount of dirt and foreign matter that can quickly destroy a chain, and the dripping lubricant will not spray off onto the track as easily. While the oil can will keep the chain lubed, it is recommended to also brush a soft grease or heavy gear oil into the chain.

Chain wear is apparent by how the chain fits the kart. It cannot be too tight, nor can it be too loose. A good guide is approximately 1/4-inch play of a new chain, installed. As the chain wears, this play will increase. The maximum acceptable before replacement for stretch alone would be 1/4

For direct-drive karts, engine sprockets are available in a wide range of ratios. RIGHT: Chain oil, a must for every karter.

inch per foot of chain. A new chain will seem to loosen up rather rapidly. This is not wear, but "bedding-down", and the final chain adjustment must be made after this initial stretching. More adjustment slack may be necessary for very long Enduro races, but normal wear may provide this. Very few competition chains run with master links, the drivers preferring to use fully rivited circles. A chain press (breaker) is available through motorcycle and kart shops.

Another type of coupling has been tried, usually referred to as a timing belt drive, but in reality it is just a Gilmer-type cog-belt similar to those used for driving dragster engine superchargers. This is a very effective type connection, but it too will stretch and has problems with the small drive cog necessary for the engine.

The beginning karter may consider the chain most susceptible to wear and failure in a chain coupling final drive, but the sprockets receive almost as much punishment. There are many different sprockets available, with emphasis on final gear ratios, but the difference is really how easy the sprocket is to change for a fast ratio switch and the type of material involved. Most kart sprockets are made

by a limited number of suppliers, and may be either steel or heat treated aluminum.

Perhaps the biggest mistake the neophyte karter makes when installing engine or rear end is sprocket misalignment. Just eyeballing the drive and driven sprockets is not enough, since the engine sprocket is so small it is almost impossible to detect slight twist. A straight edge across the two sprocket faces will show misalignment. Check the chain also. If the inner plates of each chain link are polished equally, the sprockets are running true, but if one side shows considerably more wear it indicates the sprockets are not parallel or in plane.

Sprockets which are excessively worn have a hooked appearance to the teeth, something like a power saw blade. When the sprocket is replaced, always check for proper chain fit in the teeth grooves. A new chain should fit snuggly, neither to slack nor with a tight, springy feel.

Check the sprocket runout, which will cause the chain to run tight and then loose during a single revolution. Check for side wobble, which can be caused by either the sprocket, sprocket mount, or axle.

Most karts run with fully rivet chains with no master link. Karter must include rivet breaker in tool kit. RIGHT: In some cases a double chain is used if the engine puts out high horsepower.

Talk about sprockets leads invariably to gear ratios, and this is where many karters meet a solid wall. Although two karts may be identical in every way, and the driver's may have similar weight, the gearing for maximum performance from both will not be the same. There are other variables that cannot be overlooked. Therefore, trying to get winning results by duplicating a winning kart's gear ratio is seldom successful.

As a beginning, the karter should stock his tool kit with at least three driving (engine) sprockets and five axle sprockets. This will give a reasonable series of ratios to work from, or a total of fifteen possibilities. With just five engine sprockets and eleven axle sprockets, look at the tremendous gearing flexibility.

Drive Sprocket

		8T	9T	10T	11T	12T
Axle Sprocket	64T	8:1	7.1:1	6.4:1	5.82:1	5.33:1
	66T	8.25:1	7.33:1	6.6:1	6.0:1	5.5:1
	68T	8.5:1	7.55:1	6.8:1	6.18:1	5.66:1
	70T	8.75:1	7.77:1	7.0:1	6.36:1	5.83:1
	72T	9.0:1	8.1:1	7.2:1	6.54:1	6.0:1
	74T	9.25:1	8.22:1	7.4:1	6.72:1	6.16:1
	76T	9.5:1	8.44:1	7.6:1	6.91:1	6.33:1
	78T	9.75:1	8.66:1	7.8:1	7.09:1	6.5:1
	80T	10.0:1	8.88:1	8.0:1	7.27:1	6.66:1
	82T	10.25:1	9.11:1	8.2:1	7.45:1	6.83:1
	84T	10.5:1	9.33:1	8.4:1	7.63:1	7.0:1

When selecting any gear ratio, the idea is to keep the engine working in its own best rpm range. This will vary from engine to engine as well as make to make, so the only positive proof is trial-and-error gearing. However, there is a starting point. The short stroke, loop scavenged engine

The Margay quick-change gearbox final drive offers a wide range of drive ratios.

The **STANDARD RATIO RANGE** is 4.0 thru 9.0 to 1 (Column 2). For the A-B single for sprint and enduro events. This is the most popular range and is also desirable for B-C sprint, enduro and indoor events.

The **ENDURO RATIO RANGE** is 3.0 thru 6.75 to 1 (Column 3). For B-C events on oval and road course tracks with long straight ways.

The **ALL PURPOSE RANGE** is 4.55 thru 10.25 to 1 (Column 4). This range is desirable for A-B sprint and indoor events. Also in enduro events when ratios above 4.55 are not required.

TWENTY-SIX SEPARATE RATIOS in each ratio range.

Standard Ratio Range is 4.0 thru 9.0 to 1 (Shown in Column 2). Other ratio ranges shown in Columns 3 and 4 require use of **OPTIONAL** gears as shown in column headings.

The Quick Change Cartridge consists of one change gear and two slide blocks. The change gear is stamped with the number of teeth on the gear and its mating set of slide blocks are also stamped with this number.

For any listed ratio **ALWAYS** use slide blocks and change gear both stamped with the same number.
EXAMPLE—Ratio wanted 7.6 (Column 2). Use change gear No. 38 with slide blocks No. 38.

	*Standard Ratios		Gears Marked Optional Are Required To Obtain These Ratios			
	Sprint Range		Enduro Range		All Purpose Range	
	20		20		20	
INPUT GEAR	20		25 (optional)		18 (optional)	
INTERMEDIATE GEAR	20					
OUTPUT GEAR	80		75 (optional)		82 (optional)	
Column 1	Column 2		Column 3		Column 4	
CHANGE GEAR	Slide Block	Ratio	Slide Block	Ratio	Slide Block	Ratio
20	20	4.0	20	3.0	20	4.55
21	21	4.2	21	3.15	21	4.78
22	22	4.4	22	3.3	22	5.01
23	23	4.6	23	3.45	23	5.24
24	24	4.8	24	3.6	24	5.47
25	25	5.0	25	3.75	25	5.69
26	26	5.2	26	3.9	26	5.92
27	27	5.4	27	4.05	27	6.14
28	28	5.6	28	4.2	28	6.38
29	29	5.8	29	4.35	29	6.60
30	30	6.0	30	4.5	30	6.83
31	31	6.2	31	4.65	31	7.06
32	32	6.4	32	4.8	32	7.29
33	33	6.6	33	4.95	33	7.52
34	34	6.8	34	5.1	34	7.74
35	35	7.0	35	5.25	35	7.97
36	36	7.2	36	5.4	36	8.20
37	37	7.4	37	5.55	37	8.43
38	38	7.6	38	5.7	38	8.66
39	39	7.8	39	5.85	39	8.88
40	40	8.0	40	6.0	40	9.11
41	41	8.2	41	6.15	41	9.34
42	42	8.4	42	6.3	42	9.57
43	43	8.6	43	6.45	43	9.79
44	44	8.8	44	6.6	44	10.02
45	45	9.0	45	6.75	45	10.25

*Ratio Ranges other than standard available on special order at no extra cost.

Courtesy Margay Corp.

RPM-RATIO-MPH CHART

ENGINE RPM - MPH

10.5:1	9.33:1	9.0:1	8.4:1	8.0:1	7.63:1	7.5:1	7.2:1	7.0:1	6.66:1	6.54:1	6.0:1	5.45:1	5.0:1	RATIO	REAR TIRE DIAMETER
11.8	13.3	13.8	14.8	15.6	16.3	16.6	17.3	17.8	18.7	19.1	20.8	22.9	25	10.5	4000
12.4	14.0	14.5	15.5	16.3	17.1	17.4	18.1	18.6	19.6	20.0	21.8	24.0	26.2	11	
13.6	15.2	15.8	17.0	17.8	18.7	19.0	19.8	20.4	21.4	21.8	23.8	26.2	28.5	12	
14.8	16.7	17.3	18.5	19.5	20.4	20.8	21.6	22.3	23.4	23.9	26.0	28.6	31.2	10.5	5000
15.5	17.5	18.1	19.4	20.4	21.4	21.8	22.7	23.3	24.5	25.0	27.2	30.0	32.7	11	
17.0	19.1	19.8	21.2	22.3	23.4	23.8	24.7	25.5	26.3	27.2	29.7	32.7	35.6	12	
17.8	20.0	20.8	22.2	23.4	24.5	24.9	25.9	26.7	28.0	28.6	31.2	34.3	37.5	10.5	6000
18.6	21.0	21.7	23.3	24.5	25.7	26.1	27.2	28.0	29.4	30.0	32.7	36.0	39.3	11	
20.4	22.9	23.7	25.5	26.7	28.0	28.5	29.7	30.6	32.0	32.7	35.7	39.3	42.7	12	
20.7	23.3	24.2	25.9	27.3	28.6	29.1	30.3	31.2	32.7	33.4	36.4	40.1	43.7	10.5	7000
21.7	24.5	25.4	27.2	28.6	30.0	30.5	31.7	32.6	34.3	35.0	38.1	42.0	45.8	11	
23.8	26.7	27.7	29.7	31.2	32.7	33.3	34.6	35.7	37.4	38.1	41.6	45.8	49.9	12	
23.7	26.7	27.7	29.6	31.2	32.7	33.2	34.6	35.6	37.4	38.2	41.6	45.8	49.9	10.5	8000
24.8	28.0	29.0	31.1	32.7	34.3	34.8	36.3	37.3	39.2	40.0	43.5	48.0	52.4	11	
27.2	30.5	31.6	34.0	35.6	37.4	38.0	39.6	40.6	42.8	43.5	47.5	52.4	57.0	12	
26.7	30.0	31.2	33.3	35.1	36.8	37.4	38.9	40.1	42.1	43.0	46.8	51.5	56.1	10.5	9000
27.9	31.5	32.6	35.0	36.8	38.6	39.2	40.8	42.0	44.1	45.0	48.9	54.0	58.9	11	
30.6	34.3	35.6	38.2	40.1	42.1	42.8	44.5	45.9	48.2	49.0	53.5	58.9	64.2	12	
29.7	33.4	34.7	37.1	39.0	40.9	41.6	43.3	44.5	46.8	47.8	52.0	57.3	62.3	10.5	10000
31.1	35.0	36.3	38.9	40.8	42.9	43.6	45.4	46.7	49.1	50.0	54.4	60.0	65.5	11	
34.0	38.2	39.6	42.5	44.6	46.8	47.6	49.5	51.0	53.5	54.4	59.4	65.5	71.3	12	
32.6	36.7	38.1	40.8	42.9	44.9	45.7	47.6	48.9	51.4	52.5	57.2	63.0	68.5	10.5	11000
34.2	38.5	39.9	42.7	44.9	47.1	47.9	49.9	51.3	54.0	55.0	59.9	66.0	72.0	11	
37.4	42.0	43.5	46.7	49.0	51.4	52.3	54.4	56.0	58.8	59.9	65.3	72.0	78.4	12	
35.6	40.0	41.6	44.5	46.8	49.0	49.9	51.9	53.4	56.1	57.3	62.4	68.7	74.7	10.5	12000
37.3	42.0	43.5	46.6	49.0	51.4	52.3	54.4	56.0	58.9	60.0	65.4	72.0	78.6	11	
40.8	45.8	47.5	51.0	53.5	56.1	57.1	59.4	61.0	64.2	65.3	71.3	78.6	85.6	12	
38.6	43.4	45.1	48.2	50.7	53.1	54.0	56.2	57.8	60.8	62.1	67.6	74.4	80.9	10.5	13000
40.4	45.5	47.1	50.5	53.1	56.7	56.6	59.0	60.7	63.8	65.0	70.8	78.0	85.1	11	
44.2	49.6	51.4	55.2	57.9	60.8	61.8	64.3	66.3	69.5	70.8	77.2	85.1	92.7	12	
41.5	46.7	48.5	51.9	54.6	57.2	58.2	60.6	62.3	65.5	66.8	72.8	80.2	87.1	10.5	14000
43.5	49.0	50.8	54.4	57.2	61.0	61.0	63.5	65.3	68.7	70.0	76.3	84.0	91.0	11	
47.6	53.4	55.4	59.5	62.4	65.5	66.6	69.3	71.4	74.9	76.2	83.2	91.7	99.9	12	
44.5	50.1	52.0	55.6	58.5	61.3	62.4	64.9	66.8	70.2	71.6	78.0	85.9	93.3	10.5	15000
46.6	52.5	54.4	58.3	61.3	65.3	65.4	68.1	70.0	73.6	75.0	81.7	90.0	98.0	11	
51.0	57.3	59.4	63.7	66.9	70.2	71.4	74.2	76.5	80.2	81.7	89.1	98.2	107	12	

SPROCKET RATIO

DRIVEN	60T.	72T.	84T.
8T.	7.5:1	9.0:1	10.5:1
9T.	6.66:1	8.0:1	9.33:1
10T.	6.0:1	7.2:1	8.4:1
11T.	5.45:1	6.54:1	7.63:1
12T.	5.0:1	6.0:1	7.0:1

$$MPH = ENG.\ RPM \div R \times C \times .0136$$

R = SPROCKET RATIO
C = TIRE CIRCUMFERENCE

12" = 3.1416 FT.
11" = 2.8798 FT.
10.5" = 2.7489 FT.

is usually high winding, while long stroke engines won't turn as tight. A larger bore will give more bottom end torque. The only way to find out how the gearing is working is to time the kart for a series of laps, change gears, and try again.

For short tracks, or Sprint racing, the Three-Quarter rule is valid for selecting a gear ratio. Here, the idea is to have the engine peak at three-quarters of the straightaway length. Gearing too high to get a little more straight speed will lug the engine in the tight corners, a super critical factor in Sprint racing. On the other hand, gearing too low will let a fast kart overtake and pass on the straight. Sometimes the new kart driver thinks that running a really low gear will give definite advantage in the corners. Not necessarily, because traffic here is usually so tight that passing is difficult. There is also a natural limit to how fast any particular kart will corner, and the low gearing will kill an engine with over-revs on the straights. After awhile the driver will be able to look at a course and judge a good initial gear ratio; until then he should ask other karters with similar equipment what average ratio is good and work from there. When in doubt for Sprint track gearing, go with a lower gear ratio, which translates to mean run the lowest gear possible without giving a distinct advantage to other karts on the straights.

Selecting a gear ratio for the long distance Enduro tracks is completely different. Here top speed is the only quantity, especially with slipper clutches. When in doubt about Enduro gears, go to a higher ratio, which means run the highest ratio possible without giving up acceleration out of the turns.

Rear axles are as important as any part of the final drive, yet they receive almost abusive consideration from many karters. The individual drive rear wheels have long since given way to the live axle, or a common axle for both rear wheels. That there is no differential action between rear tires is of little concern; getting maximum power on the ground at all times *is* of concern.

Axles will give little trouble if they are good to begin with and are cared for. The material in a given axle may be anything from poor malleable iron to quality steel. Always select a top quality steel or premium alloy axle. If the unit is designed for the very fastest, most powerful karts, it is good for a slower kart. Scrimping a few dollars with some kind of cheap axle will usually lead to premature metal failure.

In fact, this advice about going with the better quality items holds true with the entire final drive system. It costs very little more to get quality, but the results are considerably better, which means more time having fun and less time fixing.

Imported rotary valve engines are the fastest but they cost more than American engines in competitive form. Shown is a Saetta with huge cooling fins, no cooling fan.

8. The Engine

POUND FOR pound, the Go-Kart is far and away the highest performance "automobile" ever produced. From a tiny 6 cubic inch engine can come enough horsepower to hurtle more than 300 pounds of kart and driver at nearly 70 mph. One hundred and twenty mph is common with less than three times that engine displacement. Obviously, as utilized in karting, the two-stroke internal combustion engine has a performance history far superior to the more common four-stroke engine used in passenger cars. The two-stroke has not always been so efficient.

The four-stroke engine actually has two "idling" strokes, when nothing substantial in the way of power production is accomplished. From the beginning, late in the last century, engine designers tried to find a way to eliminate the two wasted strokes by driving out the exhaust gases at the bottom of the power stroke. If this exhausting were done by the incoming fuel mixture, the upward stroke would thus be compression following induction, the downward stroke would be power followed by exhaust. There would be no wasted motion of crankshaft and piston.

The first two-stroke was designed by an Englishman, Sir Dugald Clerk, in 1881, and was really just a conversion of the four-stroke with valves. A separate engine-driven pump forced the gas mixture through a valve into the cylinder. After compression, a cylinder wall port was opened as the piston neared bottom dead center and the exhaust gases could escape. The first two port two-stroke, which uses the crank case as the pumping system for fuel, came ten years later, followed shortly by the three port design.

It is claimed there are more patents relative to the two-stroke internal combustion engine than any other part of the automobile industry, possibly because the power device is so simple. Yet it is a very complicated engine when considerations of power, dependability, and longevity are involved. To understand the ruling factors of kart engine design, it is essential to know how the two-stroke works.

The typical American two-stroke, such as the West Bend or McCulloch, has been designed primarily for workhorse duty in industrial applications, such as electrical plants and chainsaws. Lightweight and simplicity are essential to such powerplants—features abundant in two-strokes. Because the American engines are intended for volume production and industrial use, the design utilized is considered "old fashioned" by European engineers. That the design is still competitive in a horsepower race is indicative of how good basic two-stroke engines are, "old fashioned" or not. European engines are more advanced, in that they are primarily designed as power for motorcycles or small cars. The difference is basically induction.

In the typical two-stroke, there are no poppet valves. Fuel enters the combustion chamber through ports in the cylinder walls, these ports are covered and uncovered by the piston action. At the top of any particular stroke, the bottom of the piston skirt uncovers an inlet port, allowing fuel mixture to flow into the crankcase. This feature is responsible for the unique exhaust of a two-stroke. Because the fuel mixture is to surround the crankshaft and piston assembly, it must include a lubricant. Oil is mixed with the fuel in a small quantity, lubricating the moving parts as it passes and is then burned during combustion. There is a low-pressure area in the crankcase when the piston is near top dead center, which causes a pressure differential and makes the fuel flow from the carburetor.

Opposite the fuel inlet is a transfer passage between crankcase and the cylinder, the cylinder opening being just above the piston top when the piston is at bottom dead center. As the piston has moved downward on the power stroke, high pressure has built in the crankcase. When the piston uncovers the inlet port, the fuel mixture is forced into the combustion chamber.

The piston then starts upward again, compressing the mixture. Near top dead center the mixture is ignited by a spark plug and forces the piston down on a power stroke. As the piston nears bottom dead center, an exhaust port is cleared, and the spent gases rush out the exhaust pipe.

Obviously the intake and exhaust ports are going to be open at practically the same time. To keep the intake charge from rushing directly across the piston top and out the exhaust port (trapping spent gases high in the chamber), a deflector pis-

ton is used. The piston crown is shaped to divert the incoming charge upward in the cylinder. As the charge rushes upward, it helps push the exhaust gases down the back sloping piston crown and out the exhaust port. At some phase there will be either spent gases left in the cylinder, or some of the unburned mixture will exhaust before the piston can close the exhaust port. This is true in all internal combustion engines, and is reduced to a fractional amount by engineering evolution.

Simplicity of any two-stroke is obvious, since there are no valves and attendent mechanisms. The two-stroke has only three internal moving parts; the piston, connecting rod, and crankshaft. It is relatively quiet (when muffled properly), but in direct comparison with the four-stroke it has inferior fuel consumption characteristics and comparative horsepower for the two-stroke is lower. These problems are offset by the very great savings in weight, very low-production costs, and adaptability.

Parilla engine develops in excess of 14 horsepower on gasoline. BELOW: 8.116 cubic inch B-Bomb engine imported from Italy and made by Komet.

Any internal combustion engine horsepower production will be affected by five things: *volumetric efficiency, combustion efficiency, thermal efficiency, mechanical efficiency,* and *power stroke frequency.* All but the last are directly related. How well the cylinder is refilled with a combustable mixture is volumetric efficiency, and under the best conditions the two-stroke averages only about 40 percent. Combustion efficiency means how well the fuel available is converted into heat (which is energy) and thermal efficiency means the percentage of charge converted into mechanical work. Mechanical efficiency is the percentage of work done by the expanding gases when pushing downward on the piston. Put together, it all means that a two-stroke does not govern any of these design elements perfectly, but the disadvantages are outweighed by advantages.

For the karter, the two-stroke is a dream. It takes very little initial mechanical acumen to become a two-stroke mechanic. Since the path to power on any engine is increasing the efficiencies just mentioned, the two-stroke mechanic can make a number of modifications in his basement workshop with ordinary tools and expect a significant power increase.

The two-stroke Yamaha engine has been one of the most exciting breakthroughs in karting since Art Ingels bolted the first kart together. The Yamaha was designed specifically for professional quality kart racing, and the karters have taken it to heart. Both the IKF and the WKA have box stock classes where all you have to do is put together the frame of your choice, take your Yamaha engine out of the box, bolt it on and go.

Yamaha's successful motorcycle racing program contributed a lot to the development of this engine. Large aluminum fins dissipate heat from the cylinder and cylinder head to ensure that the engine puts out its maximum in the longest races. And the cylinder head uses Yamaha's unique dome-and-squish design for highly efficient combustion. Reliability at high rpms is guaranteed by an advanced transistor controlled ignition. All in all, the Yamaha makes it possible for those who don't know a wrench from a timing light to get into racing because it offers good power and incredible reliability without breaking the family bank.

Any time a discussion is started about the two-strokes for karting, the conversation will include terms like scavenging. This might be further expounded to include cross, loop, and uniflow. Essentially, the term means how well the cylinder is cleaned of exhaust gases. However, it is an extremely vital function of high performance, on both two- and four-stroke engines.

With the deflector-type engine used in the United States, termed American Reed in kart competition rules, the intake mixture swings up and then theoretically pushes the exhaust gases out. At one time this was called Loop scavenging, but Cross scavenging is now applied to the design. The Loop name is now applied to a system developed by Schnürrle of Germany. The deflector design does not allow really high compression ratios, but the Loop system does. By directing the incoming charge into the cylinder from two sides (a split port) and having it bounce off the cylinder wall opposite the exhaust port at an upward angle, the kinetic energy of the charge is used to more effectively clean out exhaust gases. This is the kind of system used on many imported two-stroke engines.

The uniflow principle is not common to karting. It has the fresh charge entering at one end of the cylinder and the spent gases out the other end (just like that first two-stroke in 1881). This can be accomplished by ports or poppet valves.

As mentioned, two-strokes may have varied valves. In the typical American engine described, the piston will also be the valve as it opens and closes the various ports. However, the amount of time a port is open is in direct relationship to piston location and speed. More fuel mixture can be packed into the crankcase if the fuel inlet is not governed by the piston. This means some other type of fuel inlet control is needed. The most common types of valves are not valves in the four-stroke sense, but

include the *reed valve* common to American designs and the *rotary valve* widely used in Europe and Japan.

The reed valve is common to the industrial engines of this country because of production simplicity. The reed construction allows fuel to flow into the crank case on demand (when internal pressure drops below external pressure), therefore effectively increasing the amount of time fuel mixture can pack into the crank cavity. The reed(s) is quite flexible and will close the intake opening when the piston has started the downstroke and there is the slightest increase in crankcase pressure. While better than the three-port piston control, this system is not the ultimate, since more fuel could be packed into the crankcase if the reeds could stay open slightly longer.

The rotary valve design, more common to very high-performance two-strokes, will give the maximum

Komet engines are among the most popular of imported plants, can put out over 24 hp on exotic fuel blends. Note the external battery-type coil ignition. RIGHT: Guazzoni engine weighs only 24 pounds, runs fan flywheel, has ball bearing crank.

Water cooling is not new to two-strokes. This is B-Bomb Komet engine with homemade water jacket and radiator system.

amount of opening for the intake cycle. In the simplest form of rotary valve, the crankshaft is hollow on one end. A hole is drilled into this hollow center from the bearing surface. As the crankshaft rotates, this second hole aligns with a transfer passage to the combustion chamber, passing fuel mixture along with added pressurization from the crankcase. This kind of valve allows the inlet period to be lengthened considerably over the three-port and reed valve systems. In some early engines, shaft main bearing wear would effect performance as normal wear of the bearing would increase clearance around the port area, allowing crankcase pressure to escape. This has been solved to some extent by the use of roller main bearings inboard from the port bushing.

The second type of rotary valve is a flat disc located on the crankshaft beside a counterweight. A hole, or a cut-away portion of the disc, covers and uncovers the case port every crank revolution. The disc is free to move sideways on the crankshaft, so crankcase pressure will keep it sealed against the case wall and prevent pressure leakage when the port is closed.

It is apparent the rotary valve is better for the high-performance engine, but it also makes the engine more costly to manufacture. Because there is a marked difference in performance between the two types of valve systems, karting rules are broken into American reed and others (meaning rotary or poppet), which gives the reed engines a place to be competitive. The separation has proven very popular, as there are more than enough karts at any meet to fill classes in both categories.

Transfer tubes are the major problem in many two-stroke designs. Taking the fuel mixture from the crankcase to the combustion chamber may be a circuituous route for low-performance two-strokes. In practically all engines, some special handwork with grinding and polishing wheels will improve performance noticeably.

While port shape near the cylinder (which effects the direction fuel mixtures will enter the chamber) is not so critical with deflector pistons, it is very important with loop scavenging designs. The shape of the intake and exhaust port openings into the cylinder are also important, as specific shapes have a bearing on piston ring life, noise level and mixture transfer efficiency. Practically every different two-stroke engine design uses a different type of transfer tube. Transfer tubes and porting of an industrial engine will be considerably different from those in a pure racing two-stroke, but in either case the design will be adequate for intended use. In all cases, performance may be improved by special modifications; to this end all leading engine manufacturers (both domestic and foreign) publish brochures on transfer tube and port changes.

While it might seem karting and motorcycling would be the only sports to benefit from engine hop-up, loggers have adapted two-stroke power modifications to their particular equipment. High-performance engines on chainsaws increase the productivity of a cutter, while chainsaw contests are common throughout the logging country. It is a fantastic sight to see a nitromethane burning McCulloch saw slash through a giant log in seconds, sending a roostertail of sawdust 50 feet high.

While the four-stroke engine relies almost entirely on cubic inch displacement and volumetric efficiency for performance, the latter controlled by valve timing, so two-stroke performance also relates directly to port timing. The problem of getting the maximum amount of fuel mixture into the combustion chamber at any given rpm plagues engineers, and it is super critical with the two-stroke.

While the ideal transfer port would allow the fuel mixture to enter the combustion chamber through the piston top, practical experience has so far proven this difficult to achieve. The introduction of cam-operated valves, as with the four-stroke, begins to complicate the engine and the performance improvement is not worth the effort. Therefore, the long traditional method of covering and uncovering the ports with the piston remains most practical. Further, there are no specific rules on minute port timing, so each engine goes through a trial and error stage of practical engineering before production. Like the automotive valve timing where radical camshaft profiles are used to get maximum performance, port timing will be really effective only in a particular rpm range. In addition, the more performance required will narrow this rpm band accordingly.

Further complications arise from pressure and resonance waves acting on the columns of intake mixture and exhaust gases. These waves drastically effect the performance of any engine at certain rpm's, and are used to advantage in competition. Ram tuning, where the total intake air column is a certain size and length, has long been standard with competition motorcycle two-strokes, and has recently been introduced to four-stroke automobile racing engines with great success. The tuned exhaust, discussed at length in another chapter, is vital to serious kart competition. Port shape and timing will affect the carburetor, also, where a constant and smooth flow of air is desirable but seldom possible.

Because of porting restrictions inherent to the conventional two stroke, mixture turbulence must be achieved by the piston crown and cylinder head design rather than port flow direction. The mixture is squeezed out from one side of the combustion chamber at a high velocity at piston top dead center. This is called a squish chamber, and imparts considerable turbulence to the mixture, causing it to burn more completely.

Just as the porting is important to the two-stroke engine, the crankcase, called the pumping chamber, is invaluable. The more the crankcase pumping efficiency, which increases the fuel mixture pressure differential between crankcase and combustion chamber, the greater (denser) the fuel mixture charge will be. In this respect, the pumping chamber is an inherent supercharger to the two-stroke. Since all the crankcase is involved, any dead space must be eliminated, so the crankcase is often only large enough to accommodate the revolving crankshaft. Most engineers start with a practical crankcase volume of $2\frac{1}{4}$ times cylinder capacity for initial design purposes.

There are only three moving parts in the conventional two-stroke engine, and only five main assemblies: the cylinder and head, piston, connecting rod, crankshaft, and crankcase. Accessories include the carburetor, muffler, ignition, perhaps a fuel pump, and drive unit (which may include a transmission, automatic clutch, or direct connection chain sprocket). Imported engines often have a close-grained cast iron cylinder, while American industrial engines use aluminum alloy, the bore either hard chromeplated for wear resistance or fitted with a steel cylinder liner.

Cooling of the air-cooled two-stroke is accomplished by deep fins around the cylinder and head area. Those engines used in motorcycles have very large fins open to the air, while industrial engines that are essentially stationary include a flywheel with impellers and a fan shroud to force air over the fins. In competition, piston seizure due to overheating is a problem that plagues the most experienced enthusiast, but in-the-pit repair is possible.

Because the piston must be both a compression seal and a timing mechanism, the cylinder bore finish must be much better than with the typical four-stroke. The match of piston and cylinder must be better, and piston material must be premium. In competition, where precise control over fuel mixture may be a problem, burned pistons are not uncommon. The conventional two-stroke will use two rings per piston.

There are two types of connecting rods in use, dictated by the type of crankshaft involved. If the crankshaft is of the "built-up" variety, where the two counterweights are pressed onto the rod journal, the connecting rod's big end will be a straight bore fitted with needle bearings. If the crankshaft is of the one-piece design, the connecting rod's big end will separate with a cap and use either standard or needle bearings. As a rule, imported engines will use the built-up crankshaft; American engines will use the one-piece design.

The type of crankshaft also dictates the type of crankcase to some extent, but in most instances, the crankcase will be two almost identical halves. The location of an induction system may vary with production requirements, as well as intended use.

In some cases the induction may be directly to the cylinder, but usually a plate on the crankcase housing will hold the carburetor.

Two-stroke lubrication is a problem unto itself, and is of particular interest to the kart enthusiast. There are three types of lubrication systems in general use. In the most common, gas and oil are mixed since both pass through the crankcase anyway. The less volatile oil is deposited on the engine parts, with about six percent oil required for most motorcycle engines. This percentage may vary from four percent with large engines to as much as twenty percent for small engines. There are some drawbacks to this very simple approach.

The second system, patented by the British motorcycle firm Villiers, uses crankcase pressure to force oil from a separate tank to the engine bearings. The third, an engine driven pump as used in four-strokes, is used in the larger two-strokes and is showing up on some smaller, more complicated designs. Most kart engines use the oil-gas mix system.

It is an interesting aspect of two-stroke engine design that any one engine has been engineered for a specific purpose—there are no true general purpose engines. While some engines can do a variety of jobs, none can do everything extremely well. A chainsaw engine is an industrial engine no matter what the sales brochure might say, and a racing two-stroke is hardly adaptable to logging operations. Still, if the basic design is sound, it is possible to modify the engine to several applications with reasonable success.

A two-stroke used as power for a lighting generator will operate within very narrow rpm limits, usually from 3000-4000 rpm and weight is no objection. A racing two-stroke, however, may have rpm limits as high as 15,000 and must be flexible over a very wide rpm range. It must also be as light as possible. The chainsaw engine falls between these two requirements, with rpm in the 6000—8000 range. Saw engines must be operational at all temperatures, run in any position, be extremely lightweight, and be totally reliable.

Balance is a problem with any engine, but pronounced with the single-cylinder units. There are two specific balance conditions to consider, that caused by the engine lower end and that caused by the piston and upper end of the connecting rod. While this is getting more into the specifics of engine modification, it must be an important consideration of any engineering approach to an engine design. No engineer wants to create undesirable balance problems, indeed performance dictates the minimum out-of-balance condition.

How well an engine is balanced will have a direct effect on how much it shakes, and this is extremely important to the karter. Trying to drive a kart with a really bad balance condition can take away all the enjoyment. Unfortunately, there is no way to eliminate all of the balance problems of the single-cylinder engine. The solution for total balance is to build a multi-cylinder engine with opposed pistons, but then design complication and cost go up.

In karting, the least amount of vibration is desirable for more than driver comfort; excess vibration has a way of loosening every nut and bolt holding the vehicle together. To combat this severe problem, karters go to great lengths balancing the engine,

McCulloch 100 is for B Stock or modified Super classes. It is superseded by 101.

then they safety wire and Loc-Tite all fasteners. The May, 1969, issue of *Modern Karting* magazine contains an excellent article on controlling balance in the Mc-91 McCulloch engine, an approach that can apply to many two-strokes; and engineer P. E. Irving discusses the problem at length in his book *Two-Stroke Power Units.* The two articles are not dated, since the problems involved are constant with the single-cylinder engine.

It all starts with the piston and upper end of the connecting rod. While the reciprocating mass of crankshaft and lower connecting rod can be balanced perfectly, the upper mass cannot. However, by adding weight to the perfectly balanced lower end, thus creating an intended out-of-balance condition at a specific point during crankshaft rotation, upper end balance can be improved. As an example, consider the Mc-91, which in stock condition creates an average of about 600 pounds of shaking force at 10,000 rpm, with a peak shaking

force of 900 pounds. By using heavy Tungsten in the counterweights, no extra crankcase space is needed, and the shaking force is considerably lessened. The factory uses this method for later, improved engines. Production to the extreme tolerances common with race engine preparation is not going to happen in the factory, however, not even with the so-called racing engines. Kart engine specialists are available to do exacting work, such as balancing and porting, but the enthusiast will be missing out on much of the fun if he farms out all the engine work. Because of the design simplicity, the two-stroke is an excellent school for the beginning mechanic.

So now the question has arrived for the second time: Which engine? The local competition events will have shown a predominance of two or three imported designs, and a heavy number of McCulloch engines. This doesn't mean there are not other engines available; it only indicates what

McCulloch 6 cubic-inch American reed engine. This design is superseded by similar 91A that puts out over 10 horsepower on gas.

engines have proven most adaptable to current competition standards. As an example, a highly successful driver uses a modified West Bend to upset the McCulloch in some major national races, but he has concentrated on making each modification perfect after thorough experimentation. Trial and error experiments prove or dispove his theories. Still, this is the exception, and few karters could expect similar success without a long background in two-stroke engine modification. McCulloch engines have come to dominate American reed designs simply because the company has taken an active interest in kart power. While McCulloch has not produced an engine specifically for racing that incorporates all the "trick" design elements of the imported engines, they have been able to modify the "industrial" design until "box stock" power production is amazing.

That McCulloch recognizes the value of kart engine design and production is indicated by the many improvements introduced during the past five or six years. Following is a list of Mac engines as they were released after the Mc10. Note there was no systematic method of numbering or identification.

Mc 10	Mc 9
Mc 5	Mc 45
Mc 6	Mc 75
Mc 20	Mc 100
Mc 1	Mc 90
Mc 2	Mc 49A
Mc 7	Mc 91
Mc 30	Mc 101
Mc 8	Mc 91A
	Mc 49C

Like developments in the space industry, McCulloch engineers are working on many different projects at the same time, and releasing improvements as they are perfected. Incidentally, McCulloch does not make it a rule to release rpm and horsepower figures on all engine tests; but those figures that are released can be accepted as proven. The factory uses a very expensive dynamometer and controls all testing conditions rigidly.

Following is a table of performance figures compiled by John Christy, Technical Editor of *Rod & Custom Magazine*. While this test was made a couple of years past, it was done at the height of American reed engine popularity when all these engines were common to karting. Since that time few changes have been made in these engines; emphasis has been limited almost exclusively to the McCulloch line. For this reason the McCulloch figures have been updated to show how power increments are steady; and while there is not a doubling or trebling of horsepower, the small percentage of improvement is highly significant in kart performance. Racing motorcycle engineers are quick to point out that the addition of 25 horsepower may have little effect upon automobile performance; but just 1 extra horsepower usually makes a tremendous difference in motorcycle top speed.

	RPM	Torque	Power
Clinton A-400			
Peak speed:	2000	6.75	1.35
5100 rpm	3000	6.00	1.8
	4000	5.25	2.25
	5000	3.00	1.5
Clinton A-490			
Peak speed:	2000	5.75	1.25
5100 rpm	3000	5.75	1.85
	4000	4.50	1.85
	5000	3.30	1.80
Clinton E-65			
Peak speed:	3000	7.0	2.0
6000 rpm	4000	6.5	2.6
	5000	6.0	3.0
	6000	4.25	2.5

Homelite KR-92			
Peak speed:	3000	5.0	1.50
8400 rpm	4000	7.25	2.75
	5000	7.25	3.60
	6000	8.00	4.50
	7000	6.50	4.75
	8000	6.25	5.00
Power Products AH-82			
Peak speed:	4000	12.5	5.0
7200 rpm	5000	10.0	5.0
	6000	6.0	3.75
	7000	5.25	3.75
McCulloch MC-6			
Peak speed:	4000	8.25	3.5
9000 rpm	5000	8.50	4.5
	6000	8.75	5.5
	7000	8.20	6.0
	8000	7.75	6.6
	9000	7.00	6.3
McCulloch MC-10 (Standard)			
Peak speed:	4000	7.75	3.0
8100 rpm	5000	7.25	3.75
	6000	7.5	4.50
	7000	6.25	4.50
	8000	5.75	4.50
McCulloch MC-10 (Power-Pack)			
Peak speed:	4000	11.6	4.3
9000 rpm	5000	11.0	5.5
	6000	10.85	6.8
	7000	10.00	7.0
	8000	8.5	6.8
	9000	8.10	7.3

Now look at what the newer McCulloch engines can do.

	RPM	Torque	Power
MC 49	7000-7500		5.5
	5000	4.5	
MC 91	9000		10.0
	6000	6.9	
MC 101	9000		12.5
	5000-6000	8.9	

Note the horsepower is well up over earlier engines, but that the torque figures are lower than the magazine test numbers. This is accounted for by the difference in dynamometers and correction factors used by the engineers. It would be unfair to make a direct comparison of the tests, but they do serve to show how improvements have been made.

The magazine tests were made on the Tom Spaulding kart engine dynamometer. By now practically all serious kart engine specialists have dyno's available, but most use the readings for comparisons of modifications to one engine only and for tuning. It is quite likely that no two dyno's will record identical readings for any given engine; but the list gives a good indication of why the older engines will not fare competitively with the modern McCulloch's.

That does not rule them out as powerplants, however, for they can provide excellent service while the karter is learning how to drive. In most cases, starting with one of the less powerful (and tuning sensitive) engines will produce far better results in learned driver technique.

It should be obvious by now that maximum engine performance can only be achieved when the unit has been modified. A look through the rules will show a "box stock" section, however, where hop-up modifications are not allowed. Even within this section of competition, aimed at keeping the racing dollar minimal, it is possible for one engine to put out more power than many others. The secret is in blueprinting.

Essentially, blueprinting means bringing all the mechanical measurements of the engine up to the specifications listed by the manufacturer. Almost never is it possible to hold production manufacturing tolerances to these specifications, which means that most engines are on the "low" side. The compression might be a fraction lower than listed, stroke may be slightly off, machined surfaces may not be perfectly aligned. Added up, all these minor irregularities are robbing the stock engine of significant power. All engine manufacturers have design specifications available, and these same specifications are utilized by kart racing officials to determine legality of any engine. Setting up a stock engine to the precision called for by original design is a matter of patience. Following is blueprint procedure for the McCulloch recommended by Warren Christenson.

Before an engine is rebuilt to blueprint specifications, it must be "run-in", used until the metals of construction have taken a definite set, or warpage. About ten hours of break-in time is necessary, and race time is considered best.

Examine the exhaust port area, to be sure the ports are round, clean, and not chipped at the edges. With a small flashlight, examine the intake ports through the exhaust ports to make sure the intakes are free of nicks and scratches leading toward the cylinder head. These are an indication that oversize rings have been used. The gouges may be so deep that honing to more than the .010 allowable in stock class will be required.

Thoroughly clean the engine before disassembly. Remove paint from the cylinder block and head after removing the seals from the block assembly. Immersion of the block and head in any of the standard carburetor cleaners for 30 minutes will completely remove all of the paint from the engine.

Check the engine parts for alignment. First check the rod alignment. This can most easily be done by turning two pieces of steel 12 inches long so that the rod will securely clamp on the crank pin end and on the wrist pin end, relieve the rod sufficiently on both sides of the center, leaving the center area of about $3/4$ inch the same size as the wrist pin in the engine. Heat the rod with a heat lamp —don't use open flame—enough to allow the connecting rod to be centered on the two alignment shafts without force. Allow to cool and then place the assembly across two parallel level surfaces such as the ways of a lathe or parallel uprights on a surface plate. If the rod is twisted it will not touch one of the four points of contact. If this occurs it will be necessary to remove the rod from the twisted portion and straighten cold until contact is made at all four points. Caution: do not use the checking rods to straighten with as they may bend and will not give a correct reading. To check the rod for side bend, it is only necessary to use a caliper or inside micrometer.

Check the crankshaft for straightness and alignment. There is only one way to accurately do this. It cannot be done between centers in the lathe as is common practice. The shaft must be placed on V blocks that hold the crank at parallel heights to the surface plate the V blocks are on. This may be checked with a dial indicator mounted on a surface plate vernier so that the reading differential is exactly one-half of the difference of the bearing mounting surface diameters on the crankshaft. With the dial indicator, check the crankshaft by turning it to see if any surfaces are bent or out of round. If they are, have the crank straightened until the run-out is less than one ten-thousandths of an inch.

Check the block for crank alignment, head and base straightness, roundness, and port timing of the cylinders. First, turn a piece of steel ten inches long that will be a slip fit into the bearing surfaces on either side of the case. The rod will protrude from the case with both extensions from the bearing being of equal diameter.

Check the roundness and taper of the cylinder with a highly accurate instrument such as the Sunnen Master gauge. If the cylinder is more than five ten-thousandths out of round or tapered it must be honed to a true condition. One word of warning in regard to honing the cylinder: this is a precision operation and should only be done with a single-stone-type industrial hone with the work being done by a reputable machine shop. The average portable hone will not achieve the accuracy required for a perfect cylinder. The cylinder must not be enlarged more than ten-thousandths or you will not have a stock engine.

Place a large piece of steel in the lathe and turn a diameter on it so the cylinder may be slipped over it (use a light coating of oil) with no allowable movement between the arbor and cylinder wall. The arbor must have one flat and a cross hole to allow for the case head and crank alignment bar. Place the crank alignment bar in position in the crankcase, and by mounting a dial indicator on the lathe carriage, rotate the cylinder block by turning the chuck by hand and reading the dial indicator as the crankshaft bar passes the instrument. The misalignment allowable is two ten-thousandths of an inch. If the readings are larger than that it will be necessary to take the cylinder block to a machine shop and have it set up in V blocks with the crankshaft alignment bar in place and bored in a vertical mill to obtain exact perpendicular trueness of the piston-to-crank surfaces. While the block is being bored, or if this is not required, the head and base surfaces should be checked for parallel areas to the crank and if they are not within tolerances the lightest possible surfacing cut should be taken to insure proper gasket seal.

Checking of the port timing in relation to the centerline of the crankshaft is a vital step. Contact the engine manufacturer, giving them the serial number of the engine for the correct port height from the centerline of the crank to the exact top of the port. To check this use a depth mike with the extension rods so that by placing the mike on top of the cylinder and measuring to the top of the crankshaft alignment rod you will have a reading to which you must add one-half the diameter of the crankshaft alignment bar. Measure from the top of the cylinder to the exact top of both the intake and the exhaust ports. The differential

The Yamaha's dependability and power has reshaped karting.

between the first and second measurements will give the port timing. It is unfortunate that the port timing cannot be checked before the crank is in alignment with the cylinder bore, but the port timing is changed by changing the bore size. If the cylinder port timing does not conform within the allowable limits the manufacturer has placed on this engine for stock use, we are faced with the problem of obtaining a cylinder (cured and broken-in) that will meet these requirements.

Next, fit or purchase a piston that will have the proper clearance to give maximum performance without seizing or being so loose as to damage the piston. A clearance at the skirt of five-thousandths 1/8 inch below the bottom ring land and then a secondary taper to nine-thousandths at the timing edge of the piston crown is suggested. If fitting the piston becomes a problem, send the block to one of the competent independent piston manufacturers who will probably fit the piston to the cylinder bore.

Assemble the piston to the rod. For this it is necessary to use the Mc service tool which is available from your engine distributor. Press the bearings into the proper places, the closed end is the exhaust side. Place the rod under a heat lamp. Heating allows the pin to pass freely through it in order that it may lock securely to the wrist pin when it is in place. While the rod is being heated, radius the end of the wrist pin very slightly with a hand oil stone or a fine grinder. In the event the piston requires the use of thrust washers, the pin will enter through them without shaving an edge from the washers.

Assemble the crankcase. Install the needle bearing into the crankcase and case seal as outlined in the Mc service bulletin. Heat the case head with a heat lamp to a point where the ball bearing already pressed onto the crank will slip into the case head without being forced or pressed. Allow the case head to cool and (lubricate the opposite end of the crank and the seal area with a very light oil) insert a tapered thimble over the crank. These are available at your Mc distributor. This will allow the crankshaft to pass freely through the seal without injuring it. With the case head and crank in place, tighten the 5/16 head screws to 60-inch pounds and the 1/4 head screws to 45-inch pounds. Hold the case in one hand and lightly tap each end of the crank with a plastic hammer to free it of any misalignment drags.

The crank must turn freely. Reach down from the cylinder head of the block with an inside caliper and check across from the cylinder wall to the opposite side of the crank pin. Both measurements should be equal and the crank pin exactly in the middle of the cylinder bore. If misalignment is found here it will be necessary to disassemble the case and shim the ball bearing one-half of the misalignment figure. Face the thrust bronze bearing an equal amount to maintain the correct amount of end play in the crankshaft. Be sure to check Mc specifications for the allowable end play and make any corrections at this time for differences that occur between what you have and what Mc recommends.

Although you have a stock engine that will be a top performer, you must remember there are only so many good races in any engine before this entire procedure must be repeated. Use the engine only for racing and run it as little as possible so that you may be a successful competitor with a minimum of wok.

While box-stock restricts hopping-up practices, there are engine modifications allowed in the other classes. As an example, following is a typical engine hop-up guide for the Mc 20. There are excellent books on the subject of two-stroke hop-up (write to: Go-Power Systems, P. O. Box 613, Palo Alto, Calif. for West Bends), and most manufacturers furnish power hints.

Mc 20 Hop-Up

1. Remove fan housing, shroud, carburetor and manifold, magneto coil and lamination, cylinder head, and crankcase bottom. Do not remove crank, piston and rod, or side cover at this time.

2. Turn crank until piston is at bottom dead center.

3. Paint Dykem around cylinder liner above transfer ports (approximately 1/4- to 3/8-inch) and let dry.

4. Measure and mark .038/.040-inch above top of transfer ports. Turn crank until *top* of piston is flush with mark, and then scribe light (not deep), but visible line above transfer ports.
   Note: This line is a reference mark for port modification. Port timing is to be raised to 65° BBC.

5. Using small, high-speed rotary file, elongate transfer ports (both sides) until top(s) just touch the scribed reference line. This work should be carefully performed in order to maintain the individual angle of each port opening.

6. Break sharp edges of ports, and blend smoothly into casting.

7. Square exhaust ports.
   a. Do not change port timing.
   b. Square inside halves of two outer ports.
   c. Narrow bridges between ports to approximately .030-inch.
   d. Radius corners approximately .031-inch.

8. Cut out reed stops. Optionally, remove only top ¾ section, leaving approximately 1-inch of each stop to tie together upper and lower case sections.

   a. If lower sections are left in, they should be shaped for maximum air flow.

9. Gully-cut third port.
   a. Do not change port timing.
   b. Leave sufficient portion of the two center bridges to retain bottom piston ring (to avoid ring snagging).

10. Break all sharp corners inside of case (to provide maximum air flow with minimum turbulence).

11. After completion of modification work, hone cylinder.
    a. Measure piston diameter at lower (bottom) ring. Cylinder should then be honed to provide .010-inch maximum clearance, piston-to-wall (.005 on each side).
    Note: Allow cylinder to cool (room temperature)—after honing—before measuring.
    b. If maximum displacement (6.1 cubic inches/100 cc.) is desired, .050-inch oversize pistons are available.

12. Thoroughly wash cylinder after honing (do not use gasoline) to remove fines and metal dust.
    a. For maximum removal of dirt from bore (liner), wash cylinder in *hot* water and ample detergent. Use bristle brush and scrub liner thoroughly.
    b. Flush cylinder with running, hot water. Blow, or shake off excess water and dry cylinder under moderate heat.
    c. If oxidation shows on liner (when dry), clean with krokus cloth (not emery or steel wool). Use a clean, well-oiled rag to wipe out bore after clean-up.

13. Fit-up (selective fit) piston rings to cylinder bore. A minimum end gap of .007/.010-inch is recommended.

14. Reassemble engine.

15. Compression Ratio.
    a. 8:1: Use Mc-20 cylinder head (P/N 48903) and .016 gasket (P/N 48742).
    b. 10.5:1: Use Mc-6 cylinder head (P/N 55146A) and .016 gasket (P/N 48742).

16. Time engine to fire at 25° BTC. (The use of a degree wheel is highly recommended.)

17. If single-carburetor induction system is used, a Van Tech manifold is recommended.
    a. Dual carburetion has advantages if correctly adjusted. However, due to the many types available, no recommendation is made relative to dual-carburetor installations.

18. Spark Plug
    a. The HO-3 (Champion) has gained wide acceptance. However, the *correct* spark plug is the one that gives the best performance for the individual.
    1. A plug that is too cold can cause burnt pistons and sticking, if the carburetor is set *too* lean in an effort to avoid plug fouling.
    2. A plug that is too hot will also burn pistons if it causes pre-ignition and/or detonation.

19. Pre-Ignition/Detonation
    a. Spark plugs of incorrect heat range (too hot) and advanced timing (plus high compression ratio) are major causes of pre-ignition and/or detonation.
    b. Use of the Mc-6 head (P/N 55146A) and .016 head gasket

(P/N 48742), with 25° BTC timing, may result in pre-ignition under some conditions. If pre-ignition does occur, and spark plug color (tan to light brown) indicates correct heat range, retard timing in one degree increments until pre-ignition is controlled.

20. Mavrick Spark
Simply, Maverick spark is a high-energy discharge (across the spark plug electrodes) that can occur when the breaker points float (hold open at high engine rpm), and is the result of (a) the difference between the mechanical setting of the breaker points in conjunction with (b) the peak energy output of the magneto coil. The difference (advance in timing that is gained-approximate) is measured by crankpin (crankshaft throw) position, in degrees BTC.

For reference purposes, it can be assumed that maximum magneto output occurs when the center of the magnetic field (flywheel) is directly under the coil center (centerline of middle leg of lamination). Thus, minimum maverick spark adjustment may be controlled (static setting) by shifting the coil lamination. (Clockwise: Advance.)

a. Maverick spark may be manually controlled through use of a single-pole, single-throw—normally closed—switch. The switch is inserted, electrically, between the coil terminal and the breaker points. When the switch is closed (normal position), the breaker points serve to open and close the primary circuit. When depressed, the switch cuts out the breaker

122

points.

b. To avoid possible pre-ignition and/or detonation at low engine rpm, adjust the points to open at 20°—22° BTC. (Low-end performance will likely improve, also.)

As engine rpm increases, pressing the switch (opening breaker point circuit) will result in Maverick firing (advanced) of the sparkplug. The advance will be approximately 6°—10°, based on static setting of the coil and lamination assembly.

21. Modification of the Mc-6 engine is similar to that work performed on the Mc-20. However, certain steps, as follow, are not accomplished.
   a. Step 3—Not required.
   b. Step 4—Not required.
   c. Step 5—Do *not* change Mc-6 port timing.
   d. Step 11B—Use of .050 o/s piston not recommended.
   e. Step 15—If stock crankshaft is used, minimum thickness head gasket is required (individual option).

22. Displacement of Mc-6
   Displacement may be increased to 5.8 cubic inches—100 cc. through use of a stroked crankshaft.
   a. If stroked crank is used, the engine will not be eligible to run as "Stock A" under some track regulations, unless changed to stock crank.

As previously mentioned, the essential difference between American and imported engines is in the type of valving. However, most imported engines use a caged needle bearing connecting rod big end with a needle bearing or a bushing. Most imported two-strokes are designed for motorcycles, so they do not include the American style cooling fan and shroud (fans are available, however), and are more inclined toward competition of some sort.

There have been a number of imported engines used in American kart races, but only recently have they really been adapted successfully. Part of the reason is the rule outlawing gearboxes except in the open FKE class, and certainly the cost of these engines must be considered. That these engines are more powerful than the American designs is admitted; that they produce more competition or more fun is debatable. However, they are an integral part of the sport, and are teaching American tuners and designers some excellent two-stroke tricks.

Most common imported engines are the Komet, Saetta, and Parilla; all well suited to kart racing and reasonably priced. There are many more designs possible for karting as attested by the following list of engines used in English karting:

Aspera	Merlin
B.M.	Mills
Bultaco	Montesa
Guazzoni	Puch
Harper Vincent	Stihl
JLO	Villiers
Konig	Zundapp

Add to this list all those new two-stroke engines being released by talented Japanese designers and the kart world is an ideal place for the enthusiast who likes to be different. Unfortunately, there are more restrictions on American karting engines than on those used overseas. It is probable these rules will be changed to include more diversified power as more exciting engines become available.

Although there have been several small water-cooled two-stroke engine designs used in karting, the most notable being Konig and the new Vega Vic 19L, the air-cooled engines dominate the sport. There is considerable similarity between the three most popular imports, Komet, Parilla, and Saetta. All are manufactured in Italy, with power figures close enough to make selection a problem for the new buyer. As a rule, 13 horsepower in the stock version is a reasonable assumption, with over 20 horsepower established by the better modifiers.

Unfortunately, trying to compare test results reported by various kart shops is difficult, since dynamometers vary, the correction factors are different, and sometimes commercial interest supercedes reality. There can be a very definite difference in these imported engines, however. Jim Akerman of Texas, a national champion driver and NASA employee, reports that dyno tests on these imports (any engine for that matter) may be entirely misleading. What the dyno reports, and what the engine will do in actual racing conditions, are often two different things.

Jim has found the Komet K-77 engine, for instance, stronger on a fast track than the newer K-88. The latter must be tuned differently, although they are both Komet designs, and offers a broader speed range. A similar situation exists with the Saetta, with the V-18 reported to have a broad torque range (due to the longer stroke, probably) and very flexible power curve. Essentially, then, the karter is faced with the selection of one of the imports that will produce well, which means using an engine

popular with race winners. However, he must also consider the type of races being won, the kind of kart involved, and possibly, the cost.

The Parilla engine is manufactured in four basic versions, including the S 13s, BA 13, TG 14, and GP 15. The 13 and 14 series engines have 98.2 cc's displacement, a reported compression ratio of 15:1, and magneto ignition. The 14 and 15 engines have a slightly shorter stroke and slightly larger bore, but essentially the same displacement at 98.3 cc's. This displacement compares favorably with the Komet K-88 at 98.25 cc's and the Saetta (first in the line that now includes Parilla, giving rise to rumor that all three engines are made by the same factory) at 97.7 cc's.

Two-stroke engineers are quick to point out that the smallest change in design may have a tremendous effect on performance, and while these imported engines may look alike, they may perform quite differently. However, for our purposes, a description of the Saetta V-18TA will serve all three popular Italian engines.

All are of the disc valve type, use Dell'Orto carburetors, and have fuel pumps actuated by crankcase pressure variations. In modified form, all three will accept the Tillotson carburetor. All use a built-up crankshaft that must be perfectly aligned by an expert during any rebuild.

The Saetta head is held to the cylinder barrel by four long studs that terminate in the crankcase, a case that splits down the middle for mechanical work. A most distinguishing feature of all these engines is the generous fin area, obviously engineered to keep heat dissapation well under control, which is essential if no fan and shroud are uesd.

Fuel transfer in the Saetta is a bit

It is possible to build your own two-stroke engine. Tom Spalding made up this vertical twin of 12 cubic inches. On alcohol fuel it develops over 40 hp.

different than the conventional method described earlier, since this is primarily a racing engine. There is transfer port, a boost port, and two finger ports. The latter are secondary transfer ports to augment fuel charge transfer. The finger and boost ports are fed through holes in the piston, with the boost port between the finger ports. The three extra ports are designed to increase volumetric efficiency, which they do remarkably well.

The cylinder liner is cast iron, piston rings (the top ring is Dykes type, used so successfully in automobile racing engines) are chrome, and the connecting rod is a beefed I-beam section modified by the factory after testing for race dependability. The crank case has no dead air space, an obvious result of racing detail.

In the end analysis, whatever kind of engine used will have a direct bearing on the kind of racing you can expect. The imported engines may have an edge in power, but they *are* expensive. American engines are less expensive, less powerful, very plentiful and still quite popular, but the Yamaha—strong, dependable and not too expensive—is the most popular power-plant on the circuit, because with it everybody on the grid starts out just about even. And that makes for great racing.

To the serious karter, it isn't just a question of cost, since none of these engines will break the bank. It isn't even a problem of finding someone to run against (or away from). The top-notch karter becomes intimately involved with machinery whether he has a strong mechanical background or not, and with a two-stroke engine he can become an engineer or sorts—when he gets an idea the only way to find out if it will work is to try it.

Popular Kart Engines

AMERICAN	FOREIGN

AMERICAN

Lawson-Tecumseh
Tecumseh Products Co.
Lawson Products Division
Grafton, Wisconsin

McCulloch Corporation
Kart Division
6101 W. Century Blvd.
Los Angeles, Calif. 90045

West Bend (parts only)
Chrysler Marine Division
P. O. Box 2641
Detroit, Michigan 48231

FKE
Honda
American Honda
100 W. Alondra
Gardena, Calif.

Kawasaki
Kawasaki Motors Corporation
1062 McGaw Ave.
Santa Ana, Calif.

FOREIGN

Komet-Parilla-B Bomb
Russell Karting Specialties
P. O. Box 9602
Kansas City, Missouri 64134

Petry
Bley Engineering Co.
120 W. Hamilton St.
Elk Grove Village Illinois 60007

Saetta
Hartman Engineering Co.
3731 Park Place
Montrose, Calif.

Suzuki
U. S. Suzuki Motors
13767 Freeway Dr.
Santa Fe Springs, Calif.

Yamaha Motor Corp., U.S.A.
6555 Katella Avenue
Cypress, California 90630

9. The Exhaust System

UNLIKE THE four-stroke engine, the two-stroke has long enjoyed a well-engineered exhaust system. The emphasis with regard to cars has been on silence at any cost, while with the two-stroke, particularly in motorcycle applications, the importance has been on performance. For years engineers have realized the value of a high-performance exhaust system, but it has not been so important on passenger cars with an abundance of horsepower. The little two-stroke engine has never been overcome with power, so the aspects of performance exhaust have been well documented through the decades. Until the requirements for silencers (mufflers) were included in kart racing regulations and competition became exceedingly keen, American karters were inclined to overlook this prime source of power control.

There is a peculiar aspect of two-stroke engine operation that seems to run against all reason. As originally

127

Open headers, as on this West Bend engine, were used until muffler rule entered rule book. BELOW: Horstman muffler was tried when new rule came into effect. It is used on twin-engined Sprints, but not recommended for enduro karts.

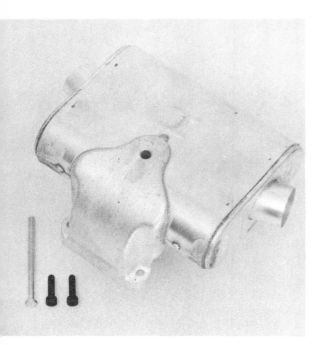

decided, the two-stroke could never be a high power, high rpm engine simply because the ports were open such a limited time. It has since been found that this time factor really works the opposite—the exhaust port opens so fast that a high degree of power is attained. All the more amazing since the port will be open for less than .003 seconds at high rpm, with only about half this time used for exhausting the cylinder.

This phenomenon is called the Kadenacy effect, and illustrates that when the exhaust port is opened quickly, the exhaust gas rushes out so fast it actually leaves a cylinder pressure lower than atmosphere. Further, the quicker the port opening rate, and the higher the initial combustion chamber pressure, the more intense the effect. A negative pressure in the chamber can be as much as 6 psi, an ideal possibility for the performance enthusiast.

In essence, the high revving two-stroke is emptying itself of its own exhaust gases rather than having the incoming charge push the gases out.

Early muffler experiments have led to some interesting designs.

Of course, the negative pressure area will fill up from somewhere, and this could be from the just released exhaust gases if a very short (or no) exhaust pipe is used. Thus the exhaust system starts with the spent gases inside the engine, not at the pipe bolt flange. The fact that no pipe at all, which should reduce back pressure to zero, may even make the engine run worse was a bit confusing until the Kadenacy effect was discovered.

This special effect can be enhanced or nullified by the exhaust system, which can include the primary pipe (the initial tubing from flange to chamber), the expansion chamber, and the tailpipe. To understand the full implications of correct two-stroke exhaust, it is necessary to understand just what happens as the exhaust travels down the pipe.

When the exhaust port opens, there is a mass of hot air suddenly shot into the pipe. This slug of air is traveling at a very rapid rate, the front portion actually reaching the speed of sound until it exits the open end of the pipe.

Inertia is involved with this mass of air, also, so that a depression forms immediately behind the slug, which tends to increase the intensity of the Kadenacy effect even more. When this happens, there is a positive pressure wave moving out toward the pipe end, and a negative wave moving back toward the exhaust port.

Now comes the difficult part. When the positive wave reaches the pipe open end, it is reflected back up the pipe as a less intense negative wave (back to the physics class and principles of acoustics). If this new negative wave arrives at the port while it is open, the new exhaust slug of air starts the trip in a lower pressure area. However, that original wave bounces off the closed cylinder area as a negative wave and returns to the pipe open end, where it is reflected back again as a positive wave. Since some of the incoming fuel mixture will be unavoidably drawn out the exhaust port with the exhaust, the new positive wave (traveling at about 1,400 ft/sec) can be used to push this unburned mixture back into the cyl-

129

TOP: Reverse megaphone muffler/tuned pipes have been common with two-stroke motorcycles for years. This is an imported unit from Italy. CENTER: Kendick Provo chamber tuned exhaust includes four different stingers (tips), works well on any 100 cc engine. LEFT: McCulloch volume-tuned muffler is different from the normal reverse-cone style, works very well.

inder just as the port is opened. An extra bit of power and economy is gained. The return pulse will have bounced around the exhaust pipe four times between the time the port just begins to open and the time it is almost closed. That is fast. The wave will continue to bounce around in the port until the port again opens and can be used to assist the new wave. When this happens, the system is working in resonance and is characterized by good performance and reasonable fuel consumption.

While the straight pipe has been associated with American racing engines for decades, engineers have found it actually harmful to potential power. If the exhaust air velocity can be slowed down before it reaches the pipe end, the tuning waves can be controlled better. Any tapering increase in pipe diameter will cause a partial wave reflection (the gas is fooled into thinking it has reached the pipe open end and changes wave type). So will a decrease in pipe diameter (a reverse cone) but the air thinks it has reached a closed end and does not change wave type. There is some effect caused by sound, but the average engineer finds this difficult to work with. The average karter finds it hopeless.

When karting was growing, the open exhaust system was everywhere, much to the chagrin of neighbors. Because the problem of tuned exhaust wasn't clearly known, only a very few drivers utilized megaphones and tuned pipe length. Of course they went fast and few owners could figure out why. Then the lightweight motorcycle, with its two-stroke engine, hit the American scene. Almost overnight, motorcycle enthusiasts took the machine to heart, and spent much time learning trade secrets for higher performance from England and Japan. The karters listened in on the exhaust discussions, and suddenly drivers with tuned exhaust and mufflers were winning all the races. They weren't really mufflers, but expansion chambers that served to reduce the noise somewhat.

The expansion chamber is a very specialized piece of equipment, and fortunately for the karter there are a number of different types sold by karting shops. In essence, the chamber is two megaphones welded together at the open end so that the pipe seems to swell in the middle before emptying through a very small, stubby tail pipe. The chamber volume is about ten times that of the cylinder. The exhaust slug travels through a very short primary pipe before entering the expansion chamber and will have drawn some of the incoming fuel mixture out into the pipe. When the exhaust wave reaches the reverse cone part of the chamber, a very powerful positive wave is reflected to push that errant fuel mixture back into the cylinder. The important part of this action is that the wave has only gone down the pipe twice, compared to the four times necessary with an open-ended megaphone.

A quick look at the accompanying photographs will reveal the difference between the earlier open-type exhaust pipes and the current expansion chambers. Immediately apparent is the longer length of the chambers, somewhere between 24 and 30 inches for most engines, necessary because of the high energy of the reflected waves. This same high energy tends to tear the chambers apart, and once the system is split horsepower falls off rapidly. This leads to some interesting

Margay custom-tuned pipe for McCulloch engines reduces total amount of overhang. RIGHT: Custom header pipes for McCulloch engines using tuned pipes.

mounting methods on both motorcycles and karts.

The big design problem of the expansion chamber is the creation of great power in a rather restricted rpm range, which may even be less than 1,000 usable rpm. For some kart tracks this is acceptable, and works especially well with the slipper clutches where engine rpm can be kept in the power range through slow corners. Then, there is the problem of true mufflers, since the expansion chamber is not really a muffler.

Which leads to some interesting looking exhaust systems on some karts. McCulloch has developed just such a system, and while it works like an expansion chamber, it is very quiet. It can also be tuned for any 5 to 8 cubic inch two-stroke. McCulloch calls it a Volume Tuned Muffler. On a test kart at Willow Springs Raceway (a long, hilly, and very fast sports car track in Southern California popular with Enduro karters), two Mc 90 engines were set up with short open exhaust. Lap time for the 2½-mile course was two minutes and three seconds. With the tuned

muffler installed, and nothing done to the engines, lap time dropped to one minute and fifty-six seconds, or 770-foot improvement per lap.

Construction of this muffler is quite simple: A seventy degree diverging megaphone empties exhaust into a semi-closed muffling chamber. There are no baffles in the chamber; a small outlet pipe controls the back pressure and noise. Because of the construction simplicity, this muffler system can be retuned for different tracks, where engine rpm requirements vary.

The adjustable components are: primary pipe length and diameter; megaphone angle and length; position of megaphone end in volume chamber; volume of the chamber; outlet pipe length; diameter, and location. Any modification must consider the IKF muffler sound ruling, which is "a maximum sound level of 109 Decibels measured at 10 feet from the sound source and 26 inches from the ground." As a guide, the primary tubing length offers the best retuning possibilities. While the McCulloch volume muffler won't win a Paris Designers' award, it does give

132

Mounting of the tuned exhaust is a great problem with karters. More races are lost because of disconnected mufflers than for any other reason except engine failure. Very little vibration damping rubber is used here. RIGHT: Rubber mounts from automotive shock absorber connections are used for cutting vibration. BELOW: Note extensive use of safety wire in addition to good mounting.

maximum performance with minimum noise.

Fortunately, the exhaust system is one place where the home-grown "engineer" can really enjoy himself. Construction is easy for anyone who can gas weld, and experiments give a good seat-of-the-pants reading. Either the engine runs better or it doesn't.

Where the engine power is, relative to the rpm scale, will be charted, and the enthusiast can try a number of different systems without laying out a bundle of cash. However, like most other aspects of kart competition, starting with something like what the winners use is the best advice.

Exhaust System Manufacturers

Cancilla Kart Sales
1445 Oakland Rd.
San Jose, Calif.

G.E.M. Products
Box 845
Carol Stream, Ill.

Hartman Engineering
3731 Park Place
Montrose, Calif.

Horstman Mfg.
730 E. Huntington Dr.
Monrovia, Calif.

K & P Engineering
330 S. Irwindale
Azusa, Calif.

Kendick Engineering
9520 DeSoto St.
Chatsworth, Calif.

Margay Products
3185 South Kingshighway
St. Louis, Mo.

McCulloch Corporation
6101 West Century Blvd.
Los Angeles, Calif.

Russell Karting Specialties
P. O. Box 9602
Kansas City, Mo.

A highly tuned kart engine must usually be spun to good rpm's before it will fire. McCulloch chain-saw motor is used to drive V-belt for this starting rig.

10. Starters

ONE OF THE most interesting, and always exciting, elements of karting has passed. Starting a kart just isn't what it used to be, to the chagrin of spectators who clogged the starting grid just to witness mass chaos in action.

Earlier competition karts were often direct drive to the rear wheels, the attitude being that a driver was either "on it or off it". Since there was no disconnect between engine

and tires, the only way to start the kart was by pushing, and this is where all the comical antics came in. Push starting any kart is an art. The driver holds the steering wheel with one hand and lifts the kart rear with the other, running to get up speed. He drops the kart, which snaps the engine to life (hopefully), and then tries to jump into the seat and apply foot throttle to keep the engine running. This bit of flamboyant acro-

The electric starters use a big capacity 12-volt battery and 6-volt starter motor for maximum revs. RIGHT: Because it has no battery to run down and boasts good torque, chain saw engine is popular.

batics is about fifty percent effective, with the kart chugging off the starting line in lunges.

Even more interesting, from a spectator standpoint anyway, was the method of push starts by crew members. At some of the larger races, bystanders were often pressed into service as push crew, with one or two men per kart. At the starter's signal, the crew would run a few steps with the kart rear end held aloft. They would drop the kart (often from a couple of feet, which was exciting to the driver) and keep pushing to give the engine some initial assistance. This was an easier method of starting for the driver, but it included the very intriguing problem of avoiding several score crews who had just started the karts in the grid ahead. This entire crew start was something

akin to a bull chase in a Spanish town and had all the earmarks of mass mayhem. Crowds loved it; drivers dreaded it; repeat push crews were rare.

Off and on through the past decade of karting, clutches have been used, which meant it was possible to flog the engine to life with a rope pull-starter. When the ignition or carburetion system were not working correctly, this type of starting could also lead to some interesting folk dances and colorful songs. Pull-starters are still available on some American reed engines, but most serious karters have discontinued this type of starting because of the popular power starter.

Because of the slipper clutches, engines can be so tuned to run only in a very narrow, and powerful, rpm band. This means the engine isn't going to run too well at lower rpm, and it may not even start at low revolutions. The engine must be spun up for starting, so the automotive starter motors are used in direct 1:1 gearing ratio, normally spinning the engine to around 1,000 rpm. There

must be no extra drag on the starter motor and it must be in excellent condition for maximum rpm and torque.

Select a starter that has a bearing or bushing in both end plates, such as a pre-1954 Ford flathead engine unit. Some starters have a nose support that reaches to the end of the Bendix drive for extra shaft support. If this can be removed without disturbing the front end plate, the starter is usable, otherwise a new end plate must be fabricated.

Twelve-volt starters may be used, but a six-volt starter connected to a twelve-volt battery will spin faster. It will also burn up under heavy continuous load. Most karters prefer the six-volt motor. There is one overdrive starter motor on the market, used in all Chrysler Corporation cars since the late 1950's. It is possible to use this starter if the Bendix drive housing (aluminum) is cut away and a special shaft support fabricated.

There are two ways to use the starter: attached to the battery cart or as a separate unit. Attached to the portable cart, the starter is above the

LEFT: **Only starter kart made by Azusa, uses kart wheels for movement on rocky ground.** ABOVE: **In this type of kart, the battery is on the pivot so no acid is spilled.**

battery. A V-belt is connected between engine and starter pulleys and the crewman pulls tension on the belt while engaging the starter motor. As soon as the engine fires, tension is released and the V-belt drops away.

In the remote starter method, the motor is connected to the battery with either 1/0 or 2/0 cable, about 6 feet long. Handles are attached to the starter and some kind of driving connection is fitted to the motor shaft. Often this is just a ratchet tool socket that fits the crankshaft nut holding the slipper clutch in place, or it may be a serrated female connector to mate with splines on the crankshaft stub. A starter button is wired to the handle for motor control.

Note how battery box pivots on small Heim rod end links here. BELOW: **This starter motor is mounted low to get into slinky FKE body with drive belt.**

Starter motor rotation may not match engine rotation, although it will be correct for at least one side in the case of twin engines. If the V-belt drive is used, the belt can be twisted to a figure-eight for rotation reversal. There will be some added drag as the belt rubs against itself. The only way to reverse the direct connection starter is by modification of the motor.

If the motor direction is to be reversed, rotate the brush end plate 90 degrees and drill new holes for the long starter assembly bolts. A new alignment notch must be filed in the starter case for indexing the little tab on the brush end plate. The ground brush leads will reach (lugs may have to be turned 180 degrees) but the field brush leads must be extended. Use leads cut from spare brushes or number 8 or 10 wire. Insulate the spliced joints well with electrical tape. The starter will now rotate in the opposite direction. This is a method used successfully by Inglewood Kart Shop.

Another method has been devised by John Hartman of Hartman Engineering when the same starter is to be used with twin engines. John extends the motor shaft out the brush end plate and equips both shafts with sockets to match crankshaft nuts. The method is ingenious and limits starting requirements to only one motor.

Another type of starter gaining favor is the converted chainsaw. Here the cutting head is removed and a direct V-belt pulley bolted to the saw crankshaft. The crewman starts the chainsaw, positions the V-belt and applies tension when the signal to start is given. Efficient and simple, but it has drawbacks.

Chainsaw motors are not inexpensive. Nor are they quiet. Sometimes the Enduro kart driver can boil an engine on the starting grid because neighboring chainsaw starter engines are so noisy he can't hear his own exhaust note. Mufflers can be installed on saw engine starters, and should be for the sake of everyone concerned.

There is a commercial starter cart for sale through kart shops, very well engineered and sturdy. Homemade carts can be welded up by the craftsman. In either case, the battery should be big and with sufficient amperage hours to last through a complete weekend of karting without recharging. Small trickle chargers are available through auto parts stores for the home shop and will bring the battery up during the week. The wise karter will not be caught without an extra starter motor. It is almost impossible to borrow a starter during the heat of competition, so a spare is recommended.

Garbage can cart is used for this battery transport.

139

Two-stroke carburetion is not nearly as complicated as for passenger car, but it does require attention during the course of a race. Carl Weeks adjusts Tillotson alcohol carburetors during hot summer day at Willow Springs sports car track.

11. The Induction System

IN ANY internal combustion engine the carburetion system is at best a compromise; for the newcomer to two-stroke engines, it is sometimes a disaster. While the two- and four-stroke engines use similar carburetion, the two-stroke is simpler but presents some very special problems. A single-cylinder engine using a piston-controlled intake port will create violent air flow impulses at all rpm, and at low rpm with open throttle the fuel mixture may even be pushed back out of the carburetor.

The automobile carburetor does not experience these violent air impulses, but it does have the extra requirement for an infinite adjustment and capability to deliver exactly the right amount of air/fuel mixture throughout the full-engine rpm range. Consequently, the car carburetor is filled with intricate measuring devices, many within the airstream. This is a fundamental difference between automotive and two-stroke carburetion.

The two-stroke carburetor will

140

have jets near the main air stream passage, a minimum number and length of drilled holes for fuel transfer, and the throttle control as a single moving part. All this tends to create a "straight bore" type carburetor with no restrictions in the air stream. In the English Amal and Italian Dell'Orto carburetors, the throttle body is a sliding tube perpendicular to the bore. American carburetors use the more traditional butterfly throttle.

Any carburetor must first vaporize the fuel and then mix this vapor with the incoming air to form a correct air/fuel ratio. It may not sound like too hard a task, and at any given engine rpm it isn't. But engine rpm is from zero to whatever, so the correct fuel mixture for the different rpm's must vary.

In the two-stroke, vacuum in the crankcase caused by a rising piston causes air to flow through the carburetor. By incorporating an adjustable venturi (slide valve) or using a fixed venturi and butterfly (fixed

bore), the air can be speeded up through a portion of the carburetor bore. At this area the suction is increased, which will pull fuel through the jet and into the air stream. The fuel is vaporized at this point. The amount of fuel vaporized relative to the amount of air flowing into the engine will determine air/fuel ratio.

Fuel does not explode inside the combustion chamber, but burns along a very definite and controllable "front". The squish combustion chamber formed by deflector pistons causes this front to streak from one side of the chamber to the other. The same kind of controlled front is helped by spark plug location and by a swirl action induction system (loop scavenging). Since not all the fuel inducted will be vaporized at the carburetor, some cooling of the chamber will be accomplished by this raw fuel before it is vaporized by the heat and burned for power.

It takes about fifteen pounds of air to thoroughly mix one pound of gasoline for total combustion. Anything

Early flatback triple-carburetor experiments for sprint kart. RIGHT: Dell Orto slide valve carburetor as used on imported engines. Most karters prefer to replace this design with American diaphragm type.

less than this, say thirteen pounds of air, will give a rich mixture leaving some unburned gas. More air will cause a lean condition, which in the case of a kart engine will leave a burned piston. The lean mixture burns with more initial heat (it doesn't have that bit of raw fuel to cool things) but will not be as powerful. Although the air/fuel ratio must be very nearly perfect for maximum engine performance, the engine will run to some degree through a very wide range of ratios, often from 8:1 through 22:1.

The kart carburetor is under rather extreme duress to produce the correct mixture ratios under the variety of loads involved in typical competition. For example, when starting a cold engine the mixture will be very rich, the ratio being about 7:1. For idling, it is leaner, but still rich at 11:1. When accelerating, where the load is very high, the mixture drops back to a richer 9:1. Running down the back straight, at a good speed and light load, but not really flat out, the ratio may be the ideal 14.8:1. But when the engine is full bore the mixture must be slightly richer to cool that combustion temperature, so the ratio is close to 13:1.

However, and this is extremely important to the karter who progresses to the stage of engine modification, the air/fuel ratio is at best a trial and error adventure even for the engineer. Therefore, any time the combustion chamber is changed, which will change the flame characteristics and burning time of the inducted mixture, the fuel ratio pattern will also change.

From the karter's viewpoint, any engine design that utilizes reed valves will be less subject to carburetor air flow upset by induction reverses, since any change in crankcase pressure will automatically seal the reeds. The suction of reed or rotary valve engines is steadier than port induction, but the high-performance rotary value engine will display some upset at low speeds.

While the straight bore slide valve imported carburetors are very popular with two-stroke motorcycle riders, they have given way almost entirely to the butterfly carburetor for American karting. The essential reason for this marked dominance of the American design is cost, availability, and a diaphragm feed system rather than a float bowl. The sliding valve in the former design controls the air flow area and speed by slide opening, while the butterly design has a fixed bore and venturi. The slide valve is very simple, with a main jet exit through a small primary choke tube into the air stream below the cross bore. Since the sliding valve is working something like a variable choke, mixture regulation is semi-automatic. More accurate fuel metering for all conditions comes usually from a tapered needle attached to the slide valve bottom, allowing more gas flow as the valve is raised.

Most American two-stroke carburetors are made by McCulloch, Tillotson, and Carter. Since they have a constant bore, the air flow speed is very low at small throttle openings which means that no fuel is drawn from the main jet. To compensate for this, a low-speed jet is included with two orifices, one for idle and one for progression, or intermediate. These holes are in the bore next to the slightly opened throttle valve, so that high air speed at the venturi will pull the fuel mixture into the engine.

New McCulloch 91A carburetor with diaphragm fuel pump included. RIGHT: American engines use reed cage to pass fuel into crankcase.

As produced for most industrial engines, these American carburetors do not have an adjustable main jet. The non-mechanical owner of a power mower tends to lean the mixture too much and burn holes in the piston. The karter must have an adjustable main jet, however, since he will want to run the engine as lean as possible without burning the piston. To this end, kart drivers develop a fine sense of "blind" tuning, reaching back over a shoulder or to one side for the carburetor. In addition, most karters will briefly hand choke the carburetor at the end of a long straight, just to pull in a little extra mixture, which will cool the combustion chamber after prolonged high speed lean conditions and give extra piston lubrication after the throttle is closed.

Although the diaphragm carburetor has been known to engineers for many years, and applied very successfully to high-performance air-

craft, it has only recently come into use on American motorcycle and kart engines. It is especially suited to both applications, since it alleviates the problems of fuel level control in a carburetor bowl. No matter what position the carburetor is in—level, tilted, or upside down—it works equally well. The design is not affected by acceleration or vibration.

An additional quality karters appreciate is the fuel pump possibilities of such a carburetor. A double diaphragm may be included in the design, the second working as a fuel pump with control pulses from the crankcase pressure.

Operation of a diaphragm carburetor is extremely simple, and is basically the same whether foreign (slide valve) or American (butterfly valve). Fuel is drawn into a chamber between the pump and carburetor diaphragms by the pump unit. As fuel is required by the engine, it passes through a flap valve to the carburetor diaphragm chamber. The carburetor (or inner) diaphragm then passes the fuel through jets as needed. Neither diaphragm moves through a big distance, as does the automotive fuel pump, rather they both quiver rapidly to keep the fuel flow constant.

Because the American diaphragm carburetors are so well suited to karting, the IKF makes a special ruling which allows use of these units on foreign engine designs. Tillotson obliges the stock classes by making certain special modifications available for the advanced kart shops. Karting specialists have been quick to create performance parts for these carbs too, with most attention focused on the popular Tillotson. Thus it is offered in modified form by Hartman Engineering, Crescent, Jeffries, and Inglewood; all are basically the same and yet all are different. Selection of one or the other rests with the karter, since he will tune according to particular modifications and type of fuel used. Like most accessory manufacturers, these shops will give detailed instructions on using their device.

How these carburetors differ from the production version is illustrated in the Hartman Engineering HL 250 (modified Tillotson). The Tillotson HL 227 is a factory unit used on many kart engines. The HL 250 is also produced by the factory, but modified to specifications of John Hartman, who is the sole distributor for the unit. Both are legal for Italian engines in the stock classes. The Hartman version is designed with slightly different internal passages for a smooth throttle response, automatic inlet tract purging, no air horn and venturi restrictions, and an adjustable position throttle arm. In essence, this is a sophisticated, or "blueprinted" version of the factory carburetor.

One of the IKF rules that may prove troublesome to the new karter is the use of any fuel that will go through the carburetor. There are tremendous differences in fuel flow, so that a stock carburetor may not be able to flow enough special fuel to make cheating possible. In the modified classes, where the carburetor may be changed, special fuel units are available. Just to make sure there is no carburetor cheating, IKF publishes a rather lengthy procedure for checking carburetors, which includes checking even the smallest drilled passage.

The two-stroke has an induction period approximately half that of the four-stroke, so it may increase the size of the carburetor bore without adversely effecting the flexibility of the engine. The three-port engine, with induction limited and controlled by the piston must use large bore sizes for high performance; rotary valve engines are not so critical.

The straight bore carburetor is superior to the modified choke carburetor common to automobiles, simply because the bore does not have as many internal obstructions to disturb the air flow. Essentially, the two-stroke bore can be approximately twice as big as the four-stroke counterpart. As a guide: The 50 cc engine can handle 15 mm; 100 cc takes an 18 mm; 125 cc should get 22 mm; and 250 cc can take 25 mm. This assumes one carburetor per cylinder.

Unless a slipper clutch is used, which allows the engine to remain in its power rpm range through low-speed corners, trying to get perfect carburetion is the most fustrating part of the sport. It is possible to

Single and dual carburetor manifolds on McCulloch engines.

mount two small carburetors with the throttles linked to open progressively. This gives small bore openings for low rpm use, and sufficient bore for the higher rpm's common on straights. The following table is a good starting point for selecting carburetion.

Engine	Carburetion Stock	Modified
Mc 49C	McCulloch 68795	—
Mc 91	McCulloch 65129	
Mc 91A	McCulloch 68886	dual Tillotsons
Mc 101	McCulloch 65929	
Komet		single
Parilla	250A	or
Saetta	or	dual
B-Bomb	227A	Tillotsons

Intake ram tuning (which is both mass and accoustic tuning) has been tried and untried so many times in karting that most enthusiasts have almost thrown the idea out the window. A long induction pipe can improve volumetric efficiency simply because it helps to overcome the problems of mixture inertia inside the inlet port. The same thing happens to the inlet charge as to the exhaust. When the inlet port opening

into the engine is shut off, a pressure wave is reflected back up the inlet port, to reverse itself at the carburetor opening. In karting the problem is that to be really effective the intake port, or manifold, would have to be quite long. Otherwise the wave is bouncing around and reversing direction so often that most of its effect is lost. As a rule, from the inlet port to carburetor air opening a length of 8 inches works well in the rpm midrange of 6000—7000. At higher speeds, the length must be less.

Pressure waves travel at the speed of sound. There are variables in the pressure wave speed, though, caused by atmospheric pressure, temperature, etc. For calculations, it can be assumed the intake wave speed is around 1100 feet per second, whereas the exhaust speed may vary from 1300-2000 ft/sec.

Pressure waves in a pipe do not look like ocean waves, but include condensations and rarefactions in the transmitting gas. When air is kicked at one end of a pipe, the air immediately ahead of the kick will be compressed. This compression moves down the pipe length, but the air

145

Special GEM intake manifold for American engines includes larger reed plate to pass extra fuel mixture.

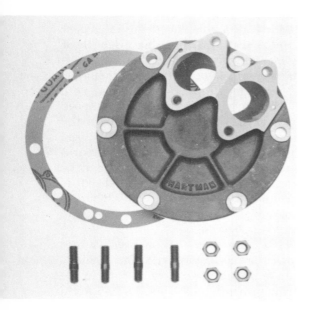

Hartman Engineering dual carburetor adapter plate for rotary valve Italian engines using Tillotson carburetors.

itself does not move. The compression pulls air molecules together then releases them as it passes.

For the sake of the mathematically inclined, following are two formulas to determine inlet tract length for ram tuning. The first was created by Chrysler and applies primarily to a mild timing:

$$L = \frac{72C}{N} \text{ where:}$$

$L =$ length of intake tract in inches

$N =$ engine speed in rpm where ram effect is desired

$C =$ velocity of wave in ft/sec (or 1100)

For an engine with longer timing duration, the following English formula may be used, but will result in a longer induction tract.

$$L = \frac{90C}{N}$$

This second formula applies more to high revving racing engines, but in either case the final result must be modified by trial and error for maximum power.

It is essential the carburetor be toward the outer end of the ram tuned inlet tract, as the pressure effect will disturb normal function of the carburetor. Ram horns for the outside of the carburetor may be used in lengths to 3 or 4 inches.

While some experiments have been tried with ram induction, nothing really substantial has come of it in karting. Motorcyclists have experienced good results with ram tuning, where engine rpm can be held relatively constant. Ram horns with the bell open end can be applied to karts by the enthusiast wishing to experiment. This makes possible use of a second unit, called a fence by bike racers, that fits near the horn opening. The fence is a piece of aluminum machined on the inner face to the same curvature as the horn opening, coming to a point. The fence is adjusted away from the horn, usually 1 to 1½ inches, and serves as a reflector for fuel charge "stand-off". When an engine is running hard, quite often some of the charge is blown out into the airstream. The fence catches it. Harley-Davidson racing engine mechanics have been enjoying success with this unit recently.

The kart engine will have a marked reluctance to idle well, seeming to skip a beat and in general act as though destruction is likely at any moment. When engines start this "four-stroking" the stacatto exhaust blatt is highly irritating. Cause of this unique two-stroke characteristic is poor scavenging of the combustion chamber at low throttle settings, and will be pronounced when the throttle is closed quickly. It cannot be eliminated entirely, although the loop scavenging chamber has less incidence than the cross-flow chamber.

It is worth noting that boat outboard engines have overcome this problem (which will actually cause an outboard engine to stall when the throttle is suddenly closed) by retarding the spark as the throttle is closed. This allows the incoming mixture more time to exhaust the cylinder before being fired, and works well.

Air cleaners are not common to competition karts, although anything entering the carburetor air flow will find its way directly to the engine heart. While this is an overlooked item for racing, where the tracks are relatively dust free, it must not be overlooked on the kart used to bang around the neighborhood dirt lots. While the cleaner will reduce power of the sensitive two-stroke, it will save an engine.

Fuel injection is not common to the two-stroke engines, although there are a number of patents registered on this subject. Injection offers a significant advantage over the traditional float-type carburetor, in that fuel metering is closely controlled under all conditions and the air/fuel mixture ratio can be consistent. However, as compared to the straight bore diaphragm-type carburetors used on karts, the advantage of injection is not great enough to offset the higher cost.

While injection systems could be introduced to place the fuel into the transfer port area, the advantage would not be appreciable on the limited kart engine. Pressure oiling might reduce the second partner to the air mixture, but crankcase pressure is still necessary to charge the cylinder, and the transfer port injection would tend to complicate the engine considerably.

Supercharging is one route to horsepower that has been overlooked by the two-stroke enthusiasts. The IKF rule book makes supercharging legal in all but the top class; but it also advances the particular engine to the next bigger class. While this might seem an undue restriction, experience has proven the classification formula sound. It is used in automobile racing, and practically all Indianapolis race cars using the Ford V8 and Offenhauser engines are equipped with exhaust turbosuperchargers. In this case, the supercharged engine must run with one-third fewer cubic inches, yet it outperforms the larger displacement engine with ease.

However, the single cylinder two-stroke engine does not produce an ample increase in horsepower through supercharging as does a typical four-stroke. The supercharger has the function of packing more mixture into the engine, which will make the charge denser. With the single-cylinder two-stroke engine, the exhaust port will be open at the same time the intake is open, so this packing effect is mostly lost motion. The problem can be overcome by incorporating a rotary valve and port where the transfer port normally is. By this method the intake port can be greater in depth than the exhaust port, so compressed mixture can be pumped after the exhaust port is closed. This is still not taking maxi-mum advantage of supercharging potential, however.

While supercharging has not been in great evidence in karting, it has been tried in traditional applications. The success has not been vivid enough to encourage much experimentation, yet it does offer some interesting possibilities to the karter who likes to work with the unusual.

If there is a single area where the two-stroke engine can be really improved, it is the induction system. Fortunately, an engineering degree from M.I.T., or the key to Fort Knox, is not required to make an experiment. While the beginning karter will tend to stay away from induction modifications, the advanced builder will delve into this problem with enthusiasm. The results will never be all good, but they do serve to whet the appetite for more karting experience. And that's good.

American Carburetors

Carter Carburetor
ACF Industries
2840 N. Spring St.
St. Louis, Mo.

McCulloch Corporation
6101 West Century Blvd.
Los Angeles, Calif.

Tillotson Mfg. Co.
761 Berdan Ave.
Toledo, Ohio

Hartman Engineering
3731 Park Place
Montrose, Calif.

Inglewood Kart Shop
1307 N. LaBrea
Inglewood, Calif.

Jeffery Industries
2425 Park St.
Findlay, Ohio

Crescent Raceway
4844 N. Detroit Ave.
Toledo, Ohio

Dick Ruzik of Kendick Engineering checks dynamometer reading on 91A McCulloch reed engine while Chuck Pittinger makes carburetor adjustments.

12. Tuning for Speed

IT IS IN the fascinating realm of kart engine performance tuning that the serious enthusiast is separated from the casual. While cubic money may help an owner *purchase* winning potential, it does not *insure* him of winning performance. No matter how good a stock or modified engine is, it will not produce maximum power unless every minute detail has been carefully plotted and executed. The tiniest fraction of horsepower usually means the difference between the winner and the pack.

Unlike the automobile four-stroke engine where tuning is understood to mean the adjustment of component parts to work in perfect harmony, two-stroke tuning also means essential adjustments to the basic engine design. In this respect, two-stroke tuning means either blueprinting for stock racing, or modification for faster classes. Further, two-stroke tuning can be divided into four categories: Reduction of mechanical friction; induction of a denser fuel mixture; burning the fuel mixture to the most

Stuffer plate bolted to bottom on McCulloch engine decreases dead space in crankcase.

time, but has not been worn excessively. If the cylinder is to be bored to a larger size, this should be farmed out to an expert machine shop, and if possible, to the shop making or supplying the larger piston. Should the stock cylinder be retained, there are some small areas near the ports that can be cleaned up. Local distortion in this area will show immediately, and can be cleaned with emery cloth.

It is in the port area where drastic changes in two-stroke tuning take place, and any alterations here are comparable to changing camshaft timing in the four-stroke. As with the four-stroke camshaft, which may produce an engine of "three-quarter, full-race, or competition" classification, two-stroke port timing may be anywhere from very mild to radical. Essentially, mild port timing will allow the engine maximum flexibility over a very broad rpm range while competition timing will restrict the engine to a very narow rpm range. As an example, the chainsaw engine works best at 6000-8000 rpm, but it will run well at lower and higher rpm. A racing motorcycle engine may work best only between 11,000 and 12,000 rpm and hardly run at all below this rpm.

The transfer and exhaust ports are mainly responsible for power and economy while the inlet port is strictly for filling the crankcase or transfer port. The former then have an entirely different function from the inlet port. Most engines are symmetical, so that the power ports operate at equal angles at each side of bottom dead center. However, the exhaust opens several degrees prior to the transfer port. Otherwise, a small percentage of exhaust will enter the transfer port. Opening the

efficient degree; and elimination of sustained back pressure at the exhaust port. Most of this can be done by the karter with simple tools, and at the limit the cost for professional help is reasonable.

There are generally three stages of tuning, or modifications, applicable to the two-stroke; but for the karter it will be assumed all these things are involved with either blueprinting or total modification.

In any modification, it is best to use an "aged" cylinder barrel. This means one that has been run for some

Tiny McCulloch piston and rod is hardly larger than a pen; piston rings are very narrow.

exhaust early is called "blow-down" and is essential. Thus the exhaust port is timed to open between 80 and 100 degrees after top dead center and the transfer port will open 15 to 30 degrees later.

If the ports are cut into the cylinder wall well up toward the combustion chamber, and are therefore opened by the piston sooner and closed later, there will be a maximum amount of cylinder exhaust scavenging and mixture intake. However, some of the power developed by the burning gas, which is expanding and pushing down on the piston, will thus escape through the exhaust port. High engine rpm will require big ports, while smaller (lower) ports will give more low-speed torque and fuel economy. Obviously, a good industrial engine can probably have the port timing altered extensively, while the high-performance two-stroke is already near optimum.

The basic problem of working with port timing is the destruction of a cylinder if the timing is incorrect. For test purposes, it is possible to modify piston crown height and piston skirt length. While this is not the best way to modify port timing, it will give an indication of what will happen if the ports are changed relative to timing.

The enthusiast does not have to charge off into port timing modifications without a guide. Most engine manufacturers will provide suggested port configurations, but these are usually for stock timings. Some kart shops have porting service, which is recommended until the new karter is thoroughly familiar with an engine.

While most engine manufacturers publish port timing data, few engines actually have this precise timing due to machining tolerances. Therefore, before any timing changes are made, it is essential to find the exact timing of the stock cylinder. Remove the cylinder head, exhaust pipe, and clean carbon from the port edges. Attach a degree wheel (sold by all speed shops) to the crankshaft and fix a pointer to some convenient bolt. Find exact top dead center of the piston and adjust the degree wheel to 0. Also mark the exact top edge of the piston in the cylinder with a depth micrometer.

Rotate the crankshaft and note the amount of degrees before top dead center the inlet port opens (on three-port engines) and closes. Do the same for exhaust and transfer ports. Also note the difference in degrees after top dead center between the opening of the exhaust and transfer ports. If there are other ports, such as boost or finger ports, note their timing also. Sometimes the piston skirt will overhang a port, so this must be considered when working on timing. Often modification to this skirt will be required along with port changes.

As a general rule, the inlet port (three-port) must not open sooner than 65 degrees before top dead center. Inlet port width can be opened slightly, but total width should not exceed 20 percent of the cylinder bore circumference. The exhaust port should open no earlier than 80-100 degrees before bottom dead center, although this will vary with different engines. The transfer ports should start to open 15 or more degrees after the exhaust port opens. In all cases, make sure the piston crown is flush with the bottom edge of both exhaust and transfer ports at full open position (bottom dead center). There must not be a ledge between cylinder and piston, as this will disturb air flow and have an adverse effect on performance.

To work on ports and passages, use rotary files and stones in a high-speed drill. These files and stones are available through most hardware stores. Getting to the transfer ports will be rather difficult, but care must be exercised to avoid scratching the cylinder bore. Generally speaking, only a small amount of metal must be taken from a port top and bottom to drastically affect timing. Some metal can be taken from the port width; but not too much, since the rings can fall into these openings and break.

Once the best porting has been achieved, it is probable this same porting will be good for other identical engines. However, trying to duplicate porting between two different engines, perhaps a Mc 91 and a Mc 101 will prove difficult. Anytime the stroke or bore is changed, the timing will change. However, there is a method to transpose a good porting system from one engine to another, a method created at California Kart Sales in San Jose, California, and reported by Bob Lawley. In this method, modification is based on port area multiplied by port opening time at a given rate of piston acceleration.

Racing mechanics have found that piston acceleration, and not piston speed, is the limit to engine performance. Ford engineers have found that piston acceleration in excess of 100,000 ft/sec squared will establish inertia forces that can destroy connecting rods and pistons. To determine piston acceleration, use the Hepworth-Grandage formula where:

$$N = \frac{A \times 2189}{\sqrt{S \ (1 \ plus \ 1/2n)}}$$

N—rpm
S—stroke length in inches
A—piston acceleration in ft/sec squared
n—ratio of connecting rod length to stroke length

California Kart Sales enthusiasts have thus found that the total exhaust port area and the blow-down area should be determined by port area multiplied by the time it takes to open the port at the limiting rpm given by the above formula. If two engines are the same displacement, the area-time figures are constant. If displacement varies, the figures are proportionally larger or smaller.

By substituting the known figures from a good performing Mc 91 engine, for instance, we have something that might read:

$$N = \sqrt{\frac{100,000 \times 2189}{1.635 \left(1 \text{ plus } \dfrac{1}{2 \times 1.53} \right)}}$$

N thus equals 10,100 rpm as a limiting factor.

To find the exhaust port opening time, use this formula:

$$T = \frac{60}{N} \times \frac{E}{360}$$

T—time in miliseconds
N—rpm for 100,000 ft/sec squared piston acceleration
E—exhaust port opening point in degrees before bottom dead center.

From the Mc 91 information this gives a formula:

$$T = \frac{60}{10,100} \times \frac{95}{360}$$

T then equals 1.57 miliseconds.

Now multiply the exhaust port area by port opening time. A quick way to find exhaust port area is to hold a piece of paper over the port and press around the opening. This gives an outline on the paper which can be measured. For the Mc 91 described, it is 1.25 square inches. So multiply:

1.25 sq/in × 1.57 milisecs.
= 1.96 sq/in milisecs.

Find the area-time for the engine blowdown period. On the Mc 91 area was figured by measuring distance from point of exhaust opening to transfer port opening, then multiplying by port width. This gave an equation:

.315-inch × 1.64-inch — .515 sq/in

Blowdown time came from the previous equation of:

$$T = \frac{60}{10,100} \times \frac{22.5}{360} = .373 \text{ milliseconds}$$

Multiply the blowdown area by the blowdown time as follows:

.515 sq/in × .373 milisecs.
— .193 sq/in milisecs.

This information, or the .193 sq/in miliseconds area-time result is from an engine that runs very well. By working with figures only for a hypothetical engine, it is then possible to find an area-time equation that is similar to the known engine. That this method works has been verified by competition results with California Kart Sales engines.

It is possible to gain more port area by squaring drilled or gabled ports, but again this must be done

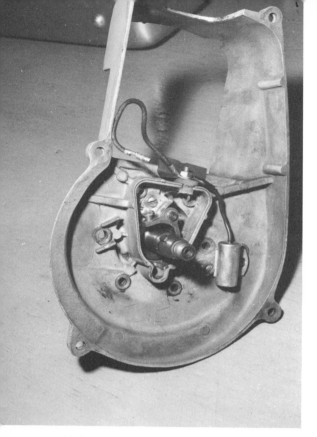

McCulloch points, condenser, and point plate operate by cam ground on crankshaft.

to a limit that will not allow the rings to hang up and break. If there are bars in the ports, these may be tapered on the backside for smooth air flow, but they should not be cut away. They are in the original design to hold the piston rings in place. It is preferable to keep the port top shape slightly curved to help guide the rings back in place as the piston rises. Since the piston rings are generally pegged in place (they cannot rotate), do not open the ports wide enough to allow the ring ends to pop into the port. With loop scavenged engines, it is essential that dual transfer ports be shaped identically to retain symmetrical mixture flow.

Improving the flow characteristics of the fuel mixture through the transfer tubes is equivalent to "porting" a four-stroke engine. Although engineers have been aware of the importance of air flow, it has only recently come into significance as a ready improvement for power. The modern racing engine, whether two- or four-stroke, will make maximum use of good port and passage shape.

Transfer passages should be so shaped to pass as great volume of air with the least amount of turbulence possible. Poorly shaped passages, with little pockets and corners that create turbulence are to be avoided, yet production engines have these very problems in abundance. Even the "racing" engines seldom have perfect passages.

Passages may be cleaned up and reshaped with simple files and stones, but merely opening up a passage or rounding a sharp corner may not actually increase the flow of fuel mixture. Here is one place some professional help can be included. Racing engine mechanics have found considerable help in porting from air flow analysis. While this service has not seen too much use in karting, it has become at least well known in automotive circles. Most speed shops can direct the enthusiast to an air flow specialist.

It has been found, for instance, that air does not necessarily flow best around a smooth bend. It might actually turn a sharp edge better. At any rate, for the really serious karter wanting to research the matter it would be a simple thing to find the optimum transfer passage shape, since the shapes can be made up from wood or clay and the air flow tested. Trying to get the perfect passage with any given engine might be impossible, but at least something better than original is usually possible.

Just how well the engine will run depends a great deal on port flow direction. Since scavenging of the exhaust gases is critical to two-stroke performance, and good combustion is vital, the air flow into the combustion chamber must be directed to get the maximum effect desired. Again, an enterprising karter might spend some time on an air flow bench and find unusual results that would enable extra power.

In any case, when a passage is reworked, the idea is to flow maximum mixture with minimum restriction. At the port the mixture must be directed to flow into the chamber at a correct angle. There are two trains of thought on passage finish. One maintains the port should be mirror smooth to reduce any extra drag to the mixture flow, the other maintains a slightly rough port finish will tend to cause just enough surface turbulence to keep the fuel in suspension. Experiments indicate the mirror finish has a flow advantage.

On engines having window and finger port holes in the piston, the inner edges of these piston holes can be chamfered to reduce any turbulence over the sharp edges. It is possible to modify three-port engines to incorporate reed or disc inlet valves, and then convert the former inlet port into a third port. While this can be done at home, it is less expensive to buy conversion kits from the kart and motorcycle shops.

Modification to the valve system, whether rotary or reed, is also simplified by kits available through kart shops. The best reed ports are of the pyramid or wedge type, which have been engineered to give maximum

External magnets are used on McCulloch flywheel. Coil and high-tension lead must be in perfect order.

gas flow. The stock reed valve bodies can be filed to remove sharp edges which impede mixture flow. Reeds are usually about .006-inch thick and some experiments with thicker reeds (.002-inch is roughly 40 percent stiffer) may give better performance. Major change to the rotary valve disc would be in degree of opening.

Crank-case pressure does not have the entire job of pumping a fuel mixture into the combustion chamber. In fact, this pressure is little more than an assist to the fuel movement. Air flow is caused primarily by the partial vacuum (depression) created in the cylinder when the piston travels downward. When this depression occurs, there is a wave effect created that travels at the speed of sound. This wave would tend to pull mixture into the cylinder even without crankcase pressure. Case pressure does help, but mostly in the higher rpm brackets.

On short stroke engines that will remain in the higher rpm ranges, the crankcase volume can be reduced to advantage. This is possible through special "stuffers"; cast and machined aluminum alloy inserts that decrease the dead space in the crankcase. However, on a long stroke engine the stuffers may prove detrimental.

Whether the stuffer is used or not, the crankcase can be cleaned and polished. Little areas or pockets where mixture can stagnate should be filled. This can be done with shaped aluminum plugs, or with a mixture of aluminum powder and epoxy. To use the epoxy, clean the area thoroughly with trichlorethylene (anything that really cleans the case will do) and then rough it up with a file or stone. If there is considerable epoxy to be used, screws threaded into the case will give a better epoxy purchase.

There is crankshaft work that should be done to the all-out competition two-stroke, but little of this is of home workshop variety. Whether the crankshaft is of the American one-piece design or the multi-piece type used with imported engines, it is a precision item and must be handled that way.

As produced for an engine of a specific purpose, the stock crankshaft is likely to last a very long time. Subjected to higher stress of just an additional 1000 rpm, the shaft may fail immediately. While many kart shops offer a special balancing service for all shafts, a few of the shops offer a special crank preparation service. The crankshaft is first inspected for straightness and trued if necessary. The metal is Magnifluxed to detect any cracks that will lead to fatigue failure. Once past this test, the crankshaft is checked on a grinding machine for perfectly true bearing surfaces. All sharp corners will be radiused to relieve stress buildup and the entire unit will be shotpeened for the same stress relief. If the enthusiast is an accomplished machinist or mechanic, he may want to disassemble and modify his own built-up crank. This is an extremely exacting business, however, and should be left to the expert.

There is not a great deal that can be done with the connecting rod, although there is at least one kart shop making special racing rods. While a billet rod might be the most desirable, cost for such an item might be more than for an entire engine. Factory rods are usually strong enough for most competition, and in the case of high-performance factory engines, the rods are satisfactory for stock classes.

It is possible to improve any factory rod, however. As noted before, it is piston acceleration that tends to break connecting rods, so maximum attention must be paid to removing any stress focal points. Always use Magniflux rods for high-performance engines. After the rod alignment has been checked and repaired as necessary, the big and little end bores should be sized. The rod surface should be ground perfectly smooth and then polished, leaving no visible scratches. This bit of work can be carried out at home and may save a good engine.

The standard piston will usually withstand higher rpm, but any form of lightening is usually a benefit, especially if in the skirt area around the ports. However, the stock piston can only do so much. It is possible to weld up an alloy piston and machine a different shape, but the cost for such a home-grown item far exceeds the cost of a special racing piston.

The major special piston manufacturer for kart two-strokes is Wiseco, at 30200 Lakeland Blvd., Wickliffe, Ohio 44092. The enthusiast with cylinder or piston problems should contact the company before making a hasty decision. The piston is vital to good kart performance, since it is involved in practically all two-stroke functions (port timing, air flow, combustion chamber, and crankcase pressure).

The high-performance piston must withstand tremendous pressures. Consider that an average engine turning 9000 rpm will have a piston speed in the neighborhood of 27,000 inches per minute! That is 450 inches per

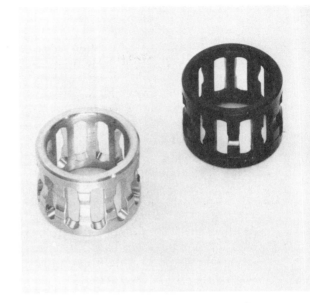

Special roller cages for imported rotary valve engines keep roller bearings from galling.

second, or nearly 40 feet a second. It is starting and stopping at these speeds (accelerating to about 70 mph in 1½ inches), so there is a tremendous load placed on the piston rings, wrist pin area, and skirt. At the same time, combustion chamber temperatures will be extremely hot.

The typical industrial engine is designed to run at relatively low speeds, around 5000—6000 rpm. Heat will be a problem, so wide rings will be used for maximum ring life and the best transfer of piston heat to the cylinder wall. In the performance engine, the rings can be much narrower, down to about .040-inch for cast iron and .024-inch for steel. The steel rings are less likely to break. Steel rings can be chromeplated for cast iron or sprayed cylinder bores; plated rings should never be used in conjunction with plated cylinders. Two rings are enough.

Competition pistons may be made of different alloys, but they almost always are created by some form of forging, either from a spanked casting or a pure billet. The lifespan of a good piston is very long, unless the crown is burned by lean fuel mixtures. Even when the piston has "stuck" in a cylinder, both cylinder and piston can normally be cleaned and reused.

It is desirable to run as high a compression ratio as possible without incurring the wrath of detonation. While most engine manufacturers will list compression ratios, this may be a dubious point. Compression ratio is calculated by the formula:

$$\frac{\text{swept vol. of cylinder} + \text{vol. of combustion chamber}}{\text{volume of combustion chamber}}$$

If the cylinder volume is not known, it may be found with the formula:

$$\frac{\text{bore} \times 7854 \times \text{stroke (millimeters)}}{1000}$$

It is easier to modify the head than the piston crown to raise compression ratio. In the case of a flat top piston, a considerable amount may be taken from the head. In the case of a deflector or dome piston, clearance between piston and head is critical (should not be less than .040-inch in any case). To find how much clearance is available, use molding wax or clay on the piston and rotate the engine several times, then measure the clay thin point.

To find the actual volume of a combustion chamber—always nice to know and essential when blueprinting an engine—remove the spark plug and turn the engine so the plug hole is vertical. Using a chemistry type measuring glass, fill the combustion chamber full of oil until the oil is halfway up the spark plug hole (piston at top dead center). The amount of oil used will give a direct reading in cc's, which is the chamber capacity.

It is interesting to note that factory quoted compression ratio may not be entirely accurate, although it may use the formula quoted above. This is for the complete piston stroke, but since compression cannot start until the exhaust port is closed, the effective stroke will be less and so will the compression. A compression ratio of 10:1 is about maximum with gasoline, upwards of 15:1 can be run with high oxygen fuels.

To determine what volume the combustion chamber must be to give a specific ratio use the formula:

$$A = \frac{\text{cylinder volume} + X}{X}$$

A—desired compression ratio
X—volume of combustion chamber

If no special high compression head is available from the kart shop, it is possible to weld up the open area of the head combustion chamber with aluminum and remachine it. However, this will change the squish characteristics of the chamber, so some thought must be given to final shape. Most kart shops can supply this service.

While a battery-type ignition is used on some motorcycle two-stroke engines, the majority of two-strokes for karting have a magneto ignition. The magneto system has a permanent magnet as the prime source of power, and is preferable in karting because of simplicity and light weight. The magnet is cast in the flywheel with

NORMAL

WET FOULING

OVERHEATING

ALUMINUM "THROW-OFF"

CORE BRIDGING

GAP BRIDGING

Learning to read the spark plugs is essential to tuning a two-stroke. RIGHT: Dunleer timing tester uses a light and horn.

both poles exposed (either on outer or inner flywheel rim). Most of these magnets are made of Alnico, a composition of aluminum, nickel, cobalt, copper, and iron. As the flywheel rotates the magnets come under a coil unit (primary and secondary windings in the coil assembly, the laminated E core, and the low and high tension leads). The magnets are placed, or timed, in the flywheel to give a high voltage spark at the correct moment on the compression cycle.

Magneto breaker points are similar to those in any ignition, adjustable to determine the moment of actual ignition. A cam on the crankshaft works the points. At the moment the points open, there is a tendency for low voltage current to continue flowing. Unchecked, this would cause an arc across the points as they open. To prevent this condition, which would burn the points, a condenser is installed.

The condenser is a capacitor that absorbs the current that would normally jump the point gap. It then releases the electrical charge in a reverse surge of current that helps to increase the voltage in the coil secondary winding. Induced voltage in the secondary winding may reach as high as 15,000 volts and is transmitted through the high tension lead to the spark plug.

There is really not a lot for the karter to do with a magneto ignition. However, since the magnetic force lines that are built up in the coil primary winding are directly related to the air gap between flywheel and the E core, the closer this gap the stronger the high voltage current to the spark plug.

There will be tolerances caused by mass production. Each engine manufacturer will have a specific gap recommendation between flywheel and lamination, but the karter can run

Modified transfer passage of McCulloch engine shows how bottom edge of transfer port is enlarged in area. Ports into cylinder are also tapered for better directional control of mixture.

the coil as close to the flywheel as possible. This will usually be between .008 and .012-inch, as set with a feeler gauge. Test the coil and condenser to manufacturer specs on any automotive tester. A bad condenser will cause the engine to pop while running. The easiest way to test a flywheel magneto is to replace the flywheel with a new one and note the performance.

On the question of fuel karters one can reach some controversial conclusions. To begin with, there is no magic fuel formula that will pour a winning championship into the gas tank. Indeed, exotic fuels are not in themselves great producers of power, but rather allow significant power producing modifications to the engine, like a higher compression ratio.

But to basics. Gasoline is perhaps one of the most powerful ingredients that can be burned in an engine, if it could be completely consumed in combustion. In searching for a "hotter" or more power producing fuel, racing

mechanics have come upon only two types of fuels: hydrocarbons and alcohols. The two categories are broken down into three main types of paraffins, aromatics, and napthenes. Gasoline is a paraffin, benzene is an aromatic, and methanol is an alcohol.

Gasoline is made up of carbon and hydrogen atoms in a ratio of approximately two hydrogen to one carbon. Hydrogen burns better than carbon, so methanol with four hydrogen atoms to one carbon atom will be a better fuel. The methanol molecule is much smaller than the gasoline molecule so it will meter and atomize better. Methanol also has a much higher latent heat of evaporation (264 calories/gram vs. gasoline at 75 calories/gram). This means it will burn much cooler. Since combustion temperature is related to compression ratio, methanol will allow a higher ratio because it does cool.

Nitromethane, a common fuel with automobile race cars, is really an oxidizer. In the car engine it might

Two-stroke cylinders are ground to perfect shape with stone.

be the major fuel (up to 98 percent of a mixture), but in karting it is more an additive. Nitro has a poor octane rating, so karters have found it best as an addition to alcohol.

Other oxidizers are hydrogen peroxide and nitric acid, both common in automobile racing. Hydrogen peroxide is unstable and nitric acid is very hard to use. The best guide to selection of an exotic fuel is to contact the special fuel companies for full information and recommendations. Ask other karters what does, and what doesn't work, and proceed with caution. About all that happens is a ruined engine, but do beware of toxic fumes from these fuels. In that respect they can be lethal.

For ignitors, there is propylene oxide and ether. Propylene oxide is about as unstable a compound as possible. Some of the greater oxygen bearing fuels tend to burn slow, and will ignite slower than gasoline. The ignitor gets things going faster and for this reason is desirable. Blenders are sometimes used when two fuels will not mix. Sometimes an additive will be selected because it will cool the combustion temperatures, and finally, it is possible to boost a fuel octane slightly with an additive.

Totaled, however, exotic fuels are principle features of the real professional or the real amateur. In the former, fuel will be used so the rest of the engine can be run at maximum potential. In the case of the latter, fuel is run as a guaranteed race winner or engine eater. It almost always ends up as an engine eater. The following data on exotic fuels has been prepared by the McCulloch corporation.

Fuel Data

1. Boiling Point
   A. Methanol, 149°F.
   B. Propylene Oxide, 80°F.
   C. Nitromethane, 214°F.

2. Nitromethane: Slow Burning (slower than methanol)

   Methanol: Slow Burning: Requires starting, igniting, and stabilizing fractions for best results.

3. Nitromethane is considered a "thermalcharger" fuel. Its chemical formula is CH_3NO_2, and it is approximately 50 percent oxygen by weight. In burning, the NO_2 group splits and the two oxygen atoms are released for combustion.

4. Air/fuel ratio—for combustible mixture—is narrower than for gasoline. a. Methanol requires approximately twice the volume of gasoline. b. Nitromethane requires approximately $\frac{1}{3}$rd again as much as methanol.

5. Cold plugs are definite requirements. Start with HO-3, and watch tips carefully. Pre-ignition will come on fast if plug is too hot. Do not overlook racing, or side electrode plugs.

   Racing fuels release more heat— thus power—than does gasoline. To avoid pre-ignition, polish head (internally) to remove sharp edges, ridges, etc. Acetone is excellent for cleaning oily plugs.

6. Ignition: Start with 25° BTDC, but watch for detonation and pre-ignition.
   A. Maverick spark advance will advance firing point by six to eight degrees.

   1. If necessary, slot laminations and move assembly to control maximum maverick advance.
   2. If detonation is present at low rpm, retard spark two to three degrees for low-end operation. Pick up maximum possible maverick advance—short of detonation —by retaining lamination position, or by advancing two to three degrees.
   3. If cut-out switch is not used, set point spring to minimum tension to bring in maverick spark at lower rpm range.

7. Mixing: Nitro blends may be mixed and stored without deterioration. Moisture, from condensation, if not excessive, will frequently improve performance.
   A. Do not exceed 15 per cent nitromethane for McCulloch engines, except at own risk. Recommend starting with a 10 percent nitro mix, and work up.

8. Storing: Nitromethane blends are corrosive.
   A. Carburetor and engine *must* be flushed after running, using gasoline base fuel mixture. Run at least a quart through the engine.
   Even with this, ultimate destruction or loss will result!
   B. Do *not* store nitro blends in metal containers. Glass or crock-type containers must be used, as corrosive action will eat out metal containers.

9. Handling: Use normal caution when handling nitromethane and methanol. They are not explosive: Nitro burns slowly, with lumin-

ous flame. Methanol burns with invisible flame.

A. For user protection:

1. Wear goggles (glass) when mixing fuel blends.

2. If racing, flameproof clothing is recommended. (With methanol you can be on fire and you won't know it until your clothing chars or it starts to hurt. By then, it's too late! Flameproofed coveralls are the simplest answer.)

3. Generally, nitro and methanol are not harmful to the skin. (Some, however, will be allergic to fuels.)

Propylene oxide does, and will harm (burn) the skin. Wear good, solid nonabsorbent gloves, of the gauntlet type when handling.

10. Compression Ratio:
A. Little is gained with fuel if stock compression ratio is used.
B. Recommended ratios are:
    9:1   10:1   11:1   12:1
Do not exceed 12:1, except at risk of engine separation.

11. Exotic fuels have solvent action on seals and gaskets and most plastics. Service life of such components will be considerably reduced and the only answer is to replace as necessary.

12. Other fuel Additives:
A. Benzol—A high-octane (108 approx.) hot-burning petroleum product. Although benzol will auto-ignite, it serves as a coolant when added to the fuel mixture (10 percent by volume).
B. Ether—a highly questionable racing fuel. Although generally used as an igniter, it serves best —if used—as a starter fraction.
C. Acetone—used generally as an igniter to boost top end rpm and acceleration. Has strong solvent action on plastics.

Acetone is also used as a blend stabilizer, plus a water tolerance booster (methanol blends, with 1 per cent to 3 per cent of distilled water added to mixture).

13. Fuel Blends (Sample Base)
A. Mild Blend
Methanol	70%
(Main power base)	
Benzol	10%
(Coolant and extender)	
Gasoline	10%
(Starter)	
Castor Oil	10%
(Lubricant)	

B. Medium Blend
Methanol	70%
(Main power base)	
Acetone	5%
(Igniter)	
Gasoline	5%
(Starter)	
Benzol	10%
(Coolant)	
Castor Oil	10%
(Lubricant)	

C. Hot Blend (Can be very wild)
Methanol	55%
(Main power base)	
Nitro Methane	15%
(Power additive)	
Acetone	5%
(Igniter)	
Gasoline	5%
(Starter)	
Benzol	10%
(Coolant)	
Castor Oil	10%
(Lubricant)	

14. Other Fuel Formulas
The following are fuel formulas which have been in existence for years; in fact, some date back to pre-WWI.

A. Methanol   75%
   Castor Oil—10:1
   Ether   10%
   Water   15%
B. Acetone   35%
   Castor Oil—10:1
   Methanol   25%
   Ethyl Acetate   5%
   Gasoline   35%
C. Ethyl-Methyl Ketone 35%
   Methanol   25%
   Ethyl Acetate   5%
   Gasoline   35%
   Castor Oil—10:1
D. Diethyl Ketone   35%
   Castor Oil—10:1
   Methanol   25%
   Ethyl Acetate   5%
   Gasoline   35%
E. Methanol   99%
   Castor Oil—10:1
   Benzol   0.75%
   Nitrons Ether   0.25%
F. Methanol   86.6%
   Benzol   5%
   Acetone   8%
   Sulfuric Ether 0.4%
   Castor Oil—10:1 Ratio

15. Carburetor and Modification

A. The high latent heat of methanol, plus the very low air/fuel ratio (4:1 to 6:1 on track, versus 12:1 for gasoline), results in a high internal cooling action with a heavy induced air/fuel charge.

B. The average carburetor calibrated for metering gasoline will not pass an adequate volume of methanol. Therefore, carburetor modification is required if methanol is to be used.

C. As a rule-of-thumb, the opening of a given passage or jet to a diameter 50% greater than that required for gasoline will suffice. However, under some conditions of engine modification it will be necessary to calibrate the carburetor for the individual installation.

There are two special heat sensing instruments for karts that rate very special attention when it comes to tuning for speed. One is called a cylinder head temperature indicator (CHT) and the other an exhaust gas temperature indicator (EGT). Both of these instruments are thermocouple millivolt pyrometers; devices to measure engine heat. Neither is especially new to internal combustion engines (the EGT is very popular with light aircraft pilots, as it allows maximum fuel economy settings for cross-country flights), but both are new to karting.

The cylinder head instrument straps around the waist (to eliminate shock and vibration damage) and includes two gauges. One reads from minus 20 to plus 320 centigrade and the other from 0 to 600 degrees Fahrenheit. The heat sensing pickup is a spark plug washer.

The EGT measures exhaust temperatures immediately behind the exhaust port, and ranges from 500 to 1,500 degrees Fahrenheit. Unlike the CHT, the exhaust meter can be mounted to the kart.

Neither of these instruments is a toy and neither is inexpensive. Still, they are ideal for finding the perfect tune of an engine under actual operating conditions, since they measure the heat the engine is producing, and this is a direct reading of how the engine is performing. Engine-operating temperatures can tell a number of things, such as how accurate is a fuel/air ratio for maximum power. Temperature instruments can also be used to compare one kind of engine tuning with another (fuel, ignition timing, compression ratio). They can also guard against destruction of an engine when unsafe temperature arises.

Following are the typical temperatures for both an ideally tuned engine and one that is about ready to burn itself up. This is for a guide only, since the temperatures will vary with different engines. However, the ratio between ideal and destruction will remain relative.

Cylinder Head Temperature
Bystrom Indicator

Engine	Ideal Temp. F	Fry Temp. F
McCulloch	375	450
West Bend	475	550
West Bend (iron sleeve)	375	425
Parilla	375	450
Komet K77	325	375
Komet K88	350	400
B-Bomb	350	400
Saetta	325	400

Exhaust Gas Temperature
EMS Industries Indicator

Engine	Ideal Temp. F	Fry Temp. F
McCulloch	1125	1200
West Bend	1150	1250
Parilla	1100	1175
Komet K88	1125	1200
B-Bomb	1100	1200
Saetta	1100	1200

Probe location in exhaust:

2½ inches—McCulloch, Komet, West Bend.

1½ inches—Parilla, Saetta, B-Bomb.

By using the combination of both CHT and EGT, it is possible to establish exactly what is the perfect tune for any particular engine, simply because the fuel mixture can be leaned until the temperature produced corresponds with maximum power. Obviously such instruments will also tell when something goes wrong. An immediate increase in

Modified full-circle crankshaft in McCulloch engine (BOTTOM) as compared to stock crankshaft (TOP).

In the field, repairs call for extensive mechanical knowledge. Here a cylinder is being honed in the pits.

temperature is a danger signal to shut off.

Not every karter is going to rush out and buy special electronic tuning instruments for his pasttime. In reality, only a few are going to be this zealous, the rest are going to rely on good old seat-of-the-pants adjustments to go fast. While not as perfect as the gauge method, it does get the job done and remarkably well.

Tuning any kart engine starts with static running tests at home or in the pits. The engine is set up to run smooth at the desired top end as well as to idle reasonably well. But no amount of throttle jockey work in the pits is going to get premium performance on the track. Only track tuning can do that, and in karterese that means "reaching around behind you at speed."

To correctly tune the average engine start in the pits begin by first closing both adjusting needles. When closing any of the carburetor adjusting needles never jam them tight— just snug. If the needles are tightened in the closed position, the needle seats may be damaged or the adjusting needle tip broken off.

From the closed position open both the high-speed jet (needle) and the low-speed needle one and one quarter (1¼) turns. This should normally have the engine running on the rich side of the best track performance. Starting rich is best because too lean might stick a piston before it even getting started.

Take the kart out on the track and make several hot laps until the engine is warm. Do not readjust the carburetor until the engine has had a chance to get warm. If the carburetor was set in the pits as described earlier, the engine will probably four

cycle (run rough or blubber) at the end of the straightaway. Begin to lean (close) the high-speed needle a little at a time until the engine runs smoothly all the way down the straightaway. After a couple more laps richen (open) the high-speed needle again, just slightly. If after just a slight richening at this point the engine goes back to four cycling, the mixture is very close to best power. Lean it again to a clean two cycle at the end of the straightaway.

The trick is to get the high-speed adjusting needle just a hair beyond the blubbering point. The engine is now at best power for the first setting.

Have a look at the low end by running a few laps at a very slow speed. If the engine has a tendency to load up (run rich) when first accelerating after running slow laps the low-speed adjustment is too rich (too open). Stop and lean (close) the low speed needle slightly, maybe an eighth (1/8) of a turn. Restart the kart and check the high-speed performance again because the low-speed needle also affects the high end. You will probably have to slightly richen the high-speed needle again. Start running your slow speed laps again to see if the engine loads up at slow speeds. If the engine runs clean and accelerates cleanly (without four cycling) your engine is probably tuned for the day. Although the engine does not four cycle or blubber, you still may not be getting top performance. Now we get down to fine tuning. If low-speed performance is sluggish coming out of the tighter turns (even though it doesn't four cycle), the low-speed adjusting needle is set too lean. Richen it slightly. Recheck the high end. It is now probably too rich (four cycling at end of

All-night overtime is not uncommon to karting, but simplicity of engine makes it possible to make immediate repairs and run the next day. RIGHT: Lightweight stands are used to get short karts up to working height.

straightaway). Lean it. The engine should be set and now ready to race.

The most important thing to remember is that when you change one needle you must then recheck because one affects the other.

Carburetor adjustments should be checked throughout the day of racing, because there are several things that will influence the carburetor. If the carburetor is adjusted early in the morning of a race day, the temperature will probably rise twenty to thirty degrees. This warming of the temperature in the afternoon will also make the engine run warmer in the afternoon, thus it requires a richer mixture for best performance. Recheck the high-speed adjustment seveal times during the day.

Another thing that effects the carburetor adjustment is the weather. If the race day starts cloudy or misty and then becomes dry the carburetor will again require a high speed adjustment (a little richer).

Engine vibration also effects the carburetor adjustment. Some engines vibrate lean and some vibrate rich. This is something you will have to find out about your particular engine. Remember also that a gear ratio change will affect the vibrations. The vibration frequency power pulse rate in the engine will change due to the gear ratio change.

Another thing that will affect adjustment is the varying amounts and kinds of oil used in the fuel mix. If the brand of oil is changed, it will change the carburetor adjustment. This is due to the difference in viscosity rating (thickness or weight) of fuel additives.

The only "don't" in carburetor adjustment is never try to tune a kart in the pits with rear wheels jacked up and running free. The engine is leaned too far.

Never use fuel that has been in storage for more than a month. The exotic fuels tend to break down dur-

167

ing storage, and the track results are usually disappointing. Keep in mind too that the tendency is to run too lean with fuel, with the only real indication being a rise in engine temperature. Some karters develop such a sensitive feel they can tell by touch when the engine temperature is right, others never can tell.

A very important factor in track tuning is ignition timing. The engine manufacturer will recommend a specific timing figure (in degrees before top dead center or in cam dimension of the breaker points) and this should be an absolute truth with the karter. It is possible to make some minor ignition tuning changes if the engine is going to be run on a kart with open spaces (extended high rpm) or a very slow track where the engine is chugging at low rpm. Advance the timing very slightly for high rpm, retard slightly for low rpm. Set timing with either a timing light or breaker point gap, but the timing light will give better performance.

Check and set the breaker points regularly and replace when signs show excessive pitting. Check the low and high tension leads to see if they are alright and making correct contact. No insulation should be worn away.

Spark plugs are a direct indication of engine performance, and no automobile racer would be caught without expert plug reading experience. The good kart tuner also learns how to make fine adjustments by reading the spark plug, as the electrode and insulator will tell whether the plug is hot or cold enough for the prevailing conditions, and something about the fuel mixture. Spark plugs are considered hot or cold according to the length of inner insulator from nose to plug shell. The longer the insulator, the longer it will take for the heat to travel to the shell for radiation, and the hotter the plug will run. Usually the engine will need a hotter plug for normal driving and banging around the neighborhood than for racing, where rpm and temperatures are higher.

There is a very pronounced difference between a two-stroke and normal automobile spark plug. The four-stroke plug has a long lower electrode that comes across the base electrode, while the two-stroke uses a short lower electrode. This means the two-stroke lower electrode covers only about half of the base so that oil cannot collect there and foul the plug so easily.

The following is an example of spark plug heat ranges for a typical McCulloch engine:

Heat Range	Plug	Running Conditions
Hotter	Champion J5J or equivalent	Average driving
	Champion J4J or equivalent	Light racing
	Champion J79 or equivalent	Lengthy racing
Cooler	Champion HO$_3$ or equivalent	Constant running

Cylinder head temperature gauge mounted to bracket. BELOW: Exotic fuels make the engines go faster, but must be used with care.

When setting a spark plug, always use just a wire gauge, as this will locate burned gaps in the electrode. Bend the lower (side) electrode only, and as a guide something in the area of .025-inch gap will work if no specifications are available.

To read a spark plug, let the engine run up to normal operating temperatures, then make a good strong pass down a high-speed straight. Pull the plug immediately and inspect the firing ends.

Normal Plug—If the firing end is light tan to gray in color, shows few deposits and the electrodes are not burned, it's a sign of a healthy engine.

Wet Fouling—This condition is symptomized by a wet, black carbon coating over the firing end. In extreme cases, the entire core nose may be sludged. Some cases of wet fouling are: (1) too cold a spark plug heat range; (2) improper carburetor adjustment; (3) wrong ratio of fuel mix or unsuitable grade of oil; (4) weak ignition; (5) dirty carburetor air filter.

Spark Plug Overheating—With this condition, electrodes erode prematurely, insulators turn light gray or chalk white and the firing end has a blistered appearance. Possible causes include: (1) too hot a plug; (2) lean carburetion; (3) overadvanced ignition timing; (4) not enough oil in gas; (5) sticking piston rings; (6) dirty cooling fins; (7) worn plug port threads or plug port bushing.

Aluminum "Throw-Off"—Here, gray pot metal is found sticking to the electrodes and plug bore, evidence that serious pre-ignition is present and the top of an aluminum piston is about to melt through. The throw-off can be caused by a combination of conditions attributed to spark plug overheating. Other possible causes are hot spots within the cylinder or carbon deposits glowing within the cylinder. *Do not install a new plug until the trouble is corrected!*

Gap and Core Bridging—Gap bridging occurs when combustion particles are wedged or fused between the electrodes, shorting out the spark gap. With core bridging, the electrodes are not burned but the plug bottom is coated with ash-like deposits and, frequently, the insulator nose is splattered with tiny beads or small chunks adhering to the firing end. Both conditions are caused by excessive deposits in the combustion chamber.

Causes of these conditions are one or more of the following defects: (1) Improper oil/gas ratios; (2) Using nonrecommended oils; (3) Clogged exhaust ports that keep the offending particles in suspension thus blocking the exit. To prevent this condition, exhaust ports should be inspected and cleaned frequently.

Sometimes, the engine will be erratic with no apparent cause, which is why the nonmechanic seems to view the two-stroke as some kind of magical contraption devised to torment the soul of man. Actually, learning to diagnose two-stroke trouble is quite simple and consists of a one-two-three step procedure of elimination. The following chart can be used as a guide to troubleshooting.

Troubleshooting The Two-Stroke

Trouble	Cause	Remedy
Engine Fails to Start	Empty fuel tank	Fill tank with right fuel mixture.
	Water or dirt in fuel	Drain fuel tank and clean carburetor. Fill tank with right fuel mixture.
	Reed valve holding open	Clean reed valve, or install new reed valve assembly.
	Closed idle fuel needle	Adjust carburetor.
	Fouled or improperly gapped spark plug	Clean and gap spark plug, or install new plug.
	Worn pushrod or breaker point rubbing block	Install new pushrod or breaker point assembly.
	Burned or pitted breaker points	Install new breaker point assembly. Check condenser or install new condenser.
	Improperly gapped breaker points	Adjust breaker points.
	Loose connections or grounded wiring	Tighten connections or insulate wiring.
	Improperly adjusted lamination-to-flywheel gap	Adjust gap.
	Coil failure	Install new coil.
Engine Hard to Start	Water or dirt in fuel	Drain fuel tank and clean carburetor. Fill tank with right fuel mixture.
	Reed valve holding open	Clean reed valve, or install new reed valve assembly.
	Improperly adjusted idle fuel needle	Adjust carburetor.
	Fouled or improperly gapped spark plug	Clean and gap spark plug or install new plug.
	Worn pushrod or breaker point rubbing block	Install new breaker point assembly. Check condenser or install new condenser.
	Burned or pitted breaker points	Install new breaker point assembly. Check condenser or install new condenser.
	Improperly gapped breaker points	Adjust breaker points.

Troubleshooting The Two-Stroke

Trouble	Cause	Remedy
Engine Hard to Start	Improperly adjusted lamination-to-flywheel gap	Adjust gap.
Engine Floods	Dirt in carburetor inlet valve seat	Clean dirt from valve seat.
	Damaged carburetor inlet control valve lever	Install new spring.
	Torn or cracked fuel pump diaphragm	Install new diaphragm.
Engine Cuts Out or Misfires	Short circuit in ignition system	Tighten connections and insulate wiring.
	Fouled or improperly gapped spark plug	Clean and gap spark plug, or install new plug.
	Reed valve seating improperly	Clean reed valve, or install new reed valve assembly.
	Worn pushrod or breaker point rubbing block	Install new pushrod or breaker point assembly.
	Burned or pitted breaker points	Install new breaker point assembly. Check condenser or install new condenser.
	Improperly gapped breaker points	Adjust breaker points.
	Improperly adjusted lamination-to-flywheel gap	Adjust gap.
Engine Falters During Acceleration	Reed valve holding open	Clean reed valve, or install new reed valve assembly.
	Improperly adjusted idle fuel needle	Adjust carburetor.
	Air leak in engine	Install new gaskets and tighten all screws to correct torque values.
	Air leak at hose connection	Check on.
	Loose exhaust stack	Install new gasket and tighten mounting screws to correct torque value.
	Worn or damaged crankcase oil seals	Install new oil seals.

Troubleshooting The Two-Stroke

Trouble	Cause	Remedy
Engine Lacks Power	Clogged air filter	Clean air filter or install new filter.
	Reed valve holding open	Clean reed valve, or install new reed valve assembly.
	Damaged fuel pump diaphragm flapper valves	Install new fuel pump diaphragm.
	Worn piston rings or cylinder and piston	Install new piston rings or new cylinder, piston and rings.
Engine Overheats and Lacks Power	Not enough oil in the fuel mixture	Use right gasoline-to-oil ratio.
	Dirty cylinder cooling fins	Clean cooling fins.
	Clogged cylinder exhaust ports	Clean exhaust ports.
	Dirty or loose exhaust ports	Clean exhaust ports.
	Dirty or loose exhaust stack	Clean exhaust stack, install new gasket and tighten mounting screws to correct torque value.
	Improperly adjusted main fuel needle	Adjust carburetor.

173

13. Fuel Tanks

Fuel tanks didn't come into prominence until Enduro racing created a need for large containers. Most tanks are made of aluminum.

ONE OF THE neatest things about early karting was the utter simplicity of the whole approach. Four old wheels, some scrap tubing, a lawnmower engine, and you were in for some hot laps at the local parking lot. Nothing fancy was likely to be found anywhere. Once in a while someone showed up with upholstery, and a few karts even had painted frames and chrome linkage. For the most part though, it was all plain piperacks.

This penchant for simplicity carried right down to the basic engine essentials. Everything was bolted to the engine necessary to make it run, and this included even a tiny gas tank. That the tank shook the gasoline to a froth didn't matter. That the tank wasn't big enough for a good race didn't matter. That the tank was already there and didn't require any effort to use did matter. Things started changing when races became longer and fuel requirements increased. That the fuel tank could also involve kart styling didn't become apparent until the modern Enduro style was created.

The original pint cans that passed for integral gas tanks were used in

TOP: **Early kart tanks were stock drums (left) and special seat hoop mountings (right).** BOTTOM: **Sprint tanks are usually mounted on or under the steering hoop area. They are usually 2-gallon maximum.**

every possible position, always with the realization that gravity feed was the essential dictate. This meant the karter could put the tank anywhere, as long as it was higher than the engine; above the engine on a bracket, or better yet, on the seat hoop. The hoop mounting became almost universal and a number of commercial tanks were quickly devised. Some are still available through kart shops, but the space limitations of the modern Sprint make most of these earlier designs obsolete. As for the Enduro, it requires far more gasoline than these tanks can hold.

Most Sprint karts will carry from 1 to 2 gallons of gas, and the average Enduro will need around 4 gallons for the minimum 1 hour racing. These are single-engine figures and they are doubled for twins. While the

Homemade tank of aluminum rests on floor boards.

kart may not use all this fuel—a single stocker Enduro will run perhaps not more than 2½ to 3½ gallons of fuel an hour—the extra gasoline is used as a weighting-up factor. In some cases, the Enduro extra tank carries water for necessary added weight. In this way, the gas tanks are not just empty baggage carried along for the ride, and at the same time they are already mounted for longer races.

With the new pumper carburetors (and individual fuel pumps on some imported engines), it is no longer mandatory to rely on gravity fuel feed. Now the gas tank can be mounted anywhere there is room, provided it is within the confines of the general kart outline. Kart rules are specific on this point. With little or no room to spare behind the seat, the modern Sprint kart usually carries the fuel tank ahead of the steering hoop and between the driver's legs. Obviously

this dictates a rather triangular shape to the container. The Enduro kart may have more width in the leg area, but not as much height, as the latter would restrict driver vision. The requirement for considerable tank capacity must also be considered, which leaves only that area alongside the frame and between front and rear wheels as a possibility.

Gas tanks are made from a variety of materials, but the consideration of weight is always a factor in decision. Thus most tanks are made from aluminum or plastic, the latter offered as options on some production Sprint karts. In any case, the requirement is for maximum capacity in minimum space, with dependability essential.

There are several commercial gas tanks available through kart shops, but the majority of karters make their own units, particularly those for Enduro racing. It is quite possible to adapt some existing shape to tank use, such as a length of cylindrical aluminum tubing. This has the advantage of ready availability and low cost, but it does not provide maximum capacity for a given area. A rectangular tank in the same general confines will hold nearly one-third more fuel. Gas tanks can be built at home by most anyone familiar with basic hand tools, and the welding of aluminum is not difficult. For the craftsman without a welding torch, the tank can be formed and taken to an aircraft mechanic for welding.

Tanks can be constructed from either aluminum or tin-plate, but aluminum is much lighter in weight and easier to form. The size of the tank will depend almost entirely on engine fuel consumption (which also includes type of fuel used. Alcohols burn much faster than gasoline, so the tanks must hold more for the same distance). While a 1½ or 2 gallon tank might be sufficient for a Sprint kart running methanol, and would allow many miles of competition, the same capacity would fall far short for a twin-engined Sprinter or for a single-engined Enduro machine.

Really serious karters are so weight conscious they figure the fuel tank size and capacity to a gnat's whisker. An extra half gallon of fuel would mean about four pounds unnecessary weight (unless the weight is needed to be class legal). A gallon of liquid displaces about 231 cubic inches, which will give an idea of how big a tank size must be.

An aluminum tank is made of 3003H14 sheet stock which is .050-inch thick. After a cardboard pattern has been made and checked in the chassis, the pattern outline is trans-ferred to the aluminum with either a scribe or legible pencil or pen. Using either an electric shear or hand snips, the flat shape is trimmed and rechecked against the original pattern.

When all cuts are perfect, a soft mallet and steel dolly are used to flatten any rolled edges (a leather or plastic mallet should always be used, as a steel hammer will scar and scratch the aluminum). The rough cut edges are smoothed with a file, necessary to get straight mating surfaces and remove nicks. The edges are also beveled slightly, thereby providing a better welding surface. All edges are rounded by hammering with the mallet over a piece of ⅜-inch diameter pipe. When these rounded edges meet for welding, they are less prone to warping.

The rest of the tank is bent to shape over a piece of larger diameter pipe, about ¾-inch being average. This is a hand operation, done carefully to make sure the bend is in the right place. When the initial lengthwise bends have been made (like the first step in making a paper box), the two longest edges should mate. Correct any small errors in alignment by sliding the tank over the big pipe and using the mallet lightly.

Brush both inside and outside surfaces of the mating edges with a good aluminum welding flux, then start at one end of the joint and tack weld the two edges together. This is an extremely important part of the operation, so go slowly, tacking every 2—3 inches. Work out any irregularities caused by the heat, using the pipe as a backup, then return and tack between the initial tack welds. Smooth welding area again with the mallet, and weld the seam.

Short, but large capacity tanks are used for enduro karts that run exotic fuels. RIGHT: Commercial tanks are made for enduro karts in many shapes and sizes.

Single large enduro tank takes advantage of special frame configuration. RIGHT: This special set of homemade enduro tanks tucks inside front wheels to get extra capacity.

Enduro tanks must give plenty of clearance for tire growth at high speeds.

Welding aluminum isn't nearly as difficult as it might seem. Aluminum welding is quite like soldering, in that a very low heat is required. Adjust the torch until the dark blue flame is soft and tapers about 1/4-inch from the torch tip. Make sure the area is clean and has enough flux, then direct the flame right at the spot to be welded. Just as the metal begins to look fluid, begin to apply the rod. Wait just a split second too long and you'll have a hole. Move along the surface slowly, tilting the flame away from the metal when the heat rises too rapidly. Don't worry so much about making a pretty weld as much as making it tight.

If facilities for heli-arc welding are available, this is preferable because the temperature and penetration is so much better. It's harder to learn, of course. If the tank welding is farmed out, it will cost about $8 an hour labor, and the average kart tank can be welded in 15 minutes.

If the tank is a perfect rectangle, the two ends may be made identical, then welded in place. When designing a tank, use only 2 or 3 pieces so there won't be as much welding as with a multi-piece unit. After the tank is entirely welded up, the fittings are installed.

The tank should have the outlet at the lowest point, but an initial filter screen is advisable. If the actual line entry point is slightly above the tank bottom, small amounts of water condensation will not enter the line. A drain plug at the very lowest point is a good bet in the latter case.

The Eelco and Moon flip-up tank caps are excellent (sold by auto speed shops), but with them a vent must be provided at the top of the tank. To keep gas from sloshing out this vent during ordinary driving, a piece of tubing is bent 360 degrees and attached to the vent fitting.

For any tank over 5 gallons it is advisable to include internal baffles

Enduro tanks are mounted in rubber compression. They must be firm, but able to flex.

which keep the gasoline from sloshing around. These baffles are usually attached on two sides only, and can be tack welded in place before the end pieces are installed. Any kind of mounting tabs welded directly to the tank should be avoided, as this would become a point of probable failure.

It is in the mounting procedure that many homemade tanks (and some commercial items) meet their doom. Kart vibrations are quite severe, and during the course of a race it is possible to rupture a tank. Generally, tank failure is caused by too solid a mounting. Perhaps the best mounting is by bungee cord and rubber bushing for Sprint karts, and the rubber bushed tubing design for Enduros.

The Enduro tank lends itself to this method, where a piece of tubing is welded through the tank front and rear, parallel with the axles. Two pieces of heavy wall tubing of a smaller diameter are welded or rubber insulated to the chassis with the exposed ends covered with rubber hose. The gas tanks then slip over these insulated ends and are held in place by bolts or nuts screwed to the tubing end. In use, these tanks will seem to be shaking off, but in reality the vibration is being absorbed in the insulation and no stress points are localizing in the tanks.

Tanks must slope to the rear to insure a constant supply of gasoline to the engine. In addition, a small trap must be built around the fuel

Cylindrical tanks are strong; these are mounted with insulation on bracket supports from frame. BELOW: Anything can be turned to good use in karting; even a beer keg for the fuel.

line fixture. This will retain gas as the kart stops and corners suddenly. If gas flows away from the outlet for just an instant, air enters the fuel line and the engine usually dies. Without rope starters and because of the slipper clutches, restarting without a special starter is impossible.

It is possible to line the tank interior with a neoprene rubber solution, and this is recommended if the welding is not good. It is also wise to carry a stick of tank sealer in the tool box. This sealer really works, and is available at most motorcycle shops, particularly those specializing in off-road bikes. The method of covering the tank with a thin fiberglass cloth impregnated with resin for strength has been discontinued as unnecessary weight.

Finally, a word about cleaning new tanks and keeping old ones clean. When a tank is first made, there will be aluminum filings inside the unit. Flush it thoroughly with a hose and water. To break loose any welding slag that might remain, throw a handful of bolts and nuts inside, then agitate. Flush again. The same treatment will dislodge corrosion from older tanks.

14. Safety Makes Sense

Karting safety record is admirable even though the rules require a minimum of basic safety equipment. Helmets and jackets are the most important.

ANY KIND of kart, racing or chugging, is like a seasoned rodeo bucking bronc; just about the time you think you have it mastered, it dumps you somewhere in a disgraceful heap. Unlike the horse, and every other form of mechanized racing, the chances of getting seriously hurt with a kart are minimal. As a sport, karting enjoys the best safety record of all motor racing, although performance is as outstanding as any car. Yet karting is safe only because drivers have taken the recommended safety precautions.

First on the list for personal safety is the helmet, and it even shows up that way in the IKF rule book. "Full coverage crash helmets of approved design . . . goggles or visors compulsory . . . jackets of heavy-weight leather or vinyl material and full-length pants. . . . Race officials may modify or supplement this rule to require additional protective clothing. . ."

Open to the elements, the kart driver is not as complacent about physical well-being as the car driver. In most respects, the karter and motorcycle racer are alike. Like the motorcycle, a kart is a precision handling piece of machinery. That the driver can make an unscheduled departure from the seat is always assumed. Experienced karters seldom blame the kart, but list driver error as the accident cause. As most karters and motorcycle riders will testify, the dangerous period of learning to handle these thoroughbred machines is the second and third weeks, when the owner feels he has learned everything. This is when the driver tends to push the kart far beyond his driving talents. A trip through the weeds is humbling.

In addition to full-coverage helmet and leather jacket for driver, the kart must be equipped with a chain guard.

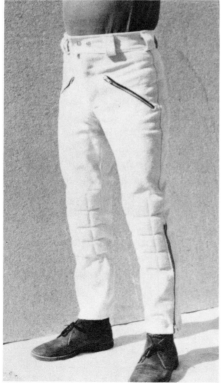

Leather pants and chaps are recommended.

Whether a kart is being driven at high speeds on a race track or just putting around the neighborhood, a helmet should be used. While it may not look quite as dashing as an Australian out-back hat, it protects the head much better. Note in the racing rules that the helmet must be the full-coverage type and of an approved design. Trying to find out what is approved may prove difficult.

Essentially, an approved helmet is one that has been fully tested and meets certain construction (and destruction) requirements. As a guide, an approved helmet will include the approving agency, which in the case of karting will be either Snell, Sema (SHCA), or Z-90. The Snell Institute was the first to become involved with helmet testing several years ago, the results leading to a rather wholesale revision of then common crash designs. Sema, which is the Speed Equipment Manufacturing Association, carries on practical application data research, working very closely with, and using recommendations of the Safety Helmet Council of America. Z-90 is a term applied to approved helmets by the U.S.A. Standards Institute.

There are many helmets available through motorcycle and kart shops, but quite a number are not approved. It isn't worth saving five dollars if the head is going to be bent up by a tiny rock. Good helmets cost $35 and up, but are often used as sales inducements by bike and kart shops. Used helmets are acceptable if they are of the approved type and have not been damaged. It is worth noting that one of the major helmet manufacturers recommends a new helmet every third year, since much strength is lost as the fiberglass resin becomes dry and brittle with age.

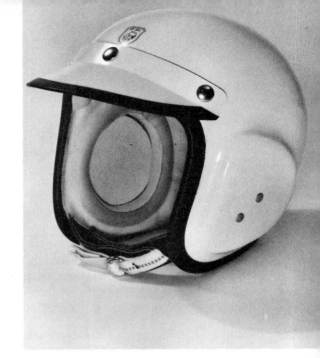

McHal Acoustablok is very popular with karters as it reduces noise level.

Bell Toptex helmet (Bell Star) protects the face with a flip-down face shield.

187

Helmets are of the full and partial coverage variety. Partial coverage is popular in Europe, and resembles an upturned bowl held in place by a leather ear covering and chin strap. They are not approved. The full-coverage helmet is more like a jet pilot helmet, with full ear coverage and an area well down the skull base. While the fiberglass shell construction is vital to a good helmet, the secret of shock absorption is in the full liner, which is where the unapproved helmets often fail. Helmet fit can be adjusted with padding, and is essential for maximum protection. The chin strap should be in place at all times.

While goggles are available, most karters prefer to run with the visor-type eye shield that snaps over the entire face area. These bubble visors give unobstructed vision and allow excellent ventilation. There is a special helmet that features a full face construction, with only a small eye cutout. It looks much like helmets worn by rocket plane pilots, but some users feel it's better suited for cars than karts.

It takes very little force to seriously damage the head; thus the requirement for a helmet cannot be overstressed. It hurts more to fall down while running than while walking. It smarts even more to dust the asphalt at 30 or 40 mph. Fortunately, the karter dressed for the occasion ends up with little more than bruised pride. Again, like the motorcycle rider, the kart driver is subject to being unloaded in strange places. To prevent skin abrasions, the rules call for a heavy leather or vinyl jacket and full-length pants. Leather and the Naugahyde type materials are

BELOW: **Bubble shield taped to helmet. This driver includes football elbow pads for extra protection. Meter strapped around waist is for cylinder head temperature readings.**

Helmets must be full-coverage type and cover ears. Bubble shield is taped on so wind will not blow it off. FAR RIGHT: Roll bars are mandatory on FKE karts because driver cannot exit the machine in case of accident.

well suited to protecting against abrasions, and they will take considerable abuse before the material fails. They can also be patched.

Selection of the jacket is an individual choice, but something relatively form fitting will give the best protection. The leather coat will be most expensive, with vinyl designs starting around $15. Vinyl has the advantage of being waterproof, and karting oils and fuels will not affect the material. Most kart shops carry a full range of jacket sizes, available in sizes from very small child to very large adult. In addition to the plain jackets, there are padded designs available at slight extra cost.

Competition rules call for full-length pants, but they do not require leather or vinyl material. Driving a kart in short pants is asking for trouble in case of upset. It is possible to protect the legs more with two

pairs of Levi's than with just one, but the vinyl pants or chaps are the best. The pants are form fitting, and sell for $25 or up. Chaps, which are zippered for tight fit and look exactly like the cowboy "shotgun chap" sell from $15.

Gloves are not common, but they should be considered as personal safety equipment. Keep in mind the possible requirement of making carburetor adjustments while driving, therefore the gloves must be flexible and tight. There are no rules concerning shoes (other than the obvious requirement to wear them), but here it is a matter of driving convenience that dictates the style. While some sort of heavy shoe would be nice for maximum protection, the driving position demands freedom for foot movements. To this end, most drivers rely on tennis or boat shoes. Fire is not much of a hazard in karting, but

to flame proof ordinary clothing, dissolve 10 ounces of Borax and 8 ounces of Boric Acid in 1 gallon of water. Dunk and dry the clothing through this solution three times.

Once the driver has been prepared, attention to safety can be turned to the kart. It would seem that anything well built would be totally safe, but this isn't the kind of attitude the serious karter takes. While commercially available, kart chassis and components are originally designed and built in the best and safest manner; they do not necessarily remain so throughout mechanical life. If there are some points on a kart chassis where stress is concentrated, fatigue failure may occur at most any time. For this reason, the race technical committee will thoroughly inspect the chassis for minute cracks that can cause an accident.

Tremendous vibrations set up by the single-cylinder engines will loosen bolts, which should be checked continually by the owner. Front spindles take a tremendous beating whether in a race or just banging around the parking lot; they should be Magnifluxed occasionally to discover hairline cracks. Nicks and scratches in alloy wheels can lead to breaks and the steering linkage must be kept in top condition with special attention to the Heim-type rod ends.

Seat upholstery will have a direct bearing on driver comfort, but it also has much to do with safety. If the seating is sloppy, allowing the driver to be tossed about, vehicle control is erratic. A good seating position will seem to fit the body, with snug sissy rails to give the hips a firm foundation. When the seat is right, especially in the upright Sprint kart, the driver feels he can actually "throw" the kart into various positions.

Very important with any kart is an adequate chain and sprocket guard. This is particularly true of the Fun kart used for neighborhood rides, where children are liable to crowd around. In racing, a driver reaching back to tune the engine while shooting down the backstretch can lose a finger(s) if there is no guard. Note also the rules call for a guard over an unused sprocket, as might happen with a twin-engined kart running minus one engine. The sharp sprocket teeth can mangle a hand.

Finally, don't overlook the steering wheel. Because there are no seat belts on karts (FKE's excepted) the body might contact the steering wheel in an accident, especially a head-on encounter. Do not use a sand cast alloy of fragile steel wheel, since they tend to fracture and can cause severe chest damage. Whether a butterfly or full-circle wheel is used, doesn't matter as much as the type of construction. The best competition wheel uses a full one-piece steel spoke with neoprene or foam rim padding.

After everything has been done to make the kart safe and protect the driver, it is up to the driver to make himself safe. This is perhaps the most difficult, and is pronounced during the first three or four rides. For this reason alone the new driver is advised to find a secluded spot to learn in. There are many such places, including dead end roads abandoned for traffic, business firm parking lots empty on weekends, even vacant dirt lots.

While asphalt is smoother, the dirt surface will be less restrictive and will allow the driver more freedom to spin out. He can spin and turn and thrash the kart to heart's content with little danger of overturning, because all the spins will come at a lower speed than on asphalt. The same is true of a frozen lake or snow-covered surface. By learning how the kart handles when out of control at reduced speeds, the beginning driver is prepared for corrective action on asphalt at much higher speeds.

When a kart is being run, it is wise to always have an observer handy, someone who can warn any traffic of the kart in use. If the kart is being run where cars are likely to travel, as on a big parking lot, some kind of buggy-whip with tip flag is recommended. This antenna should be five or six feet tall and be tipped with a colorful flag to arrest the car driver's attention. Only after the driver feels total confidence in the kart should he apply for a competition license with local organized race groups.

There are special practice sessions set aside by race organizers, a time when the neophyte competitor can get time in with other karts on the track. While on the track, he must observe all driving rules established by the organizers, allowing faster karts to pass, maintain a reasonably fast pace, keep an established path through the turns, and so on. There is no place in karting for the accident looking for a place to happen.

Helmet manufacturers are constantly updating helmet design, therefore trying to publish an always current list would be impossible. However, following is a typical grouping of helmet names with manufacturer that have been approved by the Safety Helmet Council of America.

Manufacturer	Model Name or Number	Coverage
American Sports Co.	ASC Fury 400	Full
Bell-Toptex Inc.	Bell 500TX	Full
	Bell Magnum	Full
	Bell Shorty	Partial
	Bell Star	Full
Champion Helmet Ind.	Champion	Full
D.S. Safety Helmet Corp.	D.S. "D-1"	Full
	D.S. "D-2"	Full
	D.S. "D-3"	Full
	D.S. "D-9"	Full
	D.S. "D-10"	Partial
Daytona Sports Co.	Daytona Grand Prix	Full
	Daytona 150	Partial
	Daytona 300	Full
	Daytona 500	Full
	Defensor 200	Partial
	Defensor 400	Full
McHal Enterprises	Model D	Full
	Model E	Full
	Model S	Full
Safetech	Safetech "Pro"	Full
	Safetech "Expert"	Full
	Safetech "Bearcat"	Full

15. How to Drive Karts

how a mechanical contraption works, then making a transfer to the passenger car is easy. Women, even those experienced in driving big cars, find a kart invaluable for learning how to recover from unusual positions. Men find karts keep their reactions tuned for better everyday traffic response. And in the end result, karts are perfect training for advanced automotive competition. International sports car handlers like Stirling Moss, Jim Hall, Jackie Stewart, and Dan Gurney drive karts. Dart kart manufacturer Mickey Rupp of Mansfield, Ohio, was introduced to competition through karting and found the transition to Indianapolis race cars quite easy. But driving a kart is more than plopping into the seat and mashing hard on the throttle pedal.

Essentially important to kart driving is familiarity with the machine. This starts by inspecting the vehicle from front to rear, top to bottom. Know the construction details intimately, and understand how this or that mechanical function works. Also know how it might malfunction, and what might happen should something go wrong at speed. One of the greatest road racing drivers of all time, Juan Manual Fangio of Argentina, attributed his success to a thorough mechanical knowledge of his car. American oval track racing stars Parnelli Jones and A.J. Foyt say the same thing. One of the finest kart handlers, Duffy Livingstone, is a stickler about this familiarity.

DRIVING A high-performance kart is like strapping a buzz saw to the back and challenging a moon rocket. The impression of speed is greatly magnified because of the very low seating arrangement and the outstanding power-to-weight ratio. Trying to tell someone just how fast a kart is really going, and how difficult competition can honestly be, usually ends in the statement, "try one and see."

Karts are excellent training platforms for all types of motorized vehicles. Youngsters can putt around a parking lot and gain insight into

TOP: Karts for sprint racing are designed to transfer weight to outside front wheel. Note inside wheel is off the pavement. BOTTOM: Proper driving technique calls for driving through turn with the least amount of sliding. Passing on inside is possible for better drivers.

After inspecting the kart, and doing some running-board thinking about what it probably can and can't do, take the machine out for a few hot laps of the local parking lot. It might be possible to start and learn rapidly on a regulation Sprint track. It would certainly be easier to learn on the larger Enduro tracks. But lots of wide open space for just plain wandering is recommended for the first couple of hours kart time.

Karts are extremely sensitive, both to directional control (most have a straight 1:1 steering ratio) and weight transfer. The initial few hundred feet are likely to be driven in a rather erratic manner, weaving and darting hither and yon. The problem is driver overcontrol, usually

When drivers come into turn too fast they will cause four-wheel drift just to slow kart down. It is also used to set up for coming out of turn. RIGHT: Finding the groove on a track may mean driving right on the edge of the pavement.

caused by tenseness. Relax. Take a very light grip on the steering wheel and enjoy the ride. Control will improve immediately. By comparison, the kart is steering sensitive much like a small economy car with power steering assist. At first it is almost a matter of driving with the finger tips rather than the full hand.

The seating position has much to do with learning to drive. Many be-binners, especially children and women, tend to lean forward over the steering wheel. This "elbows up and flailing" posture is tiring; it encourages muscle tightness; and the driver finds it hard to control the kart. Lean back against the seat and let the arms relax. Steering then becomes a matter of flicking the wrists and the body is not thrown about violently by direction changes.

It won't take many laps to learn that a kart is steered as much with the body as with the steering wheel, the exception being laydown Enduro designs. The center of gravity will change as the body leans to either side or forward. Weight transfer can be modified extensively by throwing the body around. As a good practice, start on a dirt surface and charge into a hard left or right turn. Keep the body rigid and note how the kart spins out. Next lean into the turn and note how the spin-out is modified. This is the beginning of body english, and the amount used will depend on the individual—some drivers are acrobats in the seat, others make almost imperceptible movements. While practicing, note how easy it is to "throw" the kart into a skid or drift. Just as the wheels are turned sharply, lean into the turn with the upper body and throw the posterior toward the outside. The lower body movement will be slight, but the sudden weight transfer will tend to break the rear wheels loose on both dirt and asphalt.

Set up an imaginary course and drive it until all reactions are smooth and coordinated. This doesn't mean

Dirt tacking is something else and requires a bit more bravado because karts are usually in a sideways skid.

gritting the teeth and boring into the corners full-steam; it means driving quickly and with finesse. A beginner can usually accomplish this after about 30 minutes preliminary practice. Now change the tire air pressure by just four pounds and try the same course with the same driving technique. It will be different. Which is the whole point of practice, learning to distinguish the difference in how a kart will handle under different conditions.

It is very easy to be overly enthusiastic about driving and spend too much time in the seat. Always take an occasional breather to relax and straighten the legs and back. As a rule, trying to drive for more than an

hour's time during any one tour will leave legs cramped and sore for several days. Several years ago a group of kart drivers embarked on a long-distance endurance test to prove the reliability of karts. After seven days and nights of constant driving they had totaled 5,240 miles around a 2½-mile road race course. No driver spent more than one hour at the wheel, most stopped for replacement after 30 minutes.

After the karter is familiar with his machine, and has some time just learning how the kart will handle, it is time to get out on the track. Things will be totally different here, because the course may be only eight or ten feet wide. Unlike the forgiving parking lot, wandering off the asphalt at speed may lead to a dusty spin-out. The detour will be bumpy at best, since the kart has no suspension and only 2½ inches ground clearance. Most courses line the tougher corners with hail bails, which aren't exactly soft but they do save bruises and pride—even the best of drivers kiss the hay occasionally.

Some tracks offer a special training period, or a time where the beginner can tootle around the course to his heart's content, at any speed he wants to travel. This usually will cost a small fee, quite reasonable, and will cover insurance. The new karter is now on his way to learning the mysteries of going slowly but quickly. At first, he will want to grip the steering wheel hard and barrel full-bore through the ᶜcorners, broadsliding in the finest A. J. Foyt dirt track fashion. Spectacular, but slow. It also tends to make the driver gun-shy. Curves become fire breathing monster pits, ready at any moment to devour kart, driver, and courage. While spin-

TOP: **Enduro racing calls for wide open spaces, such as this sports car track at Las Vegas. Plenty of room, but karts are running upward of 120 mph.** BOTTOM: **At such high speeds, techniques of drafting are used. Rear driver gets as close as possible to be pulled along in the vacuum of front car.**

outs and dumps on a corner are common, they aren't really dangerous (assuming the driver has full-protective clothing and helmet). But the pride is bruised, and the beginner begins to fight every curve, every S, every deviation in the road. He isn't relaxing.

Every successful kart driver stresses a single point about any form of competition driving—*drive around the corner, do not slide.* All the time the wheels are sliding, time is being lost on that lap. Obviously there are times when a two-or four-

wheel drift is necessary, but this won't be on every corner.

The only real way to tell how well you are improving is to time yourself around the track, and this means putting in lots of time on the course. Since most tracks have slack time, this isn't too difficult, but the beginner may be learning only that track and not learning how to drive. That is, getting around fast becomes habit, without understanding how or why. Every track is different, and every driver will tour each track in a different way. But for all, there will be a

Getting off the line, and through tight corners, usually calls for a bit of hand choking to keep mixture rich. RIGHT: Karts must go through a scoring gate in single file. Sometimes the attempt to slow down ends in a spectacular slide.

very definite "groove" which gives the fastest time. This is the place the expert driver wants to be all the time if possible. Once the karter finds the groove, he will find it requires the least amount of sliding possible. A slight improvement in kart time per lap will begin to add up to a considerable gain over the span of a normal race.

While trying to drive around a corner instead of sliding through it is the prime advice, there remains the requirement for knowing how to control a kart in all phases of drifting. It is possible to go through any given corner considerably faster than thought possible—but it takes nerve to find the ultimate limit of ability. And this is essentially the difference between champion drivers and the also-rans. There is an area of high performance where the vehicle and driver operate as an extension of each other, the place where tire adhesion is somewhere between good and none, where time seems to stand still and yet is counted in hundredths

of a second, a place where the really good driver feels completely relaxed and almost detached. When the advanced driver is in this state of competition, he reads the track and the conditions without taking time to acknowledge the assessment. He learns to act or to react to a situation, but never out of habit.

Learning how to drift a kart is a preliminary to this ultimate performance, for the sensation of a drift is very similar to that of maximum performance. Most drivers establish a reference point on the course which they use throughout a race. In some sports car races, corners are marked with signs showing how many feet remain before the actual corner begins. The driver learns during practice just how far into the chute he can go before shutting off, and he knows that this distance will change as brake fade sets in and vehicle weight lessens with gasoline consumption. Tire temperature and air density will also be factors to consider. The point is that the driver

TOP: **Coming out of a long high-speed turn, this enduro kart goes off course when corner is turned too wide.** BOTTOM: **Note body English is used even in full-bodied FKE karts.**

must constantly be making corrections for cornering technique.

To start a drifting practice, learn exactly how fast the corner can be negotiated normally. During a typically "hot" lap, note exactly where you shut off in the approach. This may be a mark on the pavement, or a hay bale, anything. It is strictly for reference. Next pick another point slightly farther into the chute, and make a few laps. Keep this up,

moving closer and closer to the actual corner at speed before getting off the throttle. It's guaranteed to cause a few gray hairs, but it will build confidence in machine and technique. The limit will show when you can't make the corner without spinning out. For the time being, that's your ultimate shut-off point. After more practice, you'll get to actually enjoy boring so deeply into the corner.

You're now going as fast as you

Getting to the race is really a part of the technique. Well-prepared transport can convince competition you mean business.

can into the corner, and driving through it smoothly. How fast you can accelerate out of the corner then becomes doubly important. Again, pick a reference point adjacent to where you normally start accelerating, then try to get on the throttle sooner. Somewhere in this practice you'll discover your own best driving technique. For some it is slowing sooner for the corner but coming out of the turn like a tiger; for others it is diving into the turn and coming out meekly. If you learn how to do both, you're ready to challenge anyone in the curves as well as on the straights.

Drifting, or sliding, around a corner is the next step up from this smooth technique just developed, and it will almost always be just a fraction second slower. However, it may be necessary to get around the entire track faster. For instance, a full four-wheel drift may position the kart with good acceleration in a better groove for snapping up competitors out of a tight turn.

To start a controlled slide, which can be practiced on dirt at much slower speeds, come to the limit of the corner approach at the normal speed. Turn the front wheels into the turn just a bit sharper than normal, which will cause the rear wheels to break loose at the beginning of a spin-out. Now turn the front wheels back in the opposite direction, just as you would when correcting for a skid on ice or snow. Since the approach will probably be from the extreme side of the track and pointing toward the inside edge of the turn, the turn exit will be at the outside edge of the track again. With the slide, the greatest amount of front wheel "correction" will come just about the time the kart approaches the inside track edge, and will begin to lessen as the kart slides toward the outside edge. It is necessary to use throttle during a slide, because traction limits are being balanced against centrifugal force. However, this is a very slight amount of throttle. Add more power and you're into a full four-wheel drift.

In the four-wheel drift situation, the kart will actually be crossed up through the corner. The front wheels will be turned into the slide, but they are also sliding sideways. It is imperative to have lots of rear tire traction and power for a full drift, and it is the ultimate in spectacular driving common to dirt trackers. Interestingly, because the four-wheel drift requires power throughout the corner, it is perhaps the fastest way to get around a turn. It is also the most delicate and will devour tires. Some kart chassis will drift much better than others, and some kart drivers never seem to learn the precise balance between too little and too much power.

The way to go to enduro kart racing in the West is by converted bus, with shade and dinner table.

National Champion Jim Akerman, NASA employee from Houston, Texas, devised unique "knees up" enduro driving technique to reduce wind resistance. BELOW: Mickey Rupp is a hot competitor in Dart karts, parlayed experience into Indianapolis 500 driving job.

How a kart will handle on a Sprint track depends on how well the chassis is set up for that track. Most drivers like to "wedge" the chassis. If the track has more right turns than left, it is possible to set the chassis on a block and jump on a corner to bend it. This will allow weight transfer earlier on a particular wheel, to take advantage of the extra right-hand curves. Nothing in the way of a fool-proof formula here, just experience.

The Enduro driver will recognize comfort as a problem, so he may carry a small plastic water bottle strapped to his waist with a flexible drinking hose attached. He may have a couple of sugar cubes for longer grinds. He'll certainly learn how to take advantage of the long straights and flex his legs, arms, and feet to circumvent cramps. Because mechanical problems always seem to occur at the furthest possible point from the pits, the Enduro driver will usually carry a spare chain, a pair of channel-lock pliers, a screwdriver, some safety wire, and a spare spark plug.

Very few karters ever drive their particular machine to its limit, because they have seldom taken the time to experiment with what it will actually do. Some time off by oneself on an empty track can be tremendously profitable. A good kart driver never stops learning.

Flags

Most automotive competition uses a set of flags to signal official information to the driver. There may be slight variations, but following is the code used by the International Kart Federation.

Green—The race has started and the course is clear.

Yellow and Red Flag Waved—Restart the race.

Yellow and Red Flags Waved—Restart the race.

Yellow Waved—Great danger, be prepared to stop. No passing.

Red—Stop immediately, clear the course as well as possible.

Blue Motionless—Another driver is following you closely.

Blue Waved—Another driver is trying to pass, make way.

Yellow with Vertical Red Stripes—Caution, oil on track somewhere.

White—One lap remaining in race.

White with Red Cross—Caution, emergency vehicle on track.

Black—Slow down for one lap, return to pit.

Checkered—Race over, slow down for one more lap.

16. *Mathematics for the Karts*

ONE OF THE most frustrating things about working with karts is the constant requirement for figuring this or that ratio or rpm or speed. The young karter thinks the math involved is some sort of advanced mental torture and the older karter has often conveniently forgotten how to solve the equation. While this particular chapter may not be used immediately to win a race, and it certainly won't give much help in buying a kart, the information is always valid and will be extremely handy at some later date.

For use in formulas, fractions should be converted to decimal equivalents. There is little need to carry the result past two or three decimal places, as the small difference will have little affect on the kart. While mathematical formulas are patterns for solving specific problems, they don't need to be relegated to memory.

U.S., British, and Metric Measuring Systems

In the following chart are the different types of measurements that apply to karts:

Type of Measurement	U.S.	BRITISH	METRIC
Linear	Foot Inch	Foot Inch	Millimeter
Area	Square Inches	Square Inches	Square Millimeters Square Millimeters
Liquid Cap.	Gallon Quart Pint Fluid Ounce	Gallon (Imp.) Quart Pint Fluid Ounce	Liter Cubic centimeter
Weight	Pound Ounce	Hundredweight Pound Ounce	Kilogram Gram
Distance	Mile	Mile	Kilometer

Some U.S. and British measures are the same and others differ; metric measures are completely different from either. For instance, the U.S. yard, which is the equivalent of 3 feet, or 36 inches, is so minutely close to the British yard that for all practical purposes the two are equal. This makes the foot and inch for the two systems equal. The metric counterpart for the yard is the "meter". It is equal to 39.37 U.S. or British inches.

For precision measurements, inches are divided into thousandths (.001). British manufacturers often use hundredths (.01) and tenths (.1) whereas U.S. manufacturers would usually use thousandths (.010 for .01 and .100 for .1) for the same measurements. For relatively crude measurements, inches are divided into fractions. The smallest commonly used being 1/64.

U.S. and British measures of area are the same. The most common one found in kart specifications is square inches.

British quarts and pints have the same relationship to the British Imperial gallon (four quarts, eight pints) as U.S. quarts and pints have to the U.S. gallon but each is larger than its U.S. counterpart because the Imperial gallon is about one-fifth larger than the U.S. gallon. However, the U.S. fluid ounce, which is 1/16-pint, is larger than the British fluid ounce, which is 1/20-Imperial pint.

U.S. and British cubic inches are equal but British manufacturers choose to use the metric cubic centimeter and the liter rather than cubic inch.

U.S. and British measures of weight are the same. Terms common to both countries are the pound and the ounce. The British also use the hundredweight, which is 112 pounds.

For distance measurements, the U.S. and British mile each contain 5,280 feet. Many British specifications also include the metric kilometer, which is .6214 mile.

In the metric system, measures that have to do with length or area are based on the meter, those that have to do with liquid capacity or volume are based on the liter, and those that have to do with weight are based on the gram. The liter is the equivalent of one kilogram (1,000 grams) of pure water at a temperature of 39.2 degrees Fahrenheit.

The metric system is built on multiples of ten. The basic measures of meter and gram are used in multiples of ten up to a thousand and in sub-divisions down to 1/1000. In other words, there are terms for measurements based on the meter that range from a thousand meters down to one-one thousandth of a meter. The thousand meter multiple is the kilometer and the thousandth division is the millimeter. The same system is used with the gram, the unit of weight. The most common of the weight terms are the gram and kilogram. The most common term for volume is cubic centimeter.

Engine dimensions, including bore and stroke, are stated in millimeters, which would indicate that cylinder displacement, which is a volume measurement, would be in cubic millimeters—but this doesn't hold true. Instead, displacement is stated in cubic centimeters. The end result is the same and because one cubic centimeter is equal to one thousandth cubic millimeters, the numbers are smaller. The smaller numbers undoubtedly are the reason for this particular usage.

Conversion Formulas

Linear

One inch equals 25.4 millimeters, and one millimeter equals .039-inch. The formula for converting millimeters to inches is millimeters ÷ 25.4 = inches

Inches are converted to millimeters with the formula

inches × 25.4 = millimeters

Area

One square inch equals 645.2 square millimeters or 6.452 square centimeters. (One square centimeter equals 100 square millimeters.) One square millimeter equals .0015 square inch, and one square centimeter equals .155 square inch. The formula for converting square millimeters to square inches is

$$\frac{\text{square millimeters}}{645.2} = \text{square inches}$$

Square inches to square millimeters is
square inches × 645.2 = square millimeters

Square inches to square centimeters is
square inches × 6.452 = square centimeters

Liquid Capacity

One U.S. gallon equals 832-British Imperial gallon. One British Imperial gallon equals 1.200 U.S. gallon.

Convert British Imperial gallons to U.S. gallons with this formula

B.I. gallons × 1.2 = U.S. gallons

A fuel tank that holds 2½ British Imperial gallons holds 3.0 U.S. gallons (2.5 × 1.2 = 3.0).

For converting U.S. gallons to British Imperial gallons the formula is

U.S. gallons ÷ 1.2 = B.I. gallons

A tank that holds 3¾ U.S. gallons holds 3.12 British Imperial gallons.

(3.75 ÷ 1.2 = 3.12)

One U.S. gallon equals 3.75 liters. One liter equals .264 U.S. gallon. The formula for converting liters to U.S. gallons is

liters ÷ 3.785 = U.S. gallons

A fuel tank that holds 12 liters holds 3.17 gallons.

(12 ÷ 3.785 = 3.17)

Convert U.S. gallons to liters with the formula

$$\text{U.S. gallons} \times 3.785 = \text{liters}$$

A tank that holds 2½ gallons holds 9.46 liters

$$(2.5 \times 3.785 = 9.46)$$

One British Imperial gallon equals 4.546 liters. One liter equals .220 British Imperial gallons. For converting liters to British Imperial gallons the formula is

$$\text{liters} \div 4.546 = \text{B.I. gallons}$$

A fuel tank that holds 14 liters holds 3.08 British Imperial gallons.

$$(14 \div 4.546 = 3.08)$$

British Imperial gallons are converted to liters with the formula

$$\text{B.I. gallons} \times 4.546 = \text{liters}$$

A tank that holds 2.9 British Imperial gallons holds 13.18 liters.

$$(2.9 \times 4.546 = 13.18)$$

U.S. and British quarts hold the same relationship to each other as U.S. and British gallons. One U.S. quart equals .832-British quart and one British quart equals 1.2 U.S. quart.

Convert British quarts to U.S. quarts with the formula

$$\text{British quarts} \times 1.2 = \text{U.S. quarts}$$

For converting U.S. quarts to British quarts, the formula is

$$\text{U.S. quarts} \div 1.2 = \text{British quarts}$$

One U.S. quart equals .946-liter (946 cc). One British quart equals 1.136 liter (1,136 cc).

Liters are converted to U.S. quarts with the formula

$$\text{liters} \div .946 = \text{U.S. quarts}$$

U.S. quarts are converted to liters with the formula

$$\text{U.S. quarts} \times .946 = \text{liters}$$

For converting liters to British quarts, the formula is

$$\text{liters} \div 1.136 = \text{British quarts}$$

British quarts are converted to liters with the formula

$$\text{British quarts} \times 1.136 = \text{liters}$$

The same formula can be used for converting from cc to U.S. quarts and vice versa by substituting 946 for .946; for British quarts substitute 1,136 for 1.136. These substitutions change the liter factor to cubic centimeters.

One U.S. pint equals .832-British pint and one British pint equals 1.2 U.S. pint.

Convert British pints to U.S. pints with this formula

$$\text{British pints} \times 1.2 = \text{U.S. pints}$$

A quantity of gasoline that requires 1½ British pints of oil for engine lubrication would require 1.80 U.S. pints

$$(1.5 \times 1.2 = 1.80)$$

Convert U.S. pints to British pints with this formula

$$\text{U.S. pints} \div 1.2 = \text{British pints}$$

A quantity of gasoline that required two U.S. pints of oil would require 1.66 British pints.

$$(2 \div 1.2 = 1.66)$$

One U.S. liquid pint equals 473.2 cc. One British pint equals 568 cc.
Convert cc to U.S. pints with this formula

$$\text{cc} \div 473 = \text{U.S. pints}$$

If 850 cc of oil were required in a quantity of fuel, 1.79 U.S. pints of oil would do the same job.

$$(850 \div 473 = 1.79)$$

For converting U.S. pints to cc, the formula is

$$\text{U.S. pints} \times 473 = .\text{cc}$$

If two U.S. pints of oil were required to do a job, 946 cc of oil would be required.

$$(2 \times 473 = 946)$$

Convert cc to British pints with this formula

$$\text{cc} \div 568 = \text{British pints}$$

This means 900 cc and 1.58 British pints are the same.

$$(900 \div 568 = 1.58)$$

Converting British pints to cc is done with this formula

$$\text{British pints} \times 568 = \text{cc}$$

This makes 1½ British pints of oil equal to 852 cc.

$$(1.5 \times 568 = 852)$$

One U.S. fluid ounce equals 29.6 cc. and one British fluid ounce equals 28.4. For converting cc to U.S. fluid ounces the formula is

$$cc \div 29.6 = \text{U.S. fluid ounces}$$

Therefore, 200 cc of a liquid is the same as 6.75 U.S. fluid ounces.

$$(200 \div 29.6 = 6.75)$$

The formula for converting U.S. fluid ounces to cc is

$$\text{ounces} \times 29.6 = cc$$

This makes five U.S. fluid ounces and 148 cc the same.

$$(5 \times 29.6 = 148)$$

For converting cc to British liquid ounces and vice versa, substitute 28.4 for 29.6 in the formulas for U.S. fluid ounces.

Volume

One cubic inch equals 16.387 cubic centimeters (cc). One cc equals .061 cubic inch. For converting cc to cubic inches, the formula is

$$cc \div 16.387 = \text{cubic inches}$$

A piston displacement of 250 cc is equal to 15.255 cubic inches.

$$(250 \div 16.387 = 15.255)$$

The formula for converting cubic inches to cc is

$$\text{cubic inches} \times 16.387 = cc$$

One liter equals 1000 cc or 61.023 cubic inches.

For converting liters to cubic inches the formula is

$$\text{liters} \times 61.023 = \text{cubic inches}$$

A 3-liter engine has a displacement of 183.069 cubic inches

$$(3 \times 61.023 = 183.069)$$

For converting cubic inches to liters the formula is

$$\text{cubic inches} \div 61.023 = \text{liters}$$
$$\text{Liters to cc's is liters} \times 1000 = \text{cc's}$$
$$\text{Cc's to liters is cc} \div 1000 = \text{liters}$$

Weight

In the U.S., kart weight would be measured in pounds, in England it would probably be measured in pounds or possibly hundredweight, abbreviated "cwt", and in countries that use metric measure it would be measured in kilograms.

One hundredweight equals 112 pounds.
For converting hundredweight to pounds, the formula is

$$cwt \times 112 = pounds$$

A kart that weighs 2 cwt weighs 224 pounds.

$$(2 \times 112 = 244)$$

The formula for converting pounds to hundredweight is

$$pounds \div 112 = cwt$$

A kart that weighs 252 pounds weighs 2.25 cwt.

$$(252 \div 112 = 2.25)$$

One kilogram equals 2.204 pounds, and one pound equals .453 kilogram. For pounds to kilograms the formula is

$$(pounds \div 2.204 = kilograms)$$

Kilograms are converted to pounds with the formula

$$kilograms \times 2.204 = pounds$$

One avoirdupois ounce equals 28.35 grams.
Convert grams to avoirdupois ounces with this formula.

$$grams \div 28.35 = ounces$$

This makes 300 grams of a substance equal to 10.58 avoirdupois ounces.

$$(300 \div 28.35 = 10.58)$$

Convert avoirdupois ounces to grams with this formula

$$ounces \times 28.35 = grams$$

Eight ounces becomes 226.8 grams.

$$(8 \times 28.35 = 226.8)$$

Distance

For distance and speed measurements, one mile equals 1.609 kilometers and one kilometer equals .6214 mile.
To convert kilometers to miles, use the formula

$$kilometers \div 1.609 = miles$$

A distance of 90 kilometers, or a speed of 90 kilometers per hour, becomes 55.9 miles, or 55.9 mph.

$$(90 \div 1.609 = 55.9)$$

To convert miles to kilometers, use the formula

$$\text{miles} \times 1.609 = \text{kilometers}$$

A distance of 80 miles, or a speed of 80 mph, becomes 128.72 kilometers, or 128.72 kilometers per hour.

$$(80 \times 1.609 = 128.72)$$

Other points of differences on karts built with different measuring standards are fasteners, which are the bolts, nuts, and cap screws that secure their parts. Parts built in the United States have fasteners that comply with U.S. standards, those built in England have "Whitworth" fasteners, and those built with the metric system have metric fasteners. However, engines built in England and other countries for export to the U.S. sometimes have fasteners that conform to U.S. standards.

U.S. nuts and bolts are sized according to the outside diameter of their threads but the size of the wrench that fits them is determined by the measurement from the flat on one side of their head to the flat on the other side. Thread diameters and head sizes vary in steps of 1/16-inch.

Whitworth bolts and nuts are sized according to the outside diameter of their threads. Wrenches for them are sized in the same way: a 5/16-inch bolt requires a 5/16-inch wrench. Bolt sizes are graduated in 1/16-inch steps.

Metric nuts and bolts are sized according to the outside diameter of their threads in millimeters. Wrench sizes for them are determined by the measurement from one flat to the other, as it is for U.S. bolts and nuts, but the measurement is in millimeters.

Although fasteners of different types may have threads of the same diameter and appear to be similar in other respects, they aren't interchangeable because of differences in thread shape and angles and possibly in the number of threads per inch.

Cylinder Displacement

The engine displacement formula is the standard formula for computing the volume of a cylinder of any type with an added factor that represents the number of cylinders in the engine. The cross-sectional area of the cylinders is determined and the volume of the individual cylinders is computed by multiplying the area by the stroke length. Multiplying the result by the number of cylinders gives the engine's total displacement.

The formula is

$$\text{bore diameter} \times \text{bore diameter} \times .7854 \times \text{stroke length}$$
$$\times \text{ number of cylinders} = \text{displacement}$$

Dimensions in inches will give the displacement in cubic inches. Dimensions in millimeters will give the displacement in cubic millimeters, which are converted to the standard measure of cubic centimeters with the formula

$$\text{cubic millimeters} \div 1000 = \text{centimeters}$$

For example, compute the displacement of a single-cylinder engine that has a bore of 52 mm and a stroke of 58 mm. The equation becomes

$$52 \times 52 \times .7854 \times 58 \times 1 = \text{displacement in cubic millimeters}$$

The equation is worked out in these steps

$$52 \times 52 = 2704$$
$$2704 \times .7854 = 2123.721$$
$$2123.721 \times 58 = 123175.818$$
$$123175.818 \times 1 = 123175.818$$
cubic millimeters displacement.

This is reduced to cubic centimeters by dividing by 1000

$$123175.818 \div 1000 = 123.175$$
cubic centimeters

Compression Ratio

Cylinder volume is determined in exactly the same manner as for the displacement formula

$$\text{bore} \times \text{bore} \times .7854 \times \text{stroke} = \text{volume of one cylinder}$$

The measurements can be in either inches or millimeters.

$$\text{combustion chamber volume} + \text{cylinder volume} \div$$
$$\text{combustion chamber volume} = \text{compression ratio}$$

For an example, consider an engine that has a final combustion chamber volume of 18cc and a cylinder volume of 125cc. These figures applied to the formula gives the equation

$$18 + 125 \div 18 = 143 \div 18 = 7.94, \text{ the engine's compression ratio.}$$

This method of computing compression ratio cannot be used accurately for engines that have pistons with either domed or irregularly shaped heads. Any irregularity on the piston heads will make it impossible, with normal means, to determine the final combustion chamber volume because the volume displaced by the piston heads cannot be readily computed. The only way to determine the final combustion chamber volume when such pistons are used is by measuring it with a liquid while the cylinder head is bolted to the cylinder block and the piston is in top dead center position.

Piston Speed

Piston speed is the distance a piston moves in its cylinder during a minute of running time. Factors involved are the length of the stroke through which the piston moves and the crankshaft speed. Crankshaft speed is measured in revolutions per minute. The stroke length must be multiplied by 2 because the piston moves from the top to the bottom of its cylinder and back again to the top each time the crankshaft revolves one revolution. If the stroke length is quoted in inches, a factor of 12 must be used in the formula to convert inches per minute to feet per minute.

The formula is

$$\text{stroke} \times 2 \times \text{rpm} \div 12 = \text{piston speed in feet per minute}$$

Horsepower and Torque

Horsepower and torque are measures of engine performance. They are related to the extent that one cannot exist without the other. Torque is the measure of the amount of work an engine can do and horsepower is the measure of the amount of work done in a given time. The time factor for horsepower computations is the engine's crankshaft speed, as measured in revolutions per minute.

In U.S. and British systems torque is measured in "foot-pounds". A foot-pound is a force of one pound exerted on a lever one foot long. Thirty-three thousand foot-pounds of work done in one minute, no matter by what means, equals one horsepower. Because the force exerted by a flywheel or crankshaft acts in a circular direction, the power formula contains the constant "2 pi" to change the rotating force to straight-line force. The formula is

$$2 \text{ pi} \times \text{torque} \times \text{rpm} \div 33,000 = \text{horsepower}$$

By eliminating the 2 pi constant and reducing the 33,000 factor accordingly, the formula is reduced to

$$\text{torque} \times \text{rpm} \div 5252 = \text{horsepower}$$

For computing torque when horsepower and rpm's are known, the formula is

$$\text{horsepower} \times 5252 \div \text{rpm} = \text{torque}$$

The metric system measure for hp is 75 kilogram-meters of work in one second. One metric hp equals .986 U.S. hp.

Power ratings derived with the metric system can be converted to U.S. hp with the formula

$$\text{metric hp} \times .986 = \text{U.S. hp}$$

Convert U.S. hp to metric hp with the formula

$$\text{U.S. hp} \div .986 = \text{metric hp}$$

Gear Ratio-Speed Relationships

There are four versions of the formula that involves the relationship of kart speed, engine speed, drive gear ratios, and rear tire size. By using the appropriate version, any of these factors can be determined for any combination of the other three.

To simplify the formulas, a representative symbol is substituted for each of the factors. There are:

> mph for kart speed
> rpm for engine speed
> r for final gear ratio
> w for tire size (rear wheel)

Tire size can be determined in several ways but the one that is easiest and as accurate as any is by measuring a wheel and tire effective radius. This is done by measuring the distance from the surface on which the tire is resting to the center of the rear axle. The tire must be inflated to its normal hot-operating pressure and the rider must be on the kart when the measurement is made. The measurement must be in inches. Any fraction of an inch involved in the measurement must be converted to a decimal equivalent to simplify the mathematics. When tire size is measured in this manner a constant of 168 is used in the formula.

To determine kart speed for a given combination of engine speed, gear ratio and tire size, the formula is

$$rpm \times w \div r \times 168 = mph$$

To determine engine speed for a given combination of the other three factors the formula is

$$mph \times r \div w \times .168 = rpm$$

To determine the final drive ratio for a combination of the other three factors, the formula is

$$rpm \times w \div mph \times 168 = r$$

To determine the tire size, the formula is

$$mph \times r \times 168 \div rpm = w$$

Speeds

Formulas for computing kart speeds are based on time and distance measurements. The time is measured in seconds and fractions of seconds and the distance is measured in miles and fractions of miles. The formulas are based on the fact that there are 3,600 seconds in an hour. Results are in miles per hour.

The formula consists of a constant over the number of seconds required to travel a certain distance. Value of the constant depends on the distance traveled.

For a mile it is 3,600. For distances longer or shorter than a mile it is the distance, in miles or fractions of miles, times 3,600. For a distance of five miles the constant would be 5 times 3,600, or 18,000. For a quarter of a mile it would be .250 times 3,600, or 900.

The formula is

$$\text{constant} \div \text{time in seconds} = \text{miles per hour}$$

For example, if a mile were traveled in 40 seconds, the equation would become

$$3600 \div 40 = 90 \text{ miles per hour}$$

For another example, a quarter-mile was traveled in 10 seconds. Applied to the formula this would be

$$900 \div 10 = 90 \text{ miles per hour}$$

Fuel Mileage

The formula for computing fuel mileage is

$$\text{distance traveled} \div \text{gallons of fuel used} = \text{miles per gallon}$$

Decimal Equivalents of Millimeters

mm.	Inches	mm.	Inches	mm.	Inches	mm.	Inches	mm.	Inches
.01	.00039	.41	.01614	.81	.03189	21	.82677	61	2.40157
.02	.00079	.42	.01654	.82	.03228	22	.86614	62	2.44094
.03	.00118	.43	.01693	.83	.03268	23	.90551	63	2.48031
.04	.00157	.44	.01732	.84	.03307	24	.94488	64	2.51968
.05	.00197	.45	.01772	.85	.03346	25	.98425	65	2.55905
.06	.00236	.46	.01811	.86	.03386	26	1.02362	66	2.59842
.07	.00276	.47	.01850	.87	.03425	27	1.06299	67	2.63779
.08	.00315	.48	.01890	.88	.03465	28	1.10236	68	2.67716
.09	.00354	.49	.01929	.89	.03504	29	1.14173	69	2.71653
.10	.00394	.50	.01969	.90	.03543	30	1.18110	70	2.75590
.11	.00433	.51	.02008	.91	.03583	31	1.22047	71	2.79527
.12	.00472	.52	.02047	.92	.03622	32	1.25984	72	2.83464
.13	.00512	.53	.02087	.93	.03661	33	1.29921	73	2.87401
.14	.00551	.54	.02126	.94	.03701	34	1.33858	74	2.91338
.15	.00591	.55	.02165	.95	.03740	35	1.37795	75	2.95275
.16	.00630	.56	.02205	.96	.03780	36	1.41732	76	2.99212
.17	.00669	.57	.02244	.97	.03819	37	1.45669	77	3.03149
.18	.00709	.58	.02283	.98	.03858	38	1.49606	78	3.07086
.19	.00748	.59	.02323	.99	.03898	39	1.53543	79	3.11023
.20	.00787	.60	.02362	1.00	.03937	40	1.57480	80	3.14960
.21	.00827	.61	.02402	1	.03937	41	1.61417	81	3.18897
.22	.00866	.62	.02441	2	.07874	42	1.65354	82	3.22834
.23	.00906	.63	.02480	3	.11811	43	1.69291	83	3.26771
.24	.00945	.64	.02520	4	.15748	44	1.73228	84	3.30708
.25	.00984	.65	.02559	5	.19685	45	1.77165	85	3.34645
.26	.01024	.66	.02598	6	.23622	46	1.81102	86	3.38582
.27	.01063	.67	.02638	7	.27559	47	1.85039	87	3.42519

(Continued)

Decimal Equivalents of Millimeters

mm.	Inches	mm.	Inches	mm.	Inches	mm.	Inches	mm.	Inches
.28	.01102	.68	.02677	8	.31496	48	1.88976	88	3.46456
.29	.01142	.69	.02717	9	.35433	49	1.92913	89	3.50393
.30	.01181	.70	.02756	10	.39370	50	1.96850	90	3.54330
.31	.01220	.71	.02795	11	.43307	51	2.00787	91	3.58267
.32	.01260	.72	.02835	12	.47244	52	2.04724	92	3.62204
.33	.01299	.73	.02874	13	.51181	53	2.08661	93	3.66141
.34	.01339	.74	.02913	14	.55118	54	2.12598	94	3.70078
.35	.01378	.75	.02953	15	.59055	55	2.16535	95	3.74015
.36	.01417	.76	.02992	16	.62992	56	2.20472	96	3.77952
.37	.01457	.77	.03032	17	.66929	57	2.24409	97	3.81889
.38	.01496	.78	.03071	18	.70866	58	2.28346	98	3.85826
.39	.01535	.79	.03110	19	.74803	59	2.32283	99	3.89763
.40	.01575	.80	.03150	20	.78740	60	2.36220	100	3.93700

Decimal Equivalents
of 8ths, 16ths, 32nds, 64ths

8ths	32nds	64ths	64ths
1/8=.125	1/32=.03125	1/64=.015625	33/64=.515625
1/4=.250	3/32=.09375	3/64=.046875	35/64=.546875
3/8=.375	5/32=.15625	5/64=.078125	37/64=.578125
1/2=.500	7/32=.21875	7/64=.109375	39/64=.609375
5/8=.625	9/32=.28125	9/64=.140625	41/64=.640625
3/4=.750	11/32=.34375	11/64=.171875	43/64=.671875
7/8=.875	13/32=.40625	13/64=.203125	45/64=.703125
16ths	15/32=.46875	15/64=.234370	47/64=.734375
1/16=.0625	17/32=.53125	17/64=.265625	49/64=.765625
3/16=.1875	19/32=.59375	19/64=.296875	51/64=.796875
5/16=.3125	21/32=.65625	21/64=.328125	53/64=.828125
7/16=.4375	23/32=.71875	23/64=.359375	55/64=.859375
9/16=.5625	25/32=.78125	25/64=.390625	57/64=.890625
11/16=.6875	27/32=.84375	27/64=.421875	59/64=.921875
13/16=.8125	29/32=.90625	29/64=.453125	61/64=.953125
15/16=.9375	31/32=.96875	31/64=.484375	63/64=.984375